CONNECTING

With Self and Others

Sherod Miller, Ph. D.
Daniel B. Wackman, Ph. D.
Elam W. Nunnally, Ph.D.
Phyllis A. Miller, Ph. D.

Printed in the United States of America
10 9 8 7 6 5

ISBN 0-917340-15-9

Design: Robert Friederichsen
Editorial Assistance: Deborah Shakeri
Typesetting Assistance: Robert Bolenbaucher and Ed Nies

**INTERPERSONAL
COMMUNICATION
PROGRAMS, INC.**
7201 South Broadway
Littleton, CO 80122
(303 794-1764)

PREFACE

In 1968 the University of Minnesota Family Studies Center was blessed with an outstanding faculty and substantial research grants from the National Institute of Mental Health for the study of family development. It was in this fertile context that two of us as graduate students, Sherod Miller and Elam Nunnally, and one of us as a post-doctoral student, Dan Wackman, met and jelled into a research and program-development team.

Our research focused initially on the transition from engagement into early marriage and on the conditions which supported successful change. We learned that effective communication was central to this process and that specific communication skills could be identified and taught to partners; these skills improved the communication and satisfaction together of the couples we studied.

Impressed by the fact that relationships are not only initiated, but are also maintained, strengthened, and destroyed through communication, we broadened our scope to include couples at all stages of development who wished to enrich their relationship by learning skills for dealing more effectively with their day-to-day concerns. We began to train others to teach the skills.

By 1972, trained and certified instructors presented the Couple Communication program in schools, churches, health centers, and private counseling practices. To date, more than 100,000 couples have participated in Couple Communication throughout the United States, Canada, Australia, Japan, South America, Scandinavia, Germany, and other European countries.

Research on the program spread to other major universities, and now over 30 studies with positive results have been conducted on Couple Communication. We three originators have been honored to receive awards for our research and development of Couple Communication from the National Council on Family Relations and the Association of Couples for Marriage Enrichment.

Our previous books — ALIVE AND AWARE, TALKING TOGETHER, STRAIGHT TALK and WORKING TOGETHER — reflect the continued development of concepts and skills and the expansion from the original couple focus to other interpersonal relationships and contexts as well. Over 500 colleges and universities have adopted these books as course texts in the areas of interpersonal communication, human relations, counseling, health care sciences, and social work, as well as in family relations. The communication skills program for business and industry, called Working Together, has been taught in small businesses, government agencies, and major corporations, including 3M, Ford Motor Company, General Foods, Tennessee Eastman, NASA, Honeywell, Bell Laboratories, Tennant Company, Inland Steel Corporation, Burroughs, and Helene Curtis Industries, to name a few.

Phyllis Miller has joined our writing team, and now after 20 years of research, extensive feedback from program participants and course instructors alike, we offer CONNECTING. It represents the updating of core communication skills with the addition and integration of relationship maps to help you connect more effectively and satisfactorily with the important people in your life.

ACKNOWLEDGMENTS

It is our pleasure to list the names of our personal mentors and friends who have contributed substantially to the creation of this book:

Reuben Hill, Virginia Satir, Gerhard Neubeck, Richard Hey, Earl Beatt, Gordon James, Sidney Jourard, Kathy Wackman, Eeva Nunnally, Karen Wampler, Patrick Carnes, David and Karen Olson, David and Vera Mace, Michael Paula, Ben Fuller, Ken Justice, George Shipiro, Richard Bandler, John Grinder, Ann Stefanson, Norman Parent, James Ayers, Carol Saline, Jack Spring, Dick Axelrod, Bob and Renee Noles, Tres and Loras Goddard, Bob Friederichsen, Ray Becker, Dallas and Nancy Demmitt, Chet Evenson, Sandra Hirsch, and James Nelson.

Our special thanks to the instructors, training associates, program participants, and students who have generously shared their stories, insights, and evaluations.

CONTENTS

ABOUT THE AUTHORS

Sherod Miller is President of Interpersonal Communication Programs, Inc., a Denver-Littleton based publishing and consulting firm. He specializes in interpersonal communication skill training and team building. Over the years he has worked with numerous business corporations, government agencies, and human service organizations. He is also a Fellow in the American Association of Marriage and Family Therapists, and was formerly a faculty member in the Department of Medicine at the University of Minnesota, School of Medicine.

Daniel B. Wackman is a Professor in the School of Journalism and Mass Communication at the University of Minnesota. Much of his research has focused on family processes. He also serves as a consultant to business, nonprofit organizations, and government agencies. His most recent book is *Managing Media Organizations: Effective Leadership of the Media*.

Elam W. Nunnally is an Associate Professor of Social Welfare at the University of Wisconsin-Milwaukee. He is a marriage and family therapist specializing in communication and in brief therapy which he teaches in Scandinavia and the USA. He has also co-authored the five-volume series on *Families in Trouble* as well as *Communication Basics for Human Services Professionals,* Sage Publications.

Phyllis A. Miller is President of Reading Development Resources in Denver, Colorado. As a consultant to business and government organizations, she specializes in adult reading, writing, and learning. She is the author of *Managing Your Reading* and developer of the video series *Flexible Reading* which airs on educational television stations throughout the United States and Canada, in addition to being used by businesses and schools. Together with her husband, Sherod Miller, she presents Couple Communication programs.

"Real freedom is the ability to pause between stimulus and response and in that pause choose."
— Rollo May

INTRODUCTION

For a number of years, before the ideas of this book began to take shape, we worked with couples in counseling. In our first meeting with a couple we listened to each person's story of what was going on between them. Often the woman would begin by telling what life was like living with her husband — how he was gone a lot, did not show her affection, and was hard on the kids. As she talked, her husband would punctuate her story with side glances and interruptions to defend himself like, "That's not true," or "who are you trying to fool?" When she ran out of ammunition, he would take over and return the fire.

Complain, blame, accuse — "you don't listen, you spend too much, you aren't faithful, you don't — you, you, you." Ninety percent of the time the focus was on the other person: "While I might need a 'tune up,' you need an 'overhaul.' "

As time passed, we began to see that as important as words are, sometimes they get in the way of resolving issues and solving problems. Some people use too many words; they speak a great deal, but say very little — their language hides their real thoughts, feelings, and wants. Other people speak very little and have difficulty putting the range and intensity of their experience into words. And so it was with most of the couples who came for counseling.

After hearing too many of these first sessions, we began experimenting to develop a better way of getting beyond words to assess accurately where couples were with each other and where they were headed in the future. What we did formed the basis for new ways of seeing relationships.

So then instead of sitting and listening to torrents of words or trying to draw out those who could not express themselves, we asked couples to *show* us, rather than *tell* us, what was going on between the two of them. They almost always looked a bit surprised and confused at first, but with minimal guidance were readily able to do what we asked.

HUMAN CHECKERS

With the couple's consent, we gave them the following instructions:

"As you stand and look at the floor, imagine that you are at the center of an enlarged checker board. Now I would like you, Jack, to face Marilyn, and pretend that you are standing on one square (a square measures about one square foot). Now Marilyn, I'd like you to continue facing Jack, but step back three squares, so that you are standing on the fourth square with two squares between you and Jack."

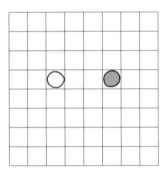

When they were in position, we gave additional instructions:

"Now, like in checkers, you take turns moving. A move can be one step forwards, backwards, sideways or diagonally. Or you may move by staying on the same square and turning sideways or completely around to face the opposite direction."

"Don't say anything. This is a nonverbal experience. Before making a move, stand quietly, look at each other, and think about where you are with each other in your relationship. When one of you feels an urge, make a move. Then without talking, the other person makes a move. Keep moving, one at a time, until one or both of you indicate you want to stop."

When both people indicated that they understood the instructions and were willing to follow through, we moved away and watched the "dance."

Within a minute or two, and often with only eight to twelve moves, the pair "danced" their basic relationship pattern. If more time elapsed, they usually repeated their original pattern. Within two minutes, they demonstrated what hours of talking would only approximate.

After the nonverbal exercise, we would go back through the "checker board" dance, step by step, letting the partners put words on their steps at each decision point.

DANCE PATTERNS

Throughout the book, we will discuss a variety of different dances (or relationship patterns) that may develop within pairs or a small group. Since each dance has its own unique steps, there are an infinite number of possible patterns. As we shall see, however, many partners have similar patterns. This is particularly the case when a relationship becomes troubled because, at that time, the pattern usually becomes more rigid and limited.

The Most Painful Dance

Occasionally, couples seek consultation when one partner has already decided to end the relationship. This was true for Ed and Judy, two seniors in college. They had been engaged for over a year but their relationship was continuously stormy — not a happy prelude to marriage. Their dance looked like this:

> The pair quietly stood facing each other for about four seconds, then Ed, who really wanted out, but had difficulty saying so, took the first step backwards. Judy, who wanted to keep the relationship going, pursued Ed with one step forward. Ed's next step was again immediately backwards. Judy's response was rather determined and she again took another step forward. Ed unwaveringly continued to back away one more step.

> Suddenly tension was running high. Judy recognized that she was at a *critical choice point*. If she moved forward she would be desperately chasing Ed, showing she had no other alternative but to pursue him unrealistically and unsatisfactorily. If she stepped backward, she would be testing the relationship and saying, "I don't need to chase you. I can make it on my own, as disappointing and difficult as that may be." Would this be Judy's first step in reordering her life apart from Ed? Judy took one step backwards and waited.

> If Ed had any interest in maintaining the relationship, he would step forward or sideways at this point. Perhaps Judy's show of strength by stepping back and giving space would be attractive to him. It wasn't. Ed took one unwaveringly final step

backward, and both partners realized their engagement was really over.

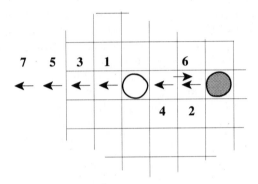

Rejection, separation, and loss are the most painful of all human dances. By the time we finish adolescence, most of us have had the music stop on a significant relationship — a pal at school, a boy or girl friend, a parent, a spouse. We all have experienced some variation of this dance. No matter what the reason for leaving — another person, a different life style, a drug, or death — it hurts.

An Intergenerational Dance: Father and Son

Many men have unfinished business with their fathers. While taking many forms, it most often revolves around power and control, closeness and distance. As a part of an assignment for a course in which students were studying their families of origin and the interpersonal dynamics which have shaped their lives, John Jr. invited his dad, John Sr. to a round of "human checkers."

John Sr. is a very successful college football coach who has taken a number of teams to championship bowls. John Jr., a physically strapping and mentally quick guy, grew up loving sports. He and his brother even played on some of their father's teams. Junior recalls playing sports both because he wanted to and because he wanted his dad's approval.

> After John Jr. explained the rules, he and his father got into place on the "checker board" and stood for a few moments looking at each other. Feeling a bit anxious and thinking, "I set this thing up," Junior made the first move — one step sideways, to his right. Senior quickly matched Junior's move — one step to his left. Wanting to avoid committing himself to any forward or backward steps, Junior moved sideways, back onto the original square again, and again his dad followed.

Junior kept the dance going by moving sideways again, only this time to his left. Senior matched him again. They stood quietly looking at each other. Now Junior decided to break the pattern and move one square backwards, hoping his dad would pursue him by taking one step towards him. But that did not happen. Senior grinned, moved one step backwards, and gave a knowing laugh. They stopped the dance.

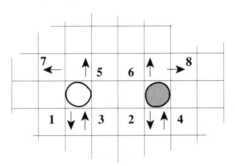

Junior and Senior did not talk much about what the dance meant. They each left the event in a friendly, knowing sort of way. John Jr. later recounted:

"The first part of the dance was tit for tat. We were doing the same thing, avoiding each other; never getting too far or too close. Then when I stepped back, I was testing him, putting the pressure on him to move forward. I hoped he would, but he didn't. I think he was thinking, 'You want me to follow but I'm not going to.' His laugh when he stepped back showed that he knew what I wanted but wouldn't go along with it. We recognize either one of us can hurt the other, and we don't know how to get closer — that's real. I'm not sure how you get closer to your dad."

This dance is more typical. Instead of father and son, they could be colleagues at work or friends. Here are two people who basically like each other but for a number of reasons — competition, embarrassment, fear of closeness, lack of communication skill, and so forth — they never really connect. As interpersonal communication trainers and team building consultants in businesses, schools, churches, and agencies, as well as in our work with couples and families, we see many of these dances.

A Decision Dance

Two very serious people found themselves caught in a dilemma. Bob, age 36, was a CPA in a well established accounting firm, with the goal of becoming a partner before he reached 40. He was putting long hours and maximum energy into his pursuit. His wife Carla, age 34, was a design engineer with an aerospace company. She too was very career oriented, loved her work, and saw good opportunities for advancement in the years ahead. Their issue was whether or not to have a baby. Carla's biological clock for a first child was rapidly ticking away. A decision had to be made soon.

> They stood on the checker board looking at each other for about 30 seconds, waiting to see who would take the first step. Then Bob took one step forward, and Carla quickly followed suit. Immediately they dissolved in each other's arms. While neither could speak, a decision had been made. As they hugged each other, Carla wept and Bob nurtured her and accepted her love as well. Both people signaled relief and release.

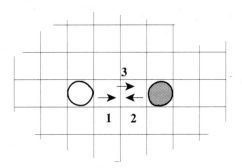

For some time they were unable to speak, and words were unnecessary. When they did talk, they had difficulty expressing what had happened inside themselves. What they expressed was that both of them had felt a shift: what they were previously thinking and feeling suddenly changed as they looked at each other and began to move physically. Suddenly they experienced a new freedom; they were no longer stuck. When the emotional climax mellowed, they sat down to reflect on what had occurred. They both felt certain that they wanted to have a child.

As a reader, you may be saying to yourself, "How foolish to base the rest of your life on a few simple steps at a highly charged moment." But it often happens like this. While we may spend more time thinking, talking, and hesitating about issues and situations, eventually we make a decision. We are continuously choreographing our own dances.

You Cannot Not Dance

Everyone is dancing. It is primal. In an interpersonal sense, nothing is more basic. Whether you are aware of it or not, every exchange you have with another person is part of a small or large dance. Whether you are asking your boss for a raise, buying a newspaper from a clerk at a 7-Eleven, negotiating with a sales person over the price of a new car, or deciding whether to marry, every move, gesture, silence, and word communicates something. While it would be crazy to be thinking about every move, you are constantly on the checker board at home, school, work, and play. You are either connecting or disconnecting in physical reality with another person or actively interacting in some mental state by recalling, anticipating, or possibly rehearsing an exchange.

WHAT MAKES HUMAN CHECKERS SO ENGAGING?

Nonverbal communication — posture, facial expression, rate of breathing, odor, and subtle body gesture — is a very powerful form of communication. When you stand face-to-face, and move step-by-step, choice-by-choice around the checkerboard, heightened awareness of yourself and your relationship develops and, without words to provide a release, strong emotions often emerge. The dance becomes a condensed analogue of real life, showing "what is" at that point in time. It has the effect of time-lapse photography, collapsing into a few steps what has actually been occurring over days, weeks, and sometimes even months or years.

The nonverbal communication dance in human checkers taps four basic elements of any interpersonal relationship — *space, energy, time, and choice.*

Space

For us space means both *physical proximity*, closeness or distance, and *mental proximity,* similarities and differences between peoples' values, emotions, beliefs, and interests. Since everybody has different parameters (ranges of the acceptable, tolerable, or comfortable beliefs, emotions, wants, and behaviors), physical and mental spaces represent individual "comfort zones."

Energy

Energy is the liveliness, vigor, drive, or vitality of a person at any point in time. Energy can be charged positively or negatively, and it varies in intensity from moment to moment. A person who is enthused about something looks and acts differently than a person who is depressed. Emotional state, body tension, rate of speech, strength, and animation are all indicators of energy. Energy can be generated, focused, diffused, dissipated, or discharged by a dance. While most people maintain a consistent energy level, their presence or involvement in an interaction rises and falls as a measure of their satisfaction with it.

Time

Time records the sequence of actions and helps us see relationships as interactional systems. Partner A's action becomes the stimulus to partner B's response which, in turn, becomes the basis for partner A's interaction (reinforcement or change of his or her previous action in light of the partner's response). When you view communication in three-act sequences, you begin to see how relationships become systems which perpetuate the status quo or initiate and incorporate change.

Choice

As "human checkers" illustrates, each step is a *choice point* either to keep a relationship continuing as it is, or to change it. *Either player can change the dance because it takes only one person to change the system.* Each new or different *action* creates the potential for a new and different *reaction,* and the potential for a new and different *interaction.* Viewed in this manner, each step in an exchange becomes a *potential turning point* for the relationship.

COMMUNICATION AND RELATIONSHIPS

Throughout CONNECTING we will be presenting communication and relationships as a dynamic dance between people in terms of space, energy, time, and choices. Think of physical and mental space between parties as movement back and forth, expanding and contracting on a *horizontal* plain. Energy, on the other hand, moves up and down, rising and falling on a *vertical* axis within each individual. Time tracks the *sequential* interactional aspects of each player's movement within a dance. Finally, choices translate space, energy, and time into *explicit actions and information.*

Communication, both nonverbal and verbal, is the "stuff" that initiates, builds, maintains, and destroys relationships. It is simultaneously a *vehicle for* relating and an *index of* the relationship. Effective communicators attend to the nonverbal aspects of space, energy, and time as well as to their choice of words and actions as they move from situation to situation, building and strengthening relationships.

The Major Purpose of This Book

Life is a series of interpersonal dances — connections and disconnections — ranging from painful, distracting, and destructive encounters to joyful, meaningful, and productive experiences. If your dance steps are not just automatic responses, but based on reflective choices, you can learn and grow with each dance.

CONNECTING will help you become a more alert and talented interpersonal dancer by *increasing*:

1. *Awareness* of self, others, and your relationships.
2. *Skills* for sending and receiving messages more clearly and accurately.
3. *Options* for building relationships.

A BRIEF OVERVIEW OF CONNECTING

CONNECTING is divided into four sections — communication maps and skills and relationship maps and skills. The maps are conceptual frameworks for expanding your awareness of communication and relationship processes. The skills are practical and specific behaviors you can learn for enriching your communication and relationships. Knowing these maps and skills gives you more interpersonal options.

The Introduction has introduced "Human checkers" as a powerful tool for capturing relationships in terms of space, time, energy, and choice.

1. **The Interpersonal Dance** views every message as one of 12 possible interpersonal steps — together or apart — in a larger dance. You cannot not dance!

I. COMMUNICATION MAPS

2. **Content, Communicycle and Change** presents and illustrates five types of content messages and issues. It also introduces the concept of communicycle — the smallest measure of a completed communication.

3. **Styles of Communication** defines style as "how" people talk. Style I is sociable, friendly, and informative. Style II either takes charge appropriately or is actively or passively aggressive.

4. **Styles of Communication** (continued) shows how Style III provides an overview of a situation and Style IV goes to the core of an issue without blaming or making demands.

5. **The Awareness Wheel** draws a map for increasing self and other awareness based on the five key pieces of information in any situation.

6. **Individual Similarities and Differences** integrates C.G. Jung's seminal work on psychological types with the Awareness Wheel to show how people are similar or different and how this impacts their relationship in fundamental ways.

7. **Partial Awareness** identifies blind spots, incongruencies, and blockages which interfere with processing information and communication.

8. **Mapping Issues** outlines and illustrates an eight-step decision-making/problem-solving model which considers and combines the best of "objective" and "subjective" information around any personal, interpersonal, or organizational issue.

II. COMMUNICATION SKILLS

9. **Speaking Skills** shows how unskilled communicators unknowingly create resistance in their listeners and teaches six specific talking skills for sending clear and effective messages which enhance the speaker's likelihood of being heard accurately.

10. **Listening Skills** demonstrates how listening impacts relationships and affects productivity. This chapter identifies three different types of listening modes — based on the listener's intentions — and

illustrates how each type influences the quality of information gathered. Five specific listening skills and an overall strategy for ensuring accurate information are presented and illustrated.

11. **Meta Talk** explains how "Pre-talk," "Now-talk," and "Post-talk" supplement the skills presented in Chapters 9 and 10 to prevent, clarify, and resolve impasses. Meta Talk — "talk about talk" — skills are necessary for monitoring and enriching relationships.

III. RELATIONSHIP MAPS

12. **Relationships As Systems** introduces the Circumplex Model of Human Systems, developed by Dr. David Olson in the Family Social Science Department at the University of Minnesota, as a framework for comparing different types of two-person and group relationships in terms of open system properties and the basic dynamics of adaptability and cohesion.

13. **Relationship Phases** describes the natural growth cycles which relationships go through — visionary, adversarial, dormant, and vital — and how each phase is characterized by a different quality of relationship.

IV. RELATIONSHIP PROCESSES

14. **Communicating Under Pressure** illustrates how most people constrict rather than expand to deal with interpersonal tension. This chapter gives practical directions for managing yourself and responding to others to turn interpersonal stress into a resource.

15. **Resolving Conflicts** interrelates conflict resolution and self/other esteem building. The chapter shows how to count self and other and work out collaborative solutions to tough conflicts.

16. **Communication Strategies** offers a menu of the major concepts and skills presented in CONNECTING and suggests how to combine and sequence them with forethought to approach different situations as effectively and satisfactorily as possible.

How To Read CONNECTING

Since CONNECTING is a book about communication and interpersonal relationships, keep the following points in mind.

Throughout the book we use a number of two-person terms to try to capture the generalizability of the maps and concepts to all sorts of relationships — friendships, married couples, colleagues, boss-employee, health practitioner-patient, consultant/counselor-client, teacher-student, parent-child, and so forth. To capture these different combinations we have used a variety of interchangeable terms: *pairs, partners, couples, parties, players, and people.* As you read CONNECTING, remember that the term being used in any section represents a dyadic relationship at home, school, work, or elsewhere.

For convenience, there are repeated references to dyads: most of the concepts and skills apply to small groups or systems as well — families, project and other work groups, committees, boards and leisure groups/teams.

Finally, as in most books, later chapters in CONNECTING build on earlier ones. However, most chapters are complete in themselves so move around in the book if you wish. Read chapters that appeal to your interests or apply to your life most directly. And when you encounter a concept that has not been covered in your reading, check the index for quick reference.

1

THE INTERPERSONAL DANCE:
Together and Apart

The Dancers — People in Relationship

The word "relationship" means different things to different people. In this book, we primarily use the term to refer to ongoing relationships which are long-lasting and important to both parties. This contrasts with short-term encounters between strangers. By this definition, a relationship increases in its significance as history builds and a future is anticipated. Examples include friendships, some business and professional relationships, and especially marital and familial relationships.

The nature of a relationship may be further delineated along a continuum from *symmetrical* to *asymmetrical*. Symmetrical relationships emphasize equality over difference; typical examples include friendships, colleagues, and spouses. They assume an equal playing field. Asymmetrical relationships, on the other hand, maximize difference over equality; they suggest superior and subordinate knowledge and power. Examples include teacher-student, doctor-patient, boss-employee, parent-child.

Historically, the distinctions between symmetrical and asymmetrical relationships have been ascribed formally to people by their positions in society or in organizations. But while formal distinctions still exist, relationships have become much more informal and symmetrical. Today the nature of a relationship is much more likely to grow out of the interaction between people. Patients, for example, are much more assertive with their doctors, students readily mix with teachers, employees are encouraged to question their bosses, and parent-child relationships are much more negotiable.

Further, when two or more people act "in relation to each other," they often attempt to influence each other. Their actions may be assertive or submissive. Assertive behaviors generally strive toward equality and symmetrical exchanges, although sometimes these behaviors are attempts to dominate. Submissive actions typically reinforce differences and asymmetrical exchanges.

The classifications of symmetrical and asymmetrical should not be confused with good or bad, strong or weak. Rather they are descriptions of how people differentiate themselves to function effectively in various situations.

A relationship then, whether brief or long-term, distant or close, symmetrical or asymmetrical, is basically people dancing with each other — coming together and moving apart, influencing and being influenced, attempting to connect and sometimes failing to connect.

THE INTERPERSONAL DANCE FRAMEWORK

While a dance proceeds one step at a time, there are four basic relationship *states* or specified postures that partners/players can adopt. Partners can be in one of these states for just a brief moment, a longer interval, or a considerable length of time — perhaps even years; there is no general notion of how long a particular relationship state may continue.

Each state may further be *charged with either positive energy or negative energy.* If a relationship is in a *positively* charged state, partners/players feel *confident and comfortable* with self and other; in a *negatively* charged state, they feel *uncertain and anxious* about each other.

FIRST STATE: TOGETHERNESS

In the first state, which we call *Togetherness,* partners are mutually engaged in the same activity, whether the relationship is charged positively or negatively.

Positive Togetherness

If you are like most people, you are drawn to the positive aspects of togetherness — people playing, sharing, laughing, caring, joking, touching, celebrating, creating, deciding, and building something together. Being with others in positive togetherness is invigorating.

Positive togetherness is the state of "we" and "us" very often seen in newly-formed relationships, as well as in mature friendships, work-groups, and marriages that have withstood the tests of time. For example, parents may feel strong togetherness and pride as they watch their child take his or her first few steps or graduate from college. Two people praying together can experience a powerful spiritual bond. Sales and athletic teams enjoy great moments of comraderie (which can even be recounted years later) when they win a particularly important contract or game.

Through the processes of attending and attuning to each other in positive togetherness, people become affirming, energizing, and productive for self and other. This state establishes a sense of belonging — being liked and included — and a powerful sense of cohesion develops. When two people positively connect in any situation, it is experienced and remembered as close, "quality time." Satisfying relationships have many and varied times like this.

Take a moment and refresh yourself by recalling some of the joyful relationship moments in your life.

Negative Togetherness

Arguing, bickering, and fighting (including physical and verbal abuse) characterize negative togetherness. In this situation, both people accuse and attack each other while they defend and protect themselves. Most people view this as a bad state to be in, and one to be avoided.

While physical abuse must always be off limits in any relationship, fear of a verbal fight — hurting or being hurt — blocks many partnerships. If, however, the pair does not deadend in a destructive dance, a "good" argument can be a catalyst to positive change and growth; energy is aroused and partially released between partners. The verbal outburst only reflects the intensity of feelings below the angry surface.

When you find yourself suddenly caught in a fight, the energy aroused can be an important first step towards alerting you to connect with your own real feelings and those of your partner. If what is really bothering you is put into words and incorporated into the longer, larger dance, temporary negative togetherness, though often painful and disconcerting, can be transformed into a positive outcome. Nevertheless, whether it is a husband and wife arguing about a purchase, or two roommates disagreeing over housekeeping responsibilities, if they spend much of their time and energy in this negative state, the relationship becomes draining.

Too much togetherness can also be repressive. Partners who insist that they must think and feel alike and must want the same things become overly enmeshed. They limit their resources, thwart productivity, and diminish their individual identities.

The overall point to remember about togetherness, regardless of its positive or negative valence, is that both partners are connecting — fully participating. They are mutually contributing, involved, and responsible for what is occurring. They are returning kind for kind.

Obviously, partners cannot be together all the time, focusing their energies on each other or on some common activity. In fact, two principal fears in getting married or establishing any partnership are (1) that there will be too much togetherness and I will lose freedom to pursue my own interests; and (2) that the relationship might end up costing me more than it is worth. The big question is, "Can I do better by myself, or with another person?"

SECOND STATE:
LEADING/FOLLOWING, PULLING/DRAGGING

Partners are not together long before they begin to try to influence each other and lead one another in new directions. They attempt to change each other's minds, interests, values, and activities.

We label the second state *Leading/Following, Pulling/ Dragging.* This state occurs when one partner attempts to take the lead and move the relationship in a different direction or focus energy on some new interest or activity outside the relationship. This attempt to change direction is usually perceived by the second person as either a good thing or as a threat to the relationship. How the second person responds to the first person's initiative determines whether the move for change is treated as a positive move or a negative one.

Leading/Following

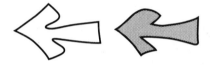

It is wonderful to take a step in a new direction and have your partner follow you with no hesitations. Likewise, it is often relieving to have your partner take the lead, and all you have to do is follow.

If one partner takes a step in a new direction, some risk is involved — the second person may either accept or reject the move. When the second person follows, showing interest, granting approval, giving support, or even encouraging the new initiative, a positive experience typically results for both people.

The classic example of the leading/following state occurs in traditional marriages where the man pursues his education and career, encouraged and supported by the woman. Another example might be when a daughter asks her parents for money to spend spring break in Florida, and they agree. Or, one partner takes care of the children while the other partner attends a conference out of town. Genuine and unwavering support, as in these situations, creates positive outcomes for everyone. However, if only grudging support is given, negative feelings often result.

Pulling/Dragging

Most partners do not always just readily follow each other. They have questions, hesitations, and doubts. Often the first partner pulls harder to sell his or her idea and the second person just drags his or her feet. At other times, the second person counters with a different proposal, trying to lead the first person in another direction. For most of us, resistance to our proposals brings disappointment, if not stronger negative feelings of frustration and anger: "Why don't you want to go along? You'd have a great time."

One important reason for the second person's resistance is that he or she feels left out or neglected. For example, the first person's activity — a hobby, work, reading, etc. — may take too much time away from the relationship and the second person resists so that he or she can remain the focus of the first person's energy. This resistance grows from the fear of becoming disconnected.

From this pulling/dragging state, the next step can be another attempt to lead, or, as often happens, the pair may get into an argument — a negative togetherness state. A more useful step, which also happens, is to begin a process of respectful negotiation.

THIRD STATE:
DIRECTING/COMPLYING, PUSHING/BLOCKING

We call the third state *Directing/Complying, Pushing/Blocking.* Situations often call for direction — someone to take charge and call the shots. Therefore, any well-functioning partnership has to determine periodically what each player will do to make the best use of its resources, including time and energy.

Directing/Complying

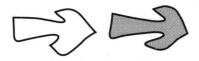

When one partner gives the other a directive, and the other readily accepts, agrees, and complies with it, there is no friction. If both are comfortable with the instruction — both with *what* is said and *how* it is said — a quick, efficient, and positive move often results.

For example, knowing they arrived late at the airport, Judy tells her husband to take the tickets, run ahead to the gate and check them in, while she returns the rented car. Or the president of a manufacturing company, making a decision based on a marketing survey, directs the vice president of production to increase the manufacturing of two products 20 percent during the next quarter. Even though his division will be pressed to increase production, the vice president accepts the directive, knowing everyone will benefit.

Pushing/Blocking

Directives are not always complied with readily; for any number of reasons, the person being directed balks. Suddenly, the directive escalates to an order, a demand, or even a threat. The first person's push turns into a verbal shove, resulting in increased friction and growing resistance.

Again, a common example of this state occurs in marriage when the more aggressive partner pushes the laid-back partner to go back to school, change jobs, or dress better so the second will become "more successful." Likewise, a teacher meets resistance with a particular student, pushing for better attendance or performance, while the student passively disattends. Salespersons lose customers by unknowingly pressing them to buy. Parents who force their child to take lessons or eat certain vegetables know how the pushing/resisting mode feels.

Sometimes resistance to the pressure for change develops because a person fears losing his or her self-identity. Complying with the pressure means acquiescing to the first person's view of *who I should be*. It may even mean succumbing to a definition of togetherness in the relationship that is suffocating — too much connectedness. Unless these partners expand their awareness and exercise communication skills, the next set of steps in their dance will revert to an argument — negative togetherness — perhaps even a raw power struggle. Occasionally a gentle push or pressure to move in a new direction can have a good outcome; later your partner thanks you for the nudge. Most often, however, it does not.

TRANSITION STATES

While change can occur in any state, states two and three are often transition states signaling and incorporating change. It should be noted that in state two (leading/following and pulling/dragging) and state three(directing/complying and pushing/blocking) either partner can take the role of leading or pulling as well as that of directing or pushing. Likewise, either partner can follow or drag, comply or block. Efforts to bring about change can flow in either direction between two partners.

It is very difficult to *make* somebody else change. Usually we can only *facilitate change in others* and *make changes in ourselves.* If you attempt to make others change, you will often find yourself negatively charged in states two and three. CONNECTING is a book about change, but most of the focus will be on what you can do to change yourself, and as a result, change the dance.

Take a couple of minutes and think about areas of your life which are changing. Think about the people involved in these changes. In which relationships are you leading or following, pulling or dragging, directing or complying, pushing or blocking? What is the range of feelings you experience as you reflect on your life?

FOURTH STATE: SEPARATENESS

The fourth relationship state is *Separateness.* As the word suggests, it is almost the opposite of togetherness. It represents the "I" and "me" in a relationship. Separateness occurs when both partners focus their interests and energies away from each other on to different activities, things, or people. The relationship is maintained, but the partners are apart.

Positive Separateness

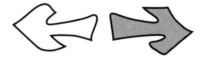

Every person on the planet has his or her own unique talents, interests, and dreams. When partners acknowledge this in each other, and encourage and support each other "to be all you can be," time and energy must be spent apart from each other. In other words, separateness may also be positive aloneness.

Partners who are comfortable with their separateness trust each other. They also discover that their separateness can make each person more interesting during their time together. Because each player generates more resources to pool — money, experience, ideas, they can be more productive and have more to talk about when they are together.

Examples of this state can be found everywhere: roommates maintaining separate circles of friends; a student doing an independent study with a professor; two project team members preparing different parts of a large report; a child spending his first week away from home at camp.

In their early months or years of marriage, many married couples believe that they should have the same friends, enjoy the same leisure-time activities, like the same foods, or perhaps make all money decisions together. Often it takes some unhappy pulling and pushing before they can allow differences. Both partners can have a good weekend if occasionally she stays in the city, and he spends a weekend with his buddies at a cabin on the lake, or vice versa. Satisfaction does not require that they both pack up for the woods every time.

To feel good about your relationship with someone while you are apart is wonderful. When partners pursue separate interests and careers in an encouraging, supportive fashion, separateness is likely to be very fulfilling for both people.

Negative Separateness

The separate state may be charged with negative energy too. When one partner views the other's separate interests as an indication of disinterest or lack of commitment to their relationship, apartness threatens and tests the relationship. Intense fear and jealousy can erupt in this state when one partner thinks he or she is excluded or liked less than the outside interest. Feeling uncertain about where the partner is and what he or she may be doing, the person becomes anxious and unsure, unable to concentrate on studies or work. It can be agonizing. In such a situation separateness may also mean loneliness.

Another negative aspect of being separate is that partners spend so much of their energy on the outside interest that when they are together again, they really are not psychologically present. They are too exhausted and unable or unwilling to tune into one another.

Too much apartness may damage and destroy a relationship just as too much togetherness can stifle it. When the negative aspects of separateness override the positive ones, the relationship is probably in serious trouble.

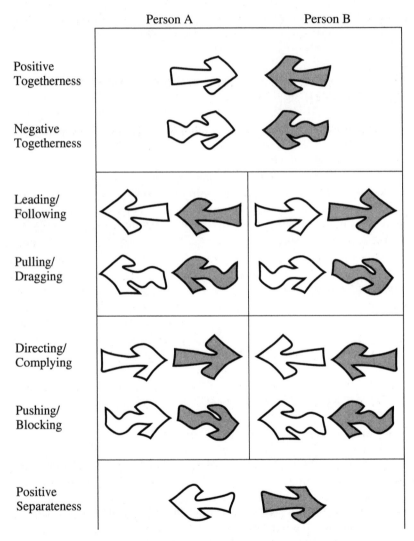

Figure 1.1 Possible Steps In An Interpersonal Dance

To summarize our discussion briefly, two people have a number of steps from which they choose their dance. At any point in time, they may be viewed in one of four basic states: (1) Togetherness; (2) Leading/Following, Pulling/Dragging; (3) Directing/Complying, Pushing /Blocking; or (4) Separateness. (In states two and three, either player can be leading/following, pulling/dragging or directing/ complying, pushing/blocking change.) All four general states have potential for generating positive or negative energy.

PRACTICAL USES OF THE INTERPERSONAL DANCE FRAMEWORK

Here are four basic ways to view relationships using the framework.

The Big Picture — Across Time

Think of some older couple (your parents, friends, or relatives) whom you know pretty well and whose relationship you have watched over the years. Use Figure 1.1 as a guide to fill in the percent of time and energy the couple have spent in each of the twelve relationship sub-states cumulatively across time. How would their percentages be distributed, making sure the figures sum to 100 percent? If their relationship was a traditional happy one, a great deal of time and energy would have accumulated in the man leading/woman following, and positive togetherness states. If their relationship appeared unhappy, perhaps a high percent of time would have been spent in a negative togetherness state or in the pushing/blocking state.

Think about your own most significant relationship. How does it distribute in Figure 1 over an extended period of time?

The Current Picture — A Cross-section

Use Figure 1.1 again to do the same mental exercise, only this time, limit the time-frame. For example, think of your relationship with someone (at home, school, or work) during the past month or week. How does your time and energy distribute in the different states? If things have been great lately, what has made it great in terms of your relationship states? If your relationship has not been good, do you find a buildup of various negative states?

If we looked at a cross-section of all our significant relationships, they would probably all have different patterns. Obviously, some patterns are more fun, productive, meaningful, or satisfying. Perhaps this helps explain why we are attracted to some relationships more than others.

A Collage — Areas of Your Life Together

You can use Figure 1.1 to look at your life together with a significant person in certain areas, such as leisure time, finances, work, friends, children, political interests, faith, and so forth. For example, a husband and wife might be positively together on faith and children, positively separate on work, pushing and blocking on finances, and in other transition states on friends and leisure time.

A Specific Moving Picture — An Issue Dance

Suppose you and your partner have a decision to make. Whether you actually stand face to face on an imaginary checker board and non-verbally dance out the decision or not, the two of you will dance out a decision. The process may involve selling, negotiating, planning, managing conflict, and decision-making.

If we videotaped the process, then ran it back in slow motion, a pattern would emerge composed of various steps from Figure 1.1. You would see a dynamic, step-by-step, sequential dance. This would occur regardless of whether you were deciding to buy a dog, planning a vacation, or looking at your schedules to determine how you could spend more time together over the next few weeks.

Let Your Fingers Do The Dancing

For fun, go back to Figure 1-1 and let your index finger represent you — Person A — in a dance, and your middle finger represent someone else — Person B — with whom you have a relationship. Now place your index finger in any state on a Person A arrow. Next, place your middle finger in the same or any other state on a Person B arrow. This represents your partner's step. Continue moving around the page alternating fingers as dance steps as you choreograph a real or imaginary dance.

VIABLE, LIMITED, AND TROUBLED RELATIONSHIPS

Over the years, we have found this relationship framework to be very helpful in understanding, assessing, and assisting in the change of relationships — our own and those of others with whom we have served as counselors, teachers, and consultants. We hope you will find it helpful too.

Our studied conclusion is that no single pattern is ideal for all relationships. Rather, we think each partnership has to find the mix that is mutually satisfying for both members.

Both partner's levels of satisfaction — your and your partner's mental, emotional, and spiritual condition — have much to do with how the two of you relate to each other. The more two people experience support, encouragement, intimacy, security, and care for each other, the more satisfying their relationship. In today's world, with all its opportunities for mobility, uncertainty, and fragmentation, we believe it takes all states to build and sustain a satisfying and productive relationship.

Viable Relationships

We have noticed that robust, viable friendships and marriages, as well as effective and productive business/professional/client relationships, work best when people move comfortably, confidently, and appropriately between all states. In these dances, partners are able to connect frequently, energize each other, lead/push, direct/pull for beneficial changes, and freely disconnect to pursue their individual work or interest separately. Most of the time the people involved are positively charged when they meet and deal with day to day issues and situations.

In viable relationships, the dance often varies across issues, because the issues vary. When the dances all start looking the same, regardless of the issues, unhappiness is likely to grow. The exception, of course, occurs when the pattern is the same across issues because both partners are satisfied with their dance.

A relationship may be quite satisfying yet have an issue around which partners keep stepping on each other's toes. However, strong partners in viable relationships do not let a difficult dance around a day-to-day issue become their dominant pattern.

Limited Relationships

Limited relationships, on the other hand, have reduced levels of mutual satisfaction or productivity and there are several reasons for this. First, in terms of the relationship framework, they do not use all available states. Second, if they do use all states, they spend disproportionate amounts of time in certain states to the regret of one or both partners.

This is true for symmetrical intimate relationships and for formal asymmetrical work and professional relationships as well. Either out of deference to authority or fear, hesitation and doubt, players only partially dance. They lack confidence together. They are too cautious, even hesitant, to connect — to exchange important information, openly disagree, yet back-up each other. Players seem shy about taking the lead, and are too kind to direct or push. In short, they fear negative consequences and, as a result, lack courage and gusto in relating to each other.

Limited relationships act more out of compulsion than choice and as a result are less flexible. Partners often feel secure but not fully pleased with their familiar routines. Some couples, for example, spend too much time together. They are afraid to act separately in more areas of their lives. Other couples hesitate to get close because they fear they will be consumed or would not be able to move apart. Still others feel guilty when they are apart, thinking they should be together. For all of these couples, life is not what it could be.

Troubled Relationships

Troubled relationships are not nurturing and satisfying relationships. Partners in these circumstances are out of step with each other — pushing and shoving, stepping on each other's toes, protecting turf, and repeatedly failing to connect. Their bodies and souls are out of sync; when they are together, they wish they were apart. They feed on negative energy and maintain a climate of tension, anger, and uncertainty.

Troubled relationships spend most of their time in negatively charged states — fighting, pushing, pulling the other to change, or remaining at a cold distance. Besides having a limited repertoire, their moves are either rigid and pressured, or chaotic and unpredictable. Expectations are either totally understood or completely unknown so there is little middle ground for negotiation. Partners frequently are either verbally or physically abusive; they are stuck, unable to effectively handle the ordinary day-to-day issues of living. Life in these relationships is not a satisfying experience; it is only a painful existence.

We will have more to say about viable, limited, and troubled relationships in Chapter 12, "Relationships As Systems."

CHANGING THE WAY YOU RELATE

From time to time we all feel frustrated with a relationship or with a particular way an issue is being decided. The Interpersonal Dance Framework helps you recognize what you specifically dislike about how you are relating (what you want to improve). It also shows you alternative states to choose from to improve things (where you want to go).

When things are not going well between partners, or an issue within a partnership is not going the way they would like it to go, the first thing each person usually tries is to change the other person. However, this creates a bigger problem: *when I am focused on changing you, and you in turn are focused on changing me, there is usually no change in our relationship-system.* As human checkers demonstrates, I cannot control you, and you cannot control me. We can only change or control our own behavior; we can only *ask for change* in the other.

ACTION, REACTION, INTERACTION

You will recall from the introductory chapter that your *action* becomes the stimulus to your partner's *reaction*. In turn, this becomes the basis for your *interaction* — your response to your partner's reaction in light of your original action. With these points in mind consider the following principles.

Principle #1 — It only takes one person to change a system — you or me — by changing the next step.

Each action, reaction, and interaction is a choice point. Therefore each person potentially has equal interactional power or control. You can either continue to act the same way, or you can choose different steps. You only give power or control to another person when you fail to exercise your own choices.

Principle # 2 — If it only takes one person to change a relationship pattern, then that person is me.

In CONNECTING, we operate on the assumption that if I change, the dance will change. When I change my typical action, reaction, or interaction, my partner will be responding to a different action.

Principle #3 — If what I am doing is not working, I should stop doing it, and do something else.

When we notice that things are not working, most of us continue doing what is not working, only we usually do it harder, longer, or louder. So if I am pushing, I push harder. If I am pulling back, I retreat further. We seem more comfortable continuing to do what we know is not working than face the uncertainty of change and this is self-defeating.

Principle # 4 — Nothing works all the time.

Sometimes even though you change your dance steps, things do not improve. Recognizing this, painful as it may be, puts you in a stronger position to manage your own life by accepting "what is" and either living with it or ending the friendship, job, or marriage. Too often, however, we take one step, see no immediate change, and say, "See, nothing's changed." Then we quit trying to change ourselves. While stunning changes can occur in a three-act sequence of action, reaction, and interaction, change typically requires a string of consistent different actions on your part — it takes time to trust real change.

COMMUNICATION MAPS

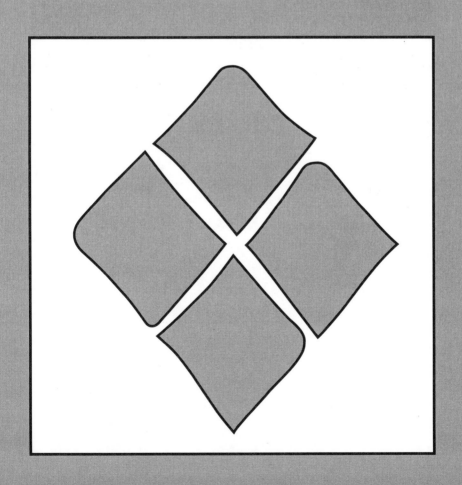

2

CONTENT, COMMUNICYCLE, AND CHANGE

CONTENT: THE FOCUS OF CONVERSATION

Think for a minute about how many different things you talk about in any one day. *What* you talk about — the content of your conversation — varies widely depending on the person with whom you are speaking. This is true because the nature of your relationship with someone — your respective positions, history, current dance, and anticipated future together — influences what you think is worthwhile and safe to discuss.

Types of Messages

The things, events, or persons referred to or talked about in your discussions are the *focus* of your conversations. We distinguish four different focuses of messages — topic, other, self, and relationship. A fifth type is a blending of topic with any of the other three.

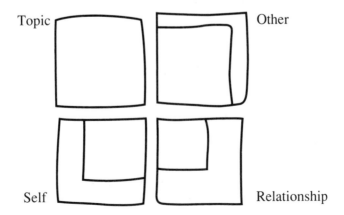

Topic Messages

A *topic message* focuses on things, events, ideas, places or people who are not immediately present. Topic messages include all statements that are not directly about you, the other person(s) present, or your relationship together — anything except me, you, us. People become a topic when they are not immediately present and you talk about them (kids, friends, parents, boss, for example):

"How much gas is in the car?"

"The game's on Friday night ."

"The kids sure have been restless today."

"The boss is back in town and seems happy."

Other Messages (Personal)

Other messages focus on the other person(s) present. They are statements you make directly to another person, such as your partner:

"What will happen if you don't hear by Wednesday?"

"How do you feel?"

"You really looked good at practice today."

"When will you be back?"

Self Messages (Personal)

A *self message* focuses on you, the speaker, as a person — your experiences, thoughts, feelings:

"I'm feeling confident."

"Guess what happened to me?"

"My leg doesn't hurt like it did."

"I'll be ready in a minute."

Self messages report some experience you have had, are having, or anticipate having.

Both self messages and other messages focus on a single person, *either you or me*. In this sense, their focus is *personal*. Because these messages are about either you or me, they express more personal involvement than topic messages.

Relationship Messages

The fourth kind of message also indicates a great deal of personal involvement. When you or the other person present say something about the two of you together — *you and me, or us* — you are expressing a *relationship message*. Relationship messages report the awareness you have *in relation to the other* and vice versa:

"I really feel pleased when you listen to me carefully."

"I think the two of us can handle any challenge."

"You think I'm stupid. Look who's talking."

"I love you."

"Do you approve of what I did?"

As a rule, relationship messages demonstrate or show evidence of relationship by talking about my/your reaction to my/your action or our interaction.

Blended-Focus Messages

We call the last type of messages *blended-focus messages*. Here topic messages are mixed with either self, other, or relationship messages. Most conversations have many blended-focus messages unless the speaker is focusing specifically on self, other, or the two of them in relationship to each other:

"I don't know if Ted saw me." (self-topic, person not present)

"What kind of car do you like best?" (other-topic)

"You surprised me by what you said about school." (relationship-topic)

It is rather difficult for two people to carry on a discussion for any length of time without bringing a third person or topic into the conversation. Like simultaneously looking into each other's eyes, purely personal and relationship messages, either as an intimate or hostile exchange, are often too close and powerful. The tendency "to bring in a third party" creates some distance and safety.

Of course, third parties are often a legitimate part of a situation, either as a source of information or a person to be considered, but the third party also provides a way of avoiding a you-me relationship issue at hand. Talking openly about someone not present is easier. Switching subjects, gossiping, blaming or scapegoating others, and sending issues to a committee can keep you off target.

Stop for a moment and recall some of the exchanges you have had recently with different people in terms of focus. Pay attention to how you feel about specific people depending on where they focus their conversations. Some connect with you; others do not. Some are energizing, others are draining. How do you think others experience you? Is your conversation balanced? In what way(s) would it be useful for you to shift your focus more often?

Topical, Personal, and Relationship Issues

Besides increasing your awareness and choice regarding what you talk about, knowing something about the difference between topic, other, self, and relationship messages has another important function. It also provides a context for understanding the types of issues which are important to your continued personal and partnership growth. Different issues correspond with different focuses.

Definition of Issue

What is meant by the term "issue?" We will be using the term frequently and our definition is as follows: *an issue may be anything which concerns one or both parties, usually involves a decision to be made, and is important for one or both of us.*

An issue is often the difference between "what is" and "what isn't" — where you are and where you want to be. Issues pop or slide into your awareness when *something changes.* Suddenly you are aware that an expectation is not being fulfilled or an unanticipated opportunity arises. You may have to understand what is going on, reflect on the implications, and decide to act or not act.

Issues arise out of normal everyday occurrences. Everyone has concerns in daily life; at different stages of development, different issues come into focus, and they may be positive or negative. For example, if my partner and I are comfortably settled in an apartment, we have no issue regarding our housing. But any number of things can change this: a decision to have a baby, a promotion opportunity in a different community, or a need for a place to study if one of us returns to school. And when something like this happens, when new pressures or options enter our life, a new set of issues emerge, such as where we are going to live, what we can afford, or how we are going to move. Sometimes issues like these raise an even more fundamental question: how we are going to make decisions about these things.

People face issues differently. Some go to great lengths to avoid them because they have never learned skills for working through issues effectively; others leave them to chance. We view issues as possibilities and challenges. Although some are painful and difficult at times, each issue is an opportunity for personal and relationship growth. Typically the earlier you can identify an issue, the more options you have for resolving it.

Our definition of issue assumes that each person is an authority on his or her own experience, so something does not have to be of concern to both partners in order for it to be an issue. If you are aware of or upset about something, it is an issue for you. Whether you disclose this concern to your partner is your choice. If you do share it, he or she in turn can acknowledge it as only your concern or as his or her concern as well.

While issues arise in any area of focus, as you move toward the core of one, you often move away from a topical focus to its impact on more personal and relational considerations. And although we make some distinction about focus of issues, we do not mean to imply that each focus is not important in its own right.

Occasionally, however, communication is confused by talking about an issue of one focus (topical for example) while your primary concern is really a personal or relationship issue. It is quite common, for example, for couples to irritate each other about money when, in fact, their conflict is really at a relationship level, a struggle for control.

Further, issues are not the same as problems. Issues are a natural part of life that come and go when they are successfully handled. In an average day you may make from fifty to a hundred decisions at work, home, school, and play. When concerns are successfully resolved they flow on through you; you may not even recall what yesterday's issues were.

Problems

If, however, you or your partner make a decision which does not work and the issue keeps unsuccessfully recycling, the issue can become a problem. For us *a problem is any issue which a person or partners are unable to resolve successfully on their own.* Frequently, parties to an issue become more rigid and polarized with each unsuccessful attempt at resolution. The problem overwhelms their use of immediate internal and external resources as means to a satisfactory solution. When this occurs, an outside expert — counselor, therapist, consultant, attorney — is often brought in to facilitate finding a solution.

An issue can also become a problem when you fail to identify it properly or simply refuse to face it. Research indicates that most families can handle their big issues (Curran, 1985). It is the little unresolved day-to-day decision-dances that can stress and destroy relationships.

To help you get a better handle on some of the issues most partnerships have to deal with at one time or another, we have grouped a number of them under three categories — topical, personal, relational.

Topical

housing	exercise	transportation
friends	drugs	contraception
education	family	pets
work	plans	moving
money	time	chores
career	space	projects
food	clothes	leisure

Personal — Other or Self (You or Me)

self-esteem	productivity	communication skills
identity	body/image	success
energy	responsibility	failure
values	expectations	appearance
freedom	faith	attitudes
recognition	habits	goals
health	creativity	death

Relational (You and Me, Us)

togetherness/apartness	celebration
closeness/distance	trust
privacy/company	affection
equality/subordination	commitment
stability/instability	sex
agreement/disagreement	acceptance
similarity/difference	rules
communication patterns	boundaries
inclusion/exclusion	conflict
collaboration/competition	power/control
understanding/misunderstanding	appreciation
decision-making	

Figure 2.1 Types of Issues

As you look over the list, think about which of the issues are important to you alone and to you with your partner? Can you identify some that you are currently dealing with and others which you find yourself avoiding? Can you locate some which have been important in the past as well as some that may become important? Perhaps you can identify some other concerns that are important to you but do not appear on this list.

The Focus of Issues: Its Effect on Risk and Intimacy

Conversations with different people take different shapes of focus. Some people's conversations are almost exclusively about topics; others attend primarily to the other person(s) present and say little or nothing about themselves. Some focus almost exclusively on themselves, with only brief interest in the other person(s) present, before shifting back to self again. Still others can talk appropriately and comfortably about topics, the other, self, and their relationship.

As you move the focus of your conversation with others away from topics and closer to the others, yourself, and your relationship, what you say becomes potentially more risky. This holds true regardless of whether an issue at hand is positive or negative. As you disclose more significant information about yourself, you reduce your control over the information by increasing options of others present for using the information for or against you. You cannot be sure how they will respond to what you say and what they will do with what you tell them.

Intimacy involves opening yourself to another person and becoming vulnerable to that person. This giving up control can be frightening, and rightly so. You must be wise and use good judgment about what you say to whom and how open you are willing to be.

A truly *intimate relationship* is one in which partners disclose themselves to each other, become mutually vulnerable, and do not take advantage of or hurt the other person. The trust that develops strengthens their relationship as they open themselves to each other.

Self-esteem influences your ability to be intimate. It is easier for people with high self-esteem to take risks because they expect to be heard and treated well; they do not expect rejection or abuse. When they are rejected, they feel its impact but are not disabled by it. They have enough confidence in their self-evaluation to deal with the situation effectively. More often the energy and confidence they bring to a situation creates payoff in the form of good connections from the risks they take.

Low self-esteem is not conducive to risk-taking. But while it is harder to take risks when you have low self-esteem, it is not impossible. Your energy is lower and your expectation of receiving a favorable response is also less. However, the choice remains yours — to risk or not to risk. Often simply the act of taking a risk leads to greater self-approval, even if you do not receive the desired response. You may just feel good about yourself for trying.

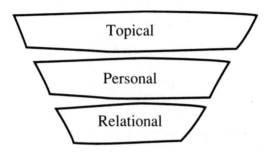

The important point is that in resolving issues and making decisions, it is crucial to recognize what is really going on, at what point of focus. Some changes necessitate work by focusing on the relationship which, in turn, can affect many topical issues. Other times it is best to focus on the topical or personal aspects of issues. In today's world, to be able to deal with the full spectrum of issues requires that couples possess awareness, skill, esteem, and even courage to risk.

COMMUNICYCLE: THE PROCESS OF CONVERSATION

Interpersonal communication is a circular, not linear, process — a communicycle. We coined the term *communicycle* to capture the essence of this circular process involving any particular message — topical, personal, or relational. If you lead a busy life, you probably complete a thousand communicycles a day.

Here is what is involved in a communicycle: (1) you verbally or nonverbally send a message to someone; (2) the other person sees or hears the message and responds (says or does something); (3) if what he or she says or does is satisfying, *you* internally close the loop and verbally or nonverbally register its completion. If for any reason the other's response is not satisfying to you, your communicycle (loop) remains open and unfinished.

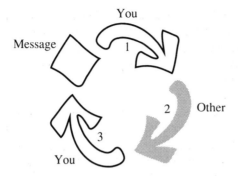

A simple example of a communicycle is asking a stranger what time it is:

"Excuse me, do you know what time it is?"

"Yes, 3:45."

"Thanks."

Your communicycle is complete. Your mind goes on to other things.

Here is an incomplete communicycle in a similar situation:

"Excuse me, do you know what time it is?"

"Late, I think. The bus already left."

"I don't want a bus. I just want the time."

Your communicycle is incomplete because you have not received the information you needed and, more important, new information has been introduced by the other person's response.

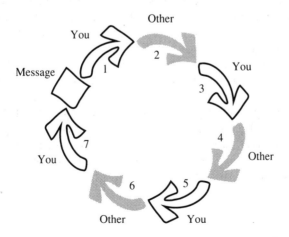

If a message is missed, misunderstood, or needs clarification, it frequently takes many more steps to complete the communicycle. Usually the cycle keeps building until the original message is satisfactorily communicated. For example, the graphic on the previous page illustrates a seven-step communicycle.

Completed communicycles punctuate conversations and move them forward. They signal confirmation and connection, but not always agreement with the message sent. Often they simply certify receipt of information or understanding of a message, which is all the sender hoped for in the first three-step communicycle above.

Effective communication is the process of closing your own loops and helping others close their loops. A key point to remember is that *the person who initiates the message is also the person who decides if the message has received an acceptable response.*

The *outcome* of any issue or relationship dance is determined to a large degree by the quality of the *process*, that is, by the way communicycles are completed or left unfinished. Incomplete communicycles can drive people nuts! People who say, "We don't communicate," often really mean, "We don't finish communicycles."

Impasse in the Communicycle

Have you ever experienced something like this — sending a message and having the other person take your message in another direction, away from your interests or expectations? Of course you have; we all have. That is what happens in the incomplete five-step impasse below. If the message has any importance, this usually leaves you feeling unfinished inside, and you typically carry this feeling until the other person eventually responds to your message in a way that enables you to close your loop.

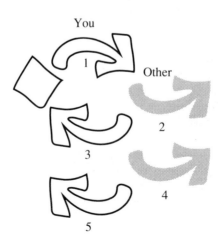

If you persist in trying to close your loop, and your partner persists in focusing in another direction, within five steps you will be in an *impasse*. The conversation can go on for nine, ninety, or three hundred and ninety exchanges across minutes, days, or months, and never change the pattern: the two of you are stuck. What began with a short five-step exchange, polarizes and solidifies into an angry standoff. Here is an example.

Tom: "I'd like to talk about that trip we are planning for early March. Are you up for that?"

Jean: "I suppose so, but only if we talk about the landscaping we want to do this summer too."

Tom: "Well I'm willing to discuss that, but not now. I want to take first things first, and the trip we planned with the Adamson's is coming up first, just a month and a half from now."

Jean: "I'm perfectly aware of that, but I insist we talk about the landscaping too because they're so closely related. First, there's the question of money. Second, we need to begin taking steps right now to line up some people to help us develop plans, figure out costs, and so forth."

Tom: "There will be plenty of money for both so let's just focus on the vacation first. I've been looking forward to this trip for a year. Do you have to mix up two things that are totally unrelated? Do you always have to make things more complicated than they are?"

Some communicycles take days or even months to complete and very important messages are often intentionally or unintentionally left as unfinished business between two people. Incomplete communicycles generate uncertainty, pressure, and stress.The misunderstandings that result from incomplete communicycles distance people, keep them from connecting, and leave people confused, frustrated, disappointed, and dissatisfied.

Pause for a few moments and think about an incomplete communicycle — some unfinished business — you may have with another person.

Complete and Incomplete Communicycles

When a response meets your expectations (thoughts, wants, and feelings), it is reflected in your facial expressions, head, and body movements. You experience an internal sense of completeness, even relaxation, at being understood and responded to adequately. If the responder misses, ignores, puts down or rejects your message, you will internally and externally register this too: your body and voice tone either increase in energy to meet the challenge or lose energy, signaling disappointment, confusion, or uncertainty.

In analyzing the effectiveness of their interpersonal communication, most people look for big changes, rather than monitor small changes in their communication-interaction. Yet, a successful conversation is really a string of small communicycles. Planning, decision-making, issue resolution, and negotiation can all be understood as a series of small complete or incomplete communicycles. When a conversation begins to go awry, it can often be traced to a particular turning point — one communicycle. Being aware of these potential turning points can make you a more effective communicator.

THE CHANGE MAP

Every relationship, group, and larger organization is constantly balancing stability with change. Issues are frequently the focal point of change. While many issues remain stable, new ones continually arise and occasionally old ones resurface. *The process of how issues are handled determines to a large extent the success of their outcome for everyone involved.*

Issues often first come up in an imbedded "pinch message." Here are several examples.

"I need the car tonight."

"Have you looked at our checking account recently?"

"I missed your call last night."

"Sales dropped last quarter."

"I saw a job posted for Phoenix today."

"Bob seemed unusually friendly with you last night."

"Tuition is going up next fall."

"Your sister called and mentioned they might drive out this way this summer."

Partners equipped with skills for monitoring their own interaction and effectively expressing their awareness are better able to spot critical issues early and, by planning change, prevent major disruptions.

When people lack the ability to deal explicitly with issues, they often act out their negative feelings and escalate a pinch message into a major disruption. On the other hand, a relatively simple personal concern is less likely to evolve into a complex relationship issue when parties are able to tune into their feelings and wants, identify the issue(s) involved, and openly discuss alternative solutions.

Figure 2.1 outlines the options for dealing with issues. Start with stability — at the middle of the figure — and trace out the options.

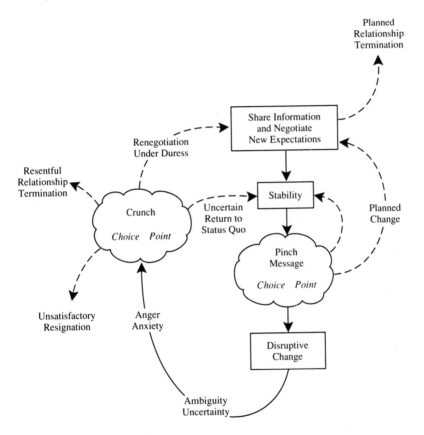

Figure 2.1 The Change Map
Adapted by the authors from Sherwood and Scherer, 1975.

The Change Map applies to any type of relationship — spouse, friend, family, boss, client, patient, colleague. Take a few minutes and compare the way you typically handle issues for two of your relationships.

The rest of CONNECTING presents additional communication and relationship maps as well as practical skills for helping you complete your own and others' communicycles as you deal with important issues and build fulfilling relationships.

3

STYLES OF COMMUNICATION:
Small and Shop Talk;
Control, Fight, and Spite Talk

Have you ever had someone talk to you about something you were interested in, but the way the person spoke to you put you off so much you could not really hear what he or she had to say? The style interfered with the message.

Each time you say something, your message contains two parts: *what* you say — the content, and *how* you say it — the style. (The *content* of a conversation can have a topical, personal, or relational focus, as described in Chapter 2, "Content, Communicycle, and Change," and it can be about any of the issues listed in Figure 2-1.) Many people think that they change the nature of their conversation by simply shifting content — the *focus of what* they talk about. But while changing *what* you talk about has an impact, your messages are most dramatically changed by shifting *style* — by shifting *how* you talk about something.*

The *style* of communication is a command message. It tells others how to "take your message" about the content — whether you are joking, serious, angry, pleased, or pressured. Style captures both the visual (nonverbal body language) and the oral (tone and inflection) aspects of a message which portray your underlying intentions. The basic function of style is to clarify and facilitate the content of a message. Style can also either help you complete communicycles or create impasses.

This Chapter introduces you to the Communication Styles Map and specifically to Styles I and II. Chapter 4 will present the remaining two communication styles, III and IV.

Because each style has its own set of characteristic intentions and behaviors, we are going to present a list of intentions and behaviors for each style. Do not try to memorize the lists — use them as a guide to help you recognize your own and others' use of styles.

---

*Material presented in Chapters 3 and 4, is based on the seminal work of William F. Hill and the *Hill Interaction Matrix*.

COMMUNICATION STYLES MAP

How you talk to someone falls into one of four major categories, as shown in The Communication Styles Map:

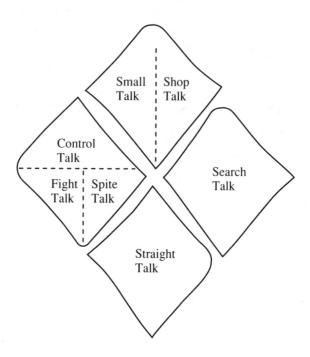

Knowing the differences between styles and being able to use each style is central to being an effective communicator. The Styles Map helps you:

1. Understand how you talk and how you can increase your conversational range by adding more styles.

2. Learn how to talk safely about explosive or delicate issues in your life by being more alert to your own style, the other person's style, and which styles to use to connect.

3. Recognize stress signals — your own and others — earlier, so that you can deal more effectively with interpersonal pressure and resistance.

4. Make deliberate connections rather than accidental ones by increasing your choices for relating.

5. Use communication to raise your self-esteem and to show esteem for others.

Different Ways to Talk About the Same Issue

Before we look at each style in more detail, notice how the same issue — money — is introduced in each style.

Style I   *Small Talk:* "It's sure hard to make ends meet these days."

Shop Talk: "Last month we spent two-hundred-fifty dollars more than we took in."

Style II   *Control Talk:* "We've got to rein in our spending, or we're going to end up with a big debt."

Fight Talk: "If you'd stop throwing away money like you do, we wouldn't have any problems."

Spite Talk: "When I do come in under budget, no one around here ever says thanks."

Style III   *Search Talk:* "I wonder what it is that causes us to have so much trouble controlling our spending. Maybe we could take a look at how we make decisions about money."

Style IV   *Straight Talk:* "I'm concerned about our spending. Last month we spent two-hundred-fifty dollars more than we took in, and we did the same thing the previous two months. I'm frightened because it's so easy to run up a big debt quickly. Would you be willing to talk with me about what we can realistically do?"

Now we will take a closer look at these different ways of communicating. Here are their characteristics and the situations in which they are useful.

STYLE I — SMALL TALK AND SHOP TALK

Small Talk and Shop Talk are the sociable styles most often used to maintain the status quo and exchange routine information. The content is common, ordinary, everyday fare; expectations are clear and tacitly agreed upon and little or no tension exists. Emotions are on an even keel. Tone of voice and pace of speech are normal and even-handed.

SMALL TALK

This friendly, conventional, and sometimes playful style keeps the world going around smoothly. When you want to relax, or keep things moving in an easy and light way, you are most likely to use Small Talk. It is the way you move in and out of conversations — in person or on the phone — with your friends, family, boss, customers, clients and strangers.

In Small Talk your intentions are to be pleasant, find out how the other person is, and not rock the boat. Conversations usually revolve around the weather, news, sports, daily routines, family, special events, and other topics of general interest.

Characteristics of Small Talk

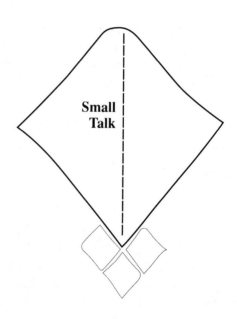

Intention to be
friendly
sociable
relaxed
playful

Intention to
build rapport
keep in touch

Actions
greetings
telling stories
playing
joking
describing
commenting

Mood/Nonverbals
relaxed
cordial
comfortable

Cues
conventional topics
daily routines
special events

Small Talk

Typical Small Talk Behaviors

Hellos and good-byes: "How are you doing today?" "See you later."

Passing the time: "Who do you think will win the election?"

Storytelling: "You wouldn't believe what happened to me last night. As I got into my car..."

Joking: "Who do you think you are — the mayor?"

Catching up: "What did you do today?"

Sharing events of the day: "Michael called from Germany today. He said that Claudia finished med school."

Observing: "I noticed there is a message for you by the phone."

Exchanging common preferences, opinions, values: "I would rather sail than camp this weekend"; "I think the media are doing a good job so far"; "My friends are really important to me."

Discussing biographical data, personal traits, habits, health, appearances: "I grew up in Denver"; "You've got a quick wit"; "I seldom miss breakfast"; "My shoulder has been sore lately"; "It looks to me like you've lost weight."

Partying: "It's time to celebrate!"

Impact

Some people think Small Talk is a waste of time and too much is. But do not underestimate its impact on people and relationships. While you are small talking, you are also letting each other know important information about yourselves: experiences, likes and dislikes, interests, values, and fantasies. With Small Talk you begin to build rapport by relating to the other person's interests and sharing your own, discovering both commonalties and interesting differences. Learning about each other as people builds comfort and paves the way for the development of trust. In a sense, Small Talk puts a deposit in your "relationship bank." Later, when you need to ask a favor or when you hit some tough times together (tension or disagreements), you have a fund of good will to draw upon.

Small Talk serves other purposes as well:

1. It can be used to shift topics, change pace, rest your mind.

2. It gives you clues to another person's current mental, physical, and emotional state. It tells you how close you can get, and whether this is a good time to bring up a certain subject.

3. Often, it suggests positive pairing between the two people in conversation, and it indirectly demonstrates the basic fondness and attraction they feel for one another. For example, if there is no hostile undercurrent as two people joke with each other, they are showing mutual affection without saying directly, "I like you — I have fun with you."

4. It is also used to ease tension or avoid issues.

Tips

1. Remember that much of Small Talk is just talking about the obvious: the weather, the news, or what is happening on your job. Other people will usually pick up on what you say. Keep this in mind if you find Small Talk hard to do. (It is surprising how many people find it difficult.)

2. Get other people to tell their stories. People's stories tell a lot about who they are and listening helps you to connect with them.

3. Tell a few stories about yourself too because almost everyone enjoys a good story. Be sure to put some energy into what you say, and watch others' responses. Some people talk too much and do not notice other people's cues to stop talking. Experiment with different ways of gaining positive responses.

4. Watch nonverbals. They give you a baseline from which you can recognize other people's moods and attitudes and the presence of unspoken issues. It is very difficult to enjoy a free and refreshing exchange if there is real tension between you and your partner. Uncomfortable silence, unusual seating arrangements, body posture, and lack of eye contact in normal Small Talk situations signal that something is wrong. Small Talk is one way to get a reading on the climate of your relationship.

5. Realize the value of Small Talk for negotiation. It is hard to negotiate effectively with others when you know little or nothing about their interests, likes, and dislikes. Small Talk provides some of this information.

6. Use jokes. Sometimes a joke (with no "zinger") is a good way to relieve tension. But Small Talk should not be used to sidetrack a serious discussion. Small Talk is inadequate and inappropriate for resolving meaty issues.

SHOP TALK

Whatever your daily "work" is — corporate, professional, homemaker, or student — Shop Talk is essential for carrying on most everyday activities. In Shop Talk you focus on work-related matters — keeping an eye on how jobs are progressing or maintaining and generating information to get tasks done. During the average day, you may have more than a hundred exchanges in Shop Talk. For example:

John (first roommate): "Did you plan to eat dinner here tonight or will you be at work?"

Hal (second roommate): "I'm hoping to get off work early, and I might eat here, but I might go straight to the library to work on my history paper."

John: "Well I was going to stop at the store, and I'd pick up some food for you if you want me to. I'm cooking spaghetti tonight, and I'm willing to cook for both of us if that would be a help."

Hal: "That would be great. I think I'll be here at six, but I've got to get to the library by seven. Does that fit your plans?"

John: "Yeah. I'll take care of dinner for us."

Characteristics of Shop Talk

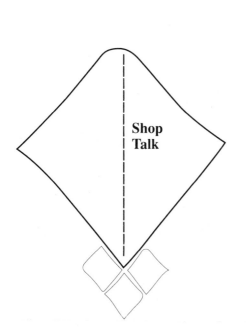

Intention to be
competent
informed
productive
profitable
cooperative

Intention to
gather/give information
monitor activities and
schedules

Actions
describing
reporting
checking up
following up

Mood
polite
matter-of-fact
business-like

Cue Words
Routine who, what, where,
when, and how questions

Typical Shop Talk Behaviors

Reporting: "The lab tests are a false positive."

Providing facts: "Growth was a modest seven percent this quarter."

Catching up: "Did anything exciting happen while I was out of town?"

Checking up: "When will the press run be finished?

Scheduling: "How about having lunch together tomorrow and going over the outline for the report?"

Making routine decisions: "John will handle A through F, Sarah G through N, and I'll do the rest."

Passing on messages or requests: "Your husband called and said he'd pick up the kids on his way home."

Impact

Shop talk is somewhat more formal than Small Talk because it can be used to maintain some distance between people in different positions — a student talking to a professor at an open-house, or a supervisor on break with employees, for example.

People like to know what each other does for a living so Shop Talk is also a comfortable way to converse in social situations. Once people sort each other out, they can risk moving to other styles. However, the content of a Shop Talk conversation usually stays topical (company politics, happenings in the organization, for instance) rather than personal (two men talking about how mid-life is impacting them).

Tips

1. Realize the difference between the two types of Style I. Shop Talk sounds a lot like Small Talk, but it focuses more on routine activities like maintenance, coordinating schedules or planning projects.

2. Notice the amount you use Shop Talk. Shop Talk is essential for functioning in our daily lives, both on and off the job. However, see if spending an excessive amount of time "talking shop" prevents you and another person from sharing your lives in other ways.

STYLE II — CONTROL TALK, FIGHT TALK, AND SPITE TALK

Even though Style II is next to Style I numerically, there is a world of difference between the two of them. The major intention behind Style II is to gain agreement or compliance, shooting for a certain outcome even if it has to be forced. The focus is on your partner, instead of yourself, on getting him or her to agree or comply. Style II is used when you want to be persuasive and control what is happening or what will happen. Most

Style II statements involve interpretations (who or what is right or wrong) and actions (what your partner should or should not do).

Basically, there are three different ways people exert their power in Style II. The first way — Control Talk — sends messages intended to be constructive. The other two — Fight Talk and Spite Talk — send negative, potentially destructive messages.

CONTROL TALK

Control Talk is very common in everyday conversations. When you want to compliment, praise, persuade, or direct, it is a natural style to use. Most selling, directing, bargaining, supervising, teaching, advocating, and preaching activities go on in Control Talk. In fact, it would be impossible for a society to exist without Control Talk. (That is a Control Talk statement in itself!)

Since the main purpose of Control Talk is to gain agreement or compliance, you know you have been effective when others follow through on your directives.

Characteristics of Control Talk

Intention to be
in charge
helpful
persuasive

Intention to
lead
direct
persuade
instruct
set expectations/limits
evaluate
positively reinforce
use legitimate authority
gain agreement/compliance

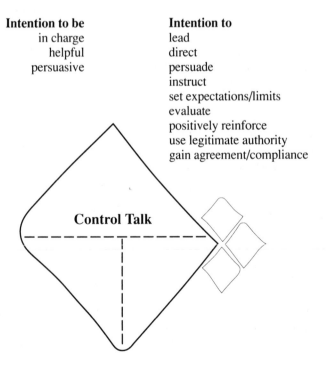

Control Talk

Actions	Cue words
directing	you, we, it pronouns
instructing	statements phrased as
advising	questions
evaluating	imperative (don't,
cautioning	should, have to)
selling	superlatives (always,
prescribing	never, super)
praising	assumptions

Mood
energized
authoritative

Typical Control Talk Behaviors

Directing: "Call the garage and tell them you need the car by 1:30."

Instructing, assigning: "There are three major classifications to look for in Chapter Six. Read the chapter and look over discussion questions, three through ten, on page 123 in preparation for Thursday's class."

Setting expectations, establishing boundaries: "You understand, don't you, that you need to be back here by 9 p.m., or we'll go without you?"

Advising: "You have to take your time with Max. You can't push him."

Challenging: "Give me one good reason why we can't finish the project on time."

Cautioning/warning: "Be careful when you lift that box. The bottom is weak."

Using statements phrased as questions: "Don't you think that...?"; "Wouldn't you agree that...?"

Advocating: "Just try it once. If you don't like it, I won't say anything more."

Assuming: "We're all morning people and could meet at 7 a.m.

Selling: "You'd have a super evening with Jack and Lynn."

Evaluating: "This procedure is twice as good as the old way."

Praising: "You look great in your new blue suit."

Pronouncing: "This is the last time we'll have to think about this."

False futuring: "If you do all your practicing, then I'll consider what you're asking."

Prescribing/Imposing solutions: "Here's how to handle it. Just call Mark and tell him to hold off one week."

Impact

Control Talk is an action-oriented communication style, proactive and efficient. When it is used in a manner that counts the other people involved, it commands respect and confidence. Unless there is some legitimate question or alternative to consider, Control Talk gains agreement and compliance when it is used appropriately.

Most people like and accept direction when it is needed. In fact, they become anxious and disorganized when they do not know what the goals are or when they do not receive feedback on progress made in achieving them. However, when Control Talk offends, it breeds resistance and resentment which usually draws Fight or Spite Talk.

Here are some tips which will help you to use Control Talk more effectively.

Tips

1. Watch others' nonverbal signs of compliance; their responses indicate the effectiveness of your directive. Nonverbals are the best indicators. You will see spontaneous, compliant head and body movements when agreement is there. Agreement comes more easily when the directive fits the situation and is not forced.

2. Notice noncongruence. People frequently say "yes" with words, but "no" with their bodies. Look and listen for "no's": a small shake of the head, a facial grimace, or a down tone in the voice. Subtle nonverbals are tough to control consciously. Consequently, they give you a more accurate reading of what another person is really thinking or feeling. If what you see does not match the words, question further. For example, "It doesn't look like you buy what I'm saying. Is that accurate?"

3. Recognize limitations of Control Talk. Most of the time when we get noncompliance, we just start pushing harder, louder, and faster in Control Talk. This only increases pressure, makes everyone more rigid, and stirs up Fight Talk. When Control Talk is not working, stop doing it! Shift to listening or talking in a more productive style.

4. Recognize the need for more information. At its best, Control Talk is brief, to the point, and efficient. But its strength is also its weakness because frequently listeners need more extensive information. People like to be included in making decisions which

affect them; no one likes to be ordered around: "Do this, do that, don't ask why, just comply." When they signal through words or nonverbals that they want more information, shift to another style. This will help you complete your Communicycle.

5. Take responsibility. To be an effective communicator, sometimes you have to set limits — say "no" or "stop" and mean it. To do this you have to feel comfortable and confident accepting responsibility for the consequences of your stand.

6. Be aware of what too much Control Talk signals. When you or your partner find yourself using a considerable amount of Control Talk, it may be an early signal that you are experiencing mounting pressures in your lives. Suddenly, most of your time together is spent directing each other around, and you are stuck in an "efficiency dance" — doing what you have to do to get through the current situation. Besides not being very nurturing to each other, you may be heading for an explosion in Fight Talk. Look at excessive Control Talk as a signal of rising tension and shift to a more self and other nurturing style.

How Does Style II Fit the Interpersonal Dance Framework?

Style II communication is used most often in the Leading/Following, Directing/Complying, Pulling/Dragging and Pushing/Blocking *transition states* of the Interpersonal Dance framework. When one person wants to lead the other in a new direction, or direct him or her to do something, and if the second resists and does not readily follow or comply, their dance can easily take a negative step. The dance will shift to Pulling/Dragging or Pushing/Blocking, using one of the next two negative styles: Fight Talk or Spite Talk. Unless they move out of these styles, they will slide into Negative Togetherness.

Our research on styles found that when one partner *acted* with a negative Style II comment, 80 percent of the time the second partner *reacted* with a negative Style II comment. If the first person *interacted* in the same style, the fight was on. Control is a powerful force. It is hard not to get hooked into fighting for it.

FIGHT TALK

Partner (fixed eyes, tightness through neck and shoulders, holding smoking cooking pot): "Now look what you've done. Our meal is ruined! You never listen to me. How could you be so stupid! I told you to turn the burner down, not up."

Sound familiar? Almost everyone has either heard or said something like this. These kinds of statements are usually made in anger and frustration when there has been some break in expectations: a change in plans, shortage of time, money, or energy. They also pop up when expectations are unclear or when partners are feeling pressure.

Fight Talk puts someone down. It masks a "you dummy" message. It attempts to force change by getting others to agree. As you verbally push and pull, emotions run high. Language is direct, aggressive, and often punitive.

In Fight Talk situations, people act out their feelings and desires instead of recognizing and coping with them. People listen to each other only to support their own view; they focus on getting their own way instead of looking for acceptable solutions. Since it is assumed only one person can be in charge, choices are eliminated. Tone of voice and choice of words signal tension and negative feelings.

Both parties try to blame each other for the problem, rather than considering how each has contributed to it; introspection is completely bypassed as both people look outside for answers. Fight Talk is a reactive, rather than a proactive, style of communication.

Characteristics of Fight Talk

Intention to be
right
justified
sometimes hurtful

Intention to
force change
defend self
avoid responsibility
hide fear or vulnerability
intimidate
bluff
compete/win

Actions
demanding
blaming
attacking
threatening
listening defensively
putting other down

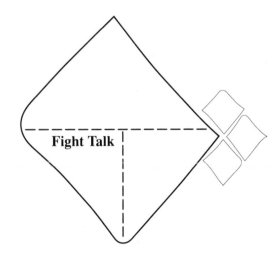

Mood	**Cue Words**
tense	you — pronoun
anxious	why questions
aggressive	don't, should, have to
hostile	always, never, every
abusive	assumptions
	labels

Typical Fight Talk Behaviors

Demanding, ordering: "Do it like I say, and don't ask me why."

Blaming, accusing, attacking: "Why'd you break it? And don't tell me you didn't. I saw you with my own eyes."

Threatening consequences: "Say that one more time and I'll ground you for a week."

Labeling: "You're lazy and irresponsible."

Name-calling, belittling, using loaded words: "Look at the way you're eating. Don't eat like a pig."

Defending: "You're not so smart yourself. Let's hear your great idea if you've got one."

Interrogating: "Tell me what you're thinking. You just sit there with that stupid smile and don't say anything."

Mind reading: "I know what you're thinking, but you're wrong!"

Judging/putting down: "You never do it right! If you had a brain, you wouldn't know what to do with it."

Taunting: "Your mother's favorite son could never do anything wrong."

Ventilating: "Why do you always do it this way?"

Falsely assuring/sympathizing: "Look, forget it! You'll get over it in no time."

Moralizing/preaching: "You shouldn't even let those thoughts enter your head."

Challenging motives: "That's not why you said that. You just want to get smart with me."

Bragging: "When I was your age, I could work three times as hard as you."

Psychologizing, diagnosing: "I suggest you find the real cause of your defensiveness. You're paranoid."

What is Behind Fight Talk?

While Fight Talk is direct, it is unclear — direct in its focus on the other person, but unclear about what is really going on beneath the anger. Often when people feel fear, frustration, or sadness they use Fight Talk to cover their vulnerability. They attack others rather than take responsibility for what they are really experiencing inside. They use Fight Talk to cover their fear of having a real or imagined weakness discovered by others:

- failing in something
- losing someone or something
- being incompetent
- being excluded, isolated
- being held responsible and blamed
- being taken advantage of
- not getting something that is important to them
- experiencing bad consequences of their actions or decisions

When your own esteem (desirability, judgment, skill, worth) is questioned, threatened, or attacked, you think you are vulnerable. That is when Fight Talk may come into play and you take a stance of superiority to cover your desperation. You try to overpower the other person because you doubt your own ability to deal candidly with your fears.

Impact

In Fight Talk you are out of control, off balance, and out of touch with your self-awareness. In your desperation, you are literally straining yourself physically and emotionally and sending stress signals to others.

The focus of Fight Talk is always on the other person, never on yourself. In your rush to get others to change, you overlook or avoid your own contribution and response to the situation. You fight fire with fire. Your *acting out* rather than *acting on* your feelings actually fans anger, fear, and resentment. While Fight Talk gets juices flowing and may break up a log jam once in awhile, its success is short-lived if it is used often. It does not promote positive long-term solutions to tough relationship issues. Instead, it can erupt in emotional and physical violence which undermines and destroys relationships.

Tips

1. Do not get caught up in Fight Talk. Since Fight Talk mainly indicates there is a deeper issue not being attended to, use it as a cue to expand your own and others' awareness about the real issue. Ask yourself, "What's behind my Fight Talk? What do I fear?"

2. Read on. If others see you as an "abrasive" person — someone who relies heavily on Fight Talk — and you want to change the way you communicate, keep reading CONNECTING. We will show you how to use your self and other awareness and new communication skills as powerful resources for connecting better with others.

3. Evaluate your impact. Fight Talk is not always loud and aggressive. What you intend as Control Talk may be taken as Fight Talk by the other person. *The meaning of a message is in its impact, not its intention.* Watch the other person's nonverbal cues to judge your impact.

4. Believe your body signals. When you feel tension in your head, neck, chest or shoulders during a conversation, check your style. You are probably already in Fight Talk, or at least headed that way. Take your internal body cues seriously; they will tell you when to shift to a more useful style.

5. Do not try to deal with others rationally when they are using Fight Talk. Instead, pick up on the underlying "sore" spot — their anger, fear, or resentment. See Chapter 14, "Communicating Under Pressure," for more information on how to respond to Fight Talk.

SPITE TALK

Partner (low energy, dejected body posture): "See if I care what you do. You don't give a hoot about what I think anyway."

If Fight Talk is conventional warfare, Spite Talk is guerrilla warfare. The first is angry, direct, and covers fear. The second is resentful, indirect, and covers hurt. Spite Talk is a passive, "powerless" way to exert power, used when people believe they have no influence. There is great power in passive spiteful non-compliance.

Spite Talk communicates a "poor me" attitude. It can represent a long-term, mind-style/lifestyle of low self-esteem, or more commonly, a temporary response to a particular situation. In either case, Spite Talk drains a partner's energy, puts him or her off, and is unattractive to be around — unless two spiteful folks get together and "enjoy" their misery.

Watch for people engaged in Fight Talk and Spite Talk. Pay particular attention to subtle facial and head gestures. You will see the energy in Fight Talk as forceful, but the energy in Spite Talk is diffused or dissipated.

In terms of a dance, the harder the aggressor pushes or pulls, the more withdrawn the passive person becomes, getting quiet or dragging along. This passivity may drive the aggressor wild, even to the point of striking out physically.

Characteristics of Spite Talk

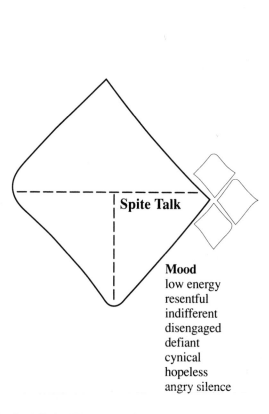

Intention to be
noticed
pitied
seen as helpless
uncooperative

Intention to
get even
make other feel guilty
protect self
thwart change
cover hurt

Actions
sniping
sulking
withholding
delaying
denying
placating
complaining
gossiping
excusing
putting self down

Mood
low energy
resentful
indifferent
disengaged
defiant
cynical
hopeless
angry silence

Cue words
they, no one
never, every

Typical Spite Talk Behaviors

Shooting zingers, taking potshots: "You do it; that's what they pay you those big bucks for. "

Implying poor me — ain't it awful: "Everyone else gets invited and has a good time. Nobody ever asks me if I want to go."

Gossiping: "Do you know what I heard? Mark is having an affair with his secretary."

Nagging: "Do I always have to remind you to take off your shoes when you come in?"

Foot-dragging: "I know I said I'd do it. When I have time, I'll get around to it."

Distracting/diverting: "How come you're talking to me about this? Mike and Jane had the idea first."

Fogging (using a lot of words that really don't make sense): "Yeah, you know what, if you want to then I will, so go ahead, until it happens."

Complaining, whining: "How come I always have to do the dirty work?"

Pouting/ignoring/withholding affection (going about business in silent unresponsiveness)

Withholding information: "I told you once. If you don't remember what I said, I'm not going to repeat it."

Lying: "I tried to call you" (when no attempt was made to call).

Withdrawing angrily: "It's not my problem. They made their own bed, now they'll just have to sleep in it."

Denying: "No, nothing's wrong. What makes you think that?"

Mean jokes: "Ann just sent the new aide down to the supply room for a couple of fallopian tubes."

Sarcasm: "Well, look who's graced us with her presence."

Placating: "No, that's all right. Let's do it your way. I'm sure it will come out better."

Being a martyr or victim (covering for others, accepting blame): "It was probably my fault again. I should have..."

Putting self down: "If I wasn't so dumb, I would have caught the mistake."

Being self-righteous: "I would never think of stooping that low."

Keeping score/reprisals: "I won't forget what you just said."

What Is Behind Spite Talk?

Spite Talk grows out of a sense of powerlessness, hurt and jealousy. When people believe they have little say and very few choices in a situation, their anger turns to spite. The passive person waits to be noticed or take a shot, rather than gather energy to express his or her thoughts, feelings,and wants in a more constructive style.

Impact

Spite Talk tries to exert control from the bottom up. It is an obtuse way to express helplessness and hopelessness. Deep sighs, down-turned eyes, slouched posture, low energy, score keeping, noncommittal answers to questions, topic changes, and silence (the quiet angry type), followed by a denial that anything is wrong are all attempts to make the other person feel guilty by saying, "Poor me, ain't it awful."

Spite Talk is also a good way to hit and run. Hitting is usually below the belt and running avoids taking responsibility. It is an underhanded way of saying, "The way I've been treated justifies my not getting involved to make positive changes."

In the long run, people hurt themselves by discounting their own power. ("Don't ask me to say anything. I'd die before I'd say anything directly to George about that.") Yet the same person may talk to all sorts of people who cannot do anything about the situation. What is the result? Again, fear undercuts the possibility of change and nothing happens for the better.

Spite Talk situations are very draining. Energy and information are dissipated rather than channeled into productive output.

Tips

1. Consider the nature of the Spite Talk situation or pattern. Spite Talk may signal a temporary situation or reflect a person's mindstyle/lifestyle. Temporary situations say, "You are overlooking me." They can be fixed rather quickly. A mind/life pattern takes more effort to alter, and perhaps it cannot be changed unless the spiteful person takes steps to help himself or herself.

2. Reflect on your own use of Spite Talk. If you find yourself in Spite Talk frequently and want to change this way of communicating, keep reading CONNECTING. We will show you how to use your self- and other-awareness and communication skills to enhance your self-esteem, increase your alternatives, and bring more positive energy to your partnerships.

3. Learn how to handle Spite Talk. When others are stuck in Spite Talk, there is a natural tendency to try to get them to talk about what is bothering them. When you ask what is wrong, you are often met with, "Nothing." The harder you try, the less you get. The more you pull, the more they resist, certainly a difficult situation. See

Chapter 14, "Communicating Under Pressure" for a detailed discussion on how to handle Spite Talk.

SIMILARITIES AND DIFFERENCES OF CONTROL, FIGHT, AND SPITE TALK

There are enough similarities among the three kinds of Style II communication that Control Talk can be confused with Fight Talk and Spite Talk. They all share a number of language cues, as indicated in the diagrams for each style:

- you-statements
- question-statements
- why-questions
- imperatives
- superlatives
- assumptions

They also share the same basic intentions: to control, persuade, and gain agreement or compliance. However, in Control Talk, the speaker wants to take the other person into account too. In Fight Talk and Spite Talk, there is no intention to do this. Rather, the speaker focuses entirely on his or her own benefit.

Given the similarities in language and intention, a fine line separates the three subtypes of Style II messages. What one partner intends as Control Talk can easily be read by the other as Fight Talk. And too much Control Talk can be overbearing, resulting in a Fight Talk reaction. While directives are necessary, too many are risky. People do not always take kindly to them.

Fight and Spite Talk are hazardous to self-esteem, your own as well as your partner's. While sometimes mistakenly used to motivate, these styles mostly just create more stress.They put down a person instead of focusing on the behavior or issue at hand. Soon the issue shifts and becomes the relationship itself.

Limited communicators get stuck in Fight or Spite Talk. They do not have the flexibility, skill, or courage to move beyond their own fears and reach out to their partner by taking responsibility for their part in an issue. Everyone gets trapped in Fight or Spite Talk from time to time. But effective communicators recognize these styles as "pinch" messages which say something needs attention. They treat Fight and Spite Talk as a signal to shift to the more constructive styles: Search Talk and Straight Talk.

4

STYLES OF COMMUNICATION:
Search Talk and Straight Talk

Most everyday exchanges are carried on in Small Talk, Shop Talk, and Control Talk. The first two keep the world running smoothly with chit chat and conversation about daily routines, and Control Talk takes charge or attempts to change things.

Fight Talk and Spite Talk signal tension and underlying issues that are going unattended. None of the styles described so far are effective for talking directly, openly, and constructively about uncertain and complex issues. This chapter introduces you to two additional styles that are appropriate and productive for these kinds of issues. We call them Search Talk and Straight Talk.

STYLE III — SEARCH TALK

The intentions involved in Style III — Search Talk — are quite different from those of Styles I and II. Rather than trying to keep things smooth or to control and create change when uncertainties arise, the intention of Style III is to stop your dance, step aside for a while, and have a look at what is happening. In doing so you overview the situation and gain perspective by seeing what surrounds the issue, what has happened in the past, or what might happen in the future.

Search Talk is sometimes confused with Small Talk or Shop Talk because their tones are similar. However, their characteristics are quite different.

Search Talk always revolves around *non-routine* matters, uncertain and complex issues that may be very fuzzy and undefined. Small and Shop Talk only consider issues insofar as it is necessary to make *routine* decisions. And though Style I may include background information, it is usually part of the reporting of an event and does not lead to the deeper understanding that occurs in Style III.

Like Styles I and II, Search Talk concentrates on other people and outside events and omits direct reporting of personal feelings. It is essentially an objective, intellectual, and rational style of communication as it explores facts and examines possibilities.

Search Talk has a tentative quality to it: in the process of gaining an overview, you can use it to speculate about causes, pose solutions, and play out various scenarios without committing yourself to any particular direction. It is a safe way to "test the water" by making observations or raising questions to get a handle on things. Though a variety of solutions may surface as part of the examination process, Search Talk avoids making a definite commitment to any one of them.

Characteristics of Search Talk

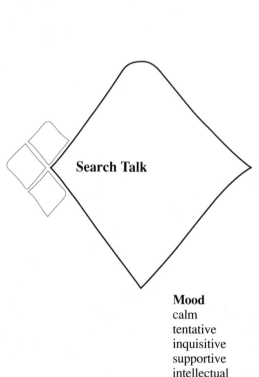

Intention to be
insightful
rational
expansive
safe

Intention to
gain overview or insight
clarify situations
search for causes
generate options
evaluate alternatives
seek or listen to advice

Actions
exploring
brainstorming
reflecting
analyzing
elaborating
reasoning

Mood
calm
tentative
inquisitive
supportive
intellectual

Cue words
past or future orientation
open questions
maybe, perhaps
could, might
possibly, probably
wonder, suppose
what if
why (with no blame)

Typical Search Talk Behaviors

Identifying issues: "I'm wondering if we are letting outside activities crowd our relationship."

Giving relevant background information: "Between us we carry about twelve credit cards."

Inviting/encouraging thinking: "What do you think?"

Searching for and analyzing causes: "Maybe you're so pooped at the end of a day because you aren't getting enough exercise."

Giving impressions/explanations: "I think maybe we eat out too much."

Making Interpretations: "Barb's phone call probably means she's convinced."

Brainstorming or generating possibilities: "Perhaps you could set a time to jog every other day? How about playing tennis together twice a week?"

Posing solutions: "Suppose you go back to school in the fall? How do you think that would work?"

Offering kindly advice: "Maybe it would be helpful to see a doctor about your knee?"

Impact

Search Talk is very helpful for reducing pressure and increasing information about an issue. In probing for information in this non-accusatory fashion, you are freed up to identify and clarify issues and events, examine relevant background information, and generate alternative courses of action. In effect, Search Talk becomes a "think tank" to play out ideas and expand options for the future.

Joan: "I got a call from Billy's teacher. He's gotten in fights three times during the past two weeks. What do you think could be bothering him?"

Mark: "When I was putting him to bed last night, he told me that he hated Jim. He wouldn't tell me why, although he mentioned some other kid that Jim was playing with. Maybe Billy is feeling jealous of this other kid for getting in the way of his friendship with Jim."

Joan: "That could be. When he came home from school today, he said he and Jim had had a great time playing at noon, and he made a big point of saying it was "just the two of them." I didn't mention the teacher's call to Billy. What do you think we should do?"

Mark: "One thing might be to talk with him about Jim and this other kid and find out what he's feeling. Or we could just leave it alone for awhile and see if they work out their difficulties."

Joan: "Maybe it's best to just let them work it out. Perhaps I should call the teacher to ask who Billy has been fighting with."

Mark: "Or we could ask Billy about that, although then he would probably wonder how we knew he had gotten into some fights."

When Search Talk is used heavily in a discussion, it gives both you and your partner a chance to be heard. The nonthreatening, nonjudgmental nature of Search Talk strengthens rapport and builds trust. However, since Search Talk is a cool, rational, and objective way to talk about an issue, crucial information may not surface. By itself, Search Talk sometimes only skims across the surface and misses the core of the issue, leaving issues unresolved and partners dissatisfied. Combining Search Talk with Straight Talk can overcome these difficulties.

Tips

1. Use Search Talk to brainstorm (raise ideas and possibilities without being censored) before settling on a particular course of action.

2. Listen for qualifiers (such as maybe, might, could) to spot Search Talk.

3. Caution: Do not let speculation, reflection, and exploration turn into just "Float Talk," where ideas sound good, but nothing happens. When no one takes responsibility for putting them into action, Search Talk can be a sophisticated way to avoid resolving issues. (How many conversations have you been involved in without any concrete results?)

4. Watch for loss of energy and involvement as signs of using too much Search Talk. Shift to a more energized style: Control Talk to lead or direct action or Straight Talk to deepen the conversation.

STYLE IV — STRAIGHT TALK

When an issue exists for you or another person, you may have a number of different intentions regarding it. One may be to avoid dealing with the issue so as not to rock the boat. You will most likely carry out this intention by communicating in Shop Talk or Small Talk. Another intention you may have is to create change in the other person. If so, it is common to use Control Talk behavior. A third intention might be to explore the issue and develop a general understanding of it, often by discussing some background information or by speculating about future possibilities. This kind of intent is typically handled with Search Talk.

Another distinct alternative for dealing with an issue is Straight Talk which communicates a different set of intentions from those in any of the previously mentioned styles. The intentions and behaviors of Style IV demonstrate a commitment to speak from both your head and heart to deal *completely* and *congruently* with the issue.

> Elaine: "I'm feeling overwhelmed with all the details on this project we're doing together for Professor Nelson. We keep finding out more and more information, and I just become more confused about how to focus it. Do you feel this way too?"

> Barb: "Not really. I feel pretty confident right now. The project might be a little too big, but I think we have enough time to handle it and make it really good. Is there anything I can do to help with your part of the project?"

> Elaine: "I'm glad you're feeling confident because I was afraid we both felt this way, and that would be hard. I think you could help me by sorting through the information I have collected and help me to organize it. It's important to me to not feel scattered — which I do now — so that would be a big help."

> Barb: "I have some time this afternoon, or I could spend most of the evening with you. Which would you like better?"

> Elaine: "Could we get together right after dinner? I really appreciate your willingness to help."

The goal of Straight Talk is to *connect* with yourself and the other person. This is done by *managing yourself* rather than by *manipulating* the other person.

Straight Talk begins where the other styles never venture. In addition to relying on external information, you use your own internal information (what you are experiencing inside yourself). In the process you focus primarily on your contribution in a situation, your own actions and interactions. Focusing primarily on the other person's reactions moves you toward Style II.

With Straight Talk, you move to the core of an issue or situation and deal with tension and differences without blaming, demanding, defending, or deceiving. Your aim is to build connections with others, not destroy them. To do this, you have a straightforward, honest and respectful interchange of thoughts, feelings, and wants. But the conversation does not stop there — you also commit yourself to future action.

Straight Talk builds on full awareness, both your own and your partner's. Therefore, when you have something to share, or there is an important issue with which to deal, Straight Talk is more complete than any other style.

In essence, Straight Talk enables you to become more responsive and responsible by:

1. *Attending* to self and other's awareness at the moment.

2. *Accepting* what you find as "what is"; often it is tempting to disregard, deny, and run from "what is" rather than accepting and dealing with it directly.

3. *Acting on*, not reacting to, this awareness.

Attending to the moment means being aware of your own incomplete communicycles and those of other people as well. What is incomplete or incongruent may be something said or done at the moment or even several minutes, days, or possibly weeks ago. If it still concerns you, then the communicycle is still in process.

Accepting "what is" means that you acknowledge and own your reality — what *you* are seeing, thinking, feeling, and wanting. In doing so, you embrace the validity of your experience as a starting point. You may try to deny your experience, perhaps repressing it with alcohol or drugs, but the reality will not go away. Instead, unacknowledged reality remains as unfinished business, as an incomplete communicycle.

Acting on your awareness means using your own and your partner's self-information to complete your communicycles.

Straight Talk can be used to communicate both *positive and negative* awareness as you and your partner work through an issue.

Characteristics of Straight Talk

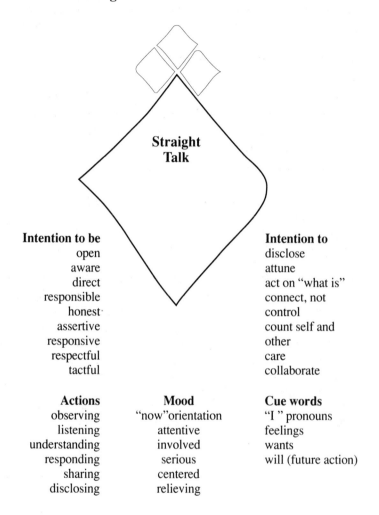

Straight Talk

Intention to be
open
aware
direct
responsible
honest
assertive
responsive
respectful
tactful

Intention to
disclose
attune
act on "what is"
connect, not
control
count self and
other
care
collaborate

Actions	**Mood**	**Cue words**
observing	"now"orientation	"I " pronouns
listening	attentive	feelings
understanding	involved	wants
responding	serious	will (future action)
sharing	centered	
disclosing	relieving	

Typical Straight Talk Behaviors

Focusing on the issue: "Here's how I see what's going on."

Identifying tension: "I'm feeling very frustrated right now."

Acknowledging differences: "Well I think we differ on this. You want to go to school full time this next year, and I think just part time would be better."

Providing feedback: "I've noticed that when you speak, you drop your voice at the end of sentences and it's difficult to hear you."

Requesting feedback: "After I ask Matt for his ideas, have you noticed whether I do something that shuts him off when he begins to speak?"

Expressing Appreciation: "Thank you for backing me up in our discussion with the kids. Your support gave me confidence to hang in there on this tough decision."

Asking for change: "We've both worked the past two weekends. Would you be willing to reserve one day this next weekend to spend together? "

Taking responsibility for your own contribution/response: "Yeah, I didn't listen to you. I assumed that I knew what you felt so I started thinking about what to do next instead of listening."

Listening effectively: "Let me see if I've got what you are telling me. You're saying that I interrupt you a lot when you are talking to me, and that this frustrates you because you are unable to complete what you want to tell me. Is that accurate?"

Encouraging disclosure: "How do you feel about this?"

Apologizing/asking for forgiveness: "I really did hurt you by cutting you out. I'm sorry I did that. I want to apologize and assure you that I will not do that again."

Sharing vulnerability: "Basically I don't feel as competent and confident as I let on."

Recognizing a harmful pattern: "I think each of us assumes the other should balance the checkbook so we end up either fighting over who will do it or letting it slide until we get an overdraft."

Recognizing impending change: "When we move to Boston, we won't know a soul. Our friends and your family will all be back here. I'm worried about that."

Anticipating future uncertainties: "Mary, there's a good chance I'll be laid off in a month, and I'd like to do some planning with you."

Affirming yourself, other, or your relationship: "Norm, I really enjoy being around you. You're interesting to talk with, but most of all I just feel comfortable around you. I don't have to perform or worry about what I'm saying or doing."

Recognizing strengths in self and others: "I think you are very good at analyzing details. I'm good at seeing their practical applications."

All the characteristic Straight Talk behaviors listed above are combinations of the Speaking and Listening Skills presented in Chapters 9 through 11.

Impact

Straight Talk is a powerful style if you are *not trying* to be powerful. As soon as you use Straight Talk to be powerful, you will slip into a control mode and lose power. In Straight Talk you can feel peaceful even though you are discussing a difficult matter *if* your intentions are to connect and collaborate rather than control and manipulate.

Straight Talk is not necessarily an easygoing style, however. You can be tough yet tender, firm yet flexible, and caring but not controlling. The real power of the style comes from putting your cards on the table without playing tricks, pushing, or shoving. As you disclose your awareness and seek the same from your partner, each of you is recognized as an authority on your own experience.

There is a risk in Straight Talk. As you disclose more about yourself, you increase choices. The information you supply can be used constructively or destructively, moving you closer together or pushing you further apart. Sometimes this makes you vulnerable. Usually disclosure begets disclosure and results in new understanding, acceptance, and intimacy between you. However, Straight Talk does not always move you into Positive Togetherness. Sometimes relationships are severed when people are straight with each other.

When you attempt use Straight Talk to try to change the other person, the result will likely be a shift into Control Talk. There is a paradox here. Genuine Straight Talk attracts when you are not trying to control. If you wish to change the other person, say so directly. That is Straight Talk! Then the other person can accept or reject your control. He or she does not have to guess where you are coming from.

Straight Talk goes to the heart of an issue by disclosing the wants and feelings that are left unsaid in other styles. In the process, it helps you and your partner connect by getting things off your chests in a productive way, working through differences and tensions directly. It generates collaborative action plans which fit for both parties.

Straight Talk affects relationships in other ways as well. As partners share their real thoughts and feelings about issues without experiencing reprisals, real trust grows. You leave conversations with good feelings about yourself and your partner because each of you understands the other's viewpoint, and both of you think that you have been understood. Without this climate of understanding and trust that develops from Straight Talk, relationships get stuck and stay stuck.

If Straight Talk Is So Useful, Why Don't More People Use It?

Many people believe Straight Talk is too risky because you cannot predict the outcome. That is true, you cannot. But the goal of Straight

Talk is not to gain a particular outcome. Rather, Straight Talk is useful for discovering "what is" and for creating alternatives which are acceptable to both parties. This may mean that the solution you and partner develop will differ from the one you had in mind at the start.

Another reason people avoid Straight Talk is a fear that someone will get hurt by something that is said. While this is possible, damage is usually done when people think they are using Straight Talk but they really are not. Instead they may be using Fight Talk to confront the other person or to "straighten them out."

Avoiding Straight Talk also happens when people skirt around the edge of the issue instead of going to the core; our experience indicates that they do so to hide a *lack of confidence* in their own communication skills. Other people sidestep Straight Talk because they prefer to work indirectly behind the scene; they believe they have more control this way. Still others avoid Straight Talk because they do not want to get involved, be responsible, or commit themselves.

Sometimes skilled communicators choose not to use Straight Talk because it is unsafe. For example, the person with whom they are speaking has demonstrated that he or she cannot be trusted to use information constructively but instead will use it destructively. Recognizing this, they either use Straight Talk to share their distrust directly, or they avoid the person and use Small Talk and Shop Talk to keep a safe distance when they do have to interact.

In today's uncertain and complex world, the ability to be straightforward to effectively process issues and create positive outcomes is a necessary skill. Because the payoffs are so great and the costs of avoiding it can be substantial, we suggest you use it when appropriate.

Therefore, we obviously do not advocate that you use Straight Talk all the time to disclose everything you know. This can be as destructive to yourself and others as never disclosing anything. It is important to respect boundaries and confidentialities and to use wisdom and tact in what you say.

The choice of a communication style to use is yours. In making your choice, pay attention to your real feelings and intentions: what do they tell you to do?

Tips

1. Use style combinations. In most situations, a combination of Straight Talk and Search Talk is the most effective and satisfying way to talk about complex and uncertain issues.

2. Know your own comfort for risk. Straight Talk talks about "what's going on below the surface": what people think, feel, and want. These kinds of information are commonplace, but many people are hesitant to talk directly about their thoughts, feelings, and wants because of the potential risks involved. Instead they use other styles to avoid disclosing self-information. Watch out for this.

3. Attend to pressure. When you feel pressure building — feelings getting stirred up — and your conversation is not getting anywhere, take a breath, bring your energy and awareness to "center" and shift to talking about "what is" at that moment. (See Chapter 14, "Communicating Under Pressure," for discussion of centering and Chapter 11, "Meta Talk" on Now Talk).

4. Caution: Do not try to use Straight Talk to pretend that you are interested in being collaborative when you are not. Others will see and hear your incongruent nonverbals signaling your desire to control, and they will distrust you. If your intention is to be in control, say so — that is Straight Talk which gives the other person the choice to go along with you or not.

5. Do not confuse Control Talk with Straight Talk. Straight Talk focuses squarely on yourself. When your focus is on the other person, telling him or her "the way things are and what the consequences will be," you are using Control Talk. There are times and places for good, clear Control Talk. Just do not confuse the two.

6. Recognize the limits. Straight Talk is not a "cure all" or "quick fix." It does not guarantee you will get your way. It demonstrates commitment to an *open process*.

MIXED MESSAGES

Mixed messages occur when any intention or behavior from Style II slips into another style. One part of the message is Style I, III, or IV, but the second Style II part is an added undercurrent which usually contradicts the other part. Mixed messages create confusion and are hard to deal with because receivers do not know whether to respond to the control part or the straight part. Mixed messages also spawn caution and resistance. If the Style II part includes elements of Fight Talk or Spite Talk, people usually just hear the negative. If the undercurrent is Control Talk, the message is more subtle.

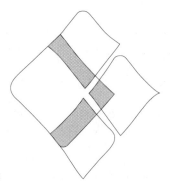

While some mixed messages can be playful and fun, they are tricky. For example, if someone mixes Small Talk with Fight Talk and says to you, "You're pretty smart for such a dumb guy," what is the message? Is it a compliment or a put-down? If you take it as a compliment, you might be naive. If you take it as a put-down, the other person might deny that was the intention and say, "What's wrong, can't you take a joke?"

Occasionally you will find yourself among people who constantly shoot zingers at each other "in fun." At first it is amusing, but soon the pattern becomes tiresome. Our experience in these situations is that usually significant issues lie just below the surface. The mixed message signals tension but keeps the real issues hidden, in a "friendly-unfriendly" sort of way. People who send many mixed messages typically lack the communication skills to give straight messages about an issue, or they fear closeness with someone. Either way they maintain a distance.

Here are some examples of mixed messages:

"I don't understand why you don't listen to me." (Search Talk mixed with blame)

"I feel pleased about my quitting smoking: now you should stop too." (Straight Talk mixed with control of other)

Most mixed messages grow out of mixed feelings or intentions, saying one thing but feeling another.

Mixed messages can take several forms:

1. An *undercurrent* as described above.

2. *Presumptions* about the other person: "I'd tell you about my day if you were really interested."

3. *But* or *yes but:* "I agree with what you're saying, but it still isn't a good idea."

4. *Condition:* "I'll treat you nice when you start treating me nice."

5. *Build-up, put-down* (*positive-negative*): "You really did a thorough job on your report, but it sure took you long enough."

A variety of behavioral cues signal mixed messages: vocal characteristics, such as a harsh voice or a whiny, sarcastic, or demanding tone; facial expressions that do not match the idea expressed, such as a smile or grin with a complaint, or a stern look with a soft, supportive statement.

The most effective way to respond to a mixed message is to acknowledge both parts and ask for clarification: the *clear style* and the *undercurrent;* the *yes* and the *but;* the *statement* and the *presumption;* the *offer* and the *condition;* the *build-up* and the *put-down*. Then ask the sender which part he or she means most. (See the section on Now Talk in Chapter 11, "Meta Talk.")

As a sender, if you find yourself slipping into mixed messages when you do not want to, look at your intentions and feelings (negative or positive) and turn them into Straight Talk.

YOU NEED ALL OF THE STYLES

No one style can do it all. You use several styles in most conversations and each style serves a special purpose and communicates something different. The key is flexibility — being able to match style and situation appropriately instead of getting stuck in just one style.

Each style is characterized by different intentions and behaviors. Most routine matters are handled in Small Talk, Shop Talk, and Control Talk. They keep the world running smoothly.

Fight and Spite Talk are transition styles. Their tension and pressure signal something bigger is going on that warrants attention. Unfortunately, some people are unable to move beyond these two "distress signals" into a combination of styles which will positively change things. Fight and Spite are as far as they ever go toward resolving issues.

Innovative and mutually satisfying solutions to most uncertain, complex, and non-routine matters call for a combination of Search Talk and Straight Talk. Search Talk overviews a situation while Straight Talk draws on critical self-other awareness to get to the core of issues. Straight Talk is also the style for expressing who you really are to significant others.

Summary Points

1. People negotiate how they are going to relate by the styles of communication they use.

2. Fight and Spite Talk try to control others by withholding information and limiting choices. Straight Talk tries to connect with others by increasing information and expanding choices

3. Control, Fight, and Spite Talk focus on others. Straight Talk focuses on yourself, on your response, and your contribution to a situation. It demonstrates self-control.

4. The style you give is generally the style you get: action, reaction, interaction.

5. The purer the style, the clearer the message. Mixed messages send unclear messages.

Tips

1. Recognize the impact and shift to another style if the style you are using is not appropriate or productive. Do not use a style that interferes with getting your message across effectively. Remember, style facilitates content.

2. Ask yourself privately during a conversation, "Is my intention to control or connect?"

3. Do not Straight Talk small issues. Do not Small Talk big issues.

Think about your own style patterns. Which style(s) do you use most frequently? Which styles do you seldom or never use? Is there a particular style you would like to learn to use more often?

5

THE AWARENESS WHEEL:
Understanding Yourself and Others

Today's technologies are impressive — computers, satellites, and electronic transmission just to mention a few. But no matter how sophisticated technology becomes, *people ultimately process the information!* People interpret printouts, listen to presentations, observe gestures, and make statements. When tense situations develop, and plans, negotiations, and projects bog down, the reason may be that key self or other information is missing or being disregarded.

The ability to process and facilitate "people information" (information about self, other, and your interaction) will bring you more meaningful experiences, good feelings, and better connections with others than any other single skill. The foundation of this skill is awareness.

The more you can know about yourself and others at any moment, the more effective you will become in completing communicycles and bridging impasses in a wide variety of critical situations. You can be the person to make the difference. You can initiate change.

Keep this is mind: *the most important resource you bring to an interpersonal situation is your ability to process your own internal and external awareness.* Your personal power increases with awareness.

IN ANY SITUATION THERE ARE
FIVE KEY PIECES OF INFORMATION

THE AWARENESS WHEEL

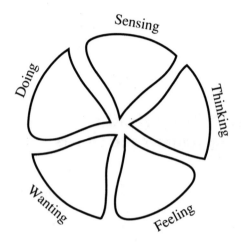

The Awareness Wheel is a map to help you become more aware of yourself or another person at any point in time. Of course no one is totally conscious of what he or she is experiencing all of the time; from moment to moment, various aspects of awareness come in and out of focus. However, the five dimensions in this tool will give you a comprehensive framework for discovering and understanding crucial information inside yourself and others. As such it increases your choices — to enjoy yourself and the other person as you each are, or to make changes.

The Awareness Wheel includes five "zones": sensing, thinking, feeling, wanting, and doing. All five parts are distinct yet interact with each other. All five are constantly present in your experience even though you may not be consciously aware of them. They become available when you tune in to them and use them. To help you understand the Awareness Wheel better and capture its usefulness, we will examine each part more closely.

SENSATIONS — Your Sensory Data

Your five senses — sight, sound, smell, taste, and touch — are your immediate points of contact with the outside world. Through these channels, you collect raw data:

observations	facts
descriptions	recollections
visualizations	fantasies
stories	

Other people's actions, both verbal and nonverbal behavior, become your sensory input. So do other contextual cues. The more you pay attention to the subtleties of what you see, hear, smell, taste, and touch, the more you will be aware of what is going on around you. Your senses are like a good journalist; they observe, report, and describe, but they do not interpret.

Verbal and Nonverbal Input

Sensory "input" basically falls into two categories — words and non-words.

As we grew up, we learned how to read, write, and speak. Throughout this formal training, the focus was on words, words, words. Research indicates, however, that in spoken communication, other aspects are much more important than words. Dr. Albert Mehrabian, a UCLA communications researcher, startled the communication field some years ago with the findings below.

Of the three major elements in spoken communications, each has the following impact on what is received and believed:

Verbal messages — what is said — account for 7 percent.

Vocal and tonal messages — the way it is said — account for 38 percent.

Visual messages — what is seen — account for a whopping 55 percent.

Mehrabian's research indicates that the nonverbal aspects of other's messages have a great impact on the meaning you make. The accompanying nonverbals become the basis for believing, disbelieving, or reinterpreting the words you hear. As we saw in the discussion of communication styles, tonal and visual cues contribute substantially to the style of a communication.

Sources of Nonverbal Data

Nonverbals are the non-word messages we receive.
Without ever hearing a word, you make meaning from these kinds of *sight data:*

- context — location and who is present
- time — when in the day and promptness or delay in response
- space — physical position of people (closeness or distance), furniture and machines
- paper — reports, memos, printouts
- props — clipboard, pencil, coffee cup
- clothing — formal or informal, neat or unkempt
- body language — posture, eye contact, facial expressions, hand and arm gestures
- energy level — alertness, involvement, fatigue

Sound data includes:

- background noise — machines running, people talking
- rate and pace of speech — slow, medium or fast; steady or halting
- pitch and tone — low, medium, or high; flat, fluctuating, strained, strong, or confident
- loudness of voice — soft, medium, loud
- diction and clarity — precise, mumbling

Touch data (hard, soft; hot, cold; rigid, flexible; smooth, scratchy), smell, and taste are important sources of nonverbal data too.

> ## THE BODY SPEAKS ITS MIND

Specific Nonverbals to Monitor

You can train yourself to be more conscious of other people's nonverbal cues. Just as an artist or actor does, pay attention to small details of facial and speech patterns.

Look for

1. Changes in skin color: different shades in various parts of the face, blushing, or paleness provide clues to emotional states.
2. Small facial muscles: tension and relaxation around the corner of the eyes and around the mouth signal how much pressure the other person is experiencing.
3. Lower lip: this is very hard to control consciously so the lower lip offers good clues to tension, relaxation, and other states.
4. Breathing patterns: shifts in breathing rate and depth signal mood changes and are usually followed by other changes in facial patterns.

Listen for

1. Rate of speech: rapid speech signals nervousness, perhaps indicating speakers think they are not being understood or gaining agreement.
2. Pace and rhythm: halting speech often indicates lack of confidence in what is being said or, perhaps, some withholding of information.
3. Loudness of voice: increases in the loudness of the voice often signal an intention to persuade or gain compliance.

Reading Nonverbals

Nonverbal communication data pose a special dilemma — you can read too much or too little into them. Since they are a very powerful and informative mode of communication, you need to attend to them and sometimes "read between the lines." To most people, reading nonverbals means focusing on the other person and interpreting what is going on with him or her. You can read books that tell you how to interpret different postures and gestures, but there is a real danger in this.

Any posture, gesture, or action can have many meanings, and your guess about what is going on with someone else may be accurate or inaccurate. When you forget this and begin thinking that you know for certain what the other person is thinking or feeling, damage can be done to the interaction. You can slip into believing you know more about other people than they know about themselves. For example, arms folded across the chest is often associated with being closed or defensive. Often this is true. But people also sit this way when they are cold or relaxed. As an alternative to acting on an assumption, we prefer asking others what their nonverbal message means, if this is important in a particular situation.

In CONNECTING we urge you to take a different perspective than you are used to taking. In interpersonal situations, other people's unconscious nonverbals often occur as a response to your stimulus. *Thinking of their reaction as a response to your action provides information about how effective you are being with them.* Following this perspective, other people are your immediate data base, providing you with ongoing feedback about how you are doing in the interaction.

Did you ever play "hide the thimble" when you were a child? If so, you will recall leaving the room, while those remaining in the room hid an object for you to find upon reentering the room. When you returned, others guided you to find the object simply by using gradations of two basic words: "You're hot" or "You're cold."

Reading other's nonverbals is like playing "hot and cold." *Nonverbals tell you how well you are doing (dancing) with the other person.* When a relationship is cooling off, you will first notice cool responses to your usual behaviors. Later you might explicitly talk about the change you have observed.

Take a look at how nonverbals typically occur in an interaction with the example below.

> Suppose the two of us are rolling along in a Small Talk conversation, standing comfortably at arms length. I shift to Shop Talk and ask you if you would be willing to edit a paper I am writing. (Remember Human Checkers? Verbally, I just took one step forward.) Before you comment, I notice you take a slight step backwards. (If I do not see your step, I might be missing important data.) If I see the step, it is easy to jump to the conclusion you are not interested. Then you say,

> "Yeah, I've got a lot to do right now, maybe I could. When would you need it?"

> Not hearing a clear no, unconsciously I take a slight step forward, slide into Control Talk and say, "It wouldn't be a big job. You could do it in an hour."

> You move back again. In my desperation to get you to say, "yes," my awareness drops. I start pressing you, crowding your space, and verbally pushing you to comply. Finally, you say,

> "I really can't do it."

In this scenario, what I am doing is not working. But instead of paying attention to your nonverbal *reaction* to my *action* and changing my dance steps (body and words) to give you more choice, I blindly pursue. A different dance, based on the recognition that I was not being effective, might have resulted in a different outcome. And even if "no" was really "no," and I had to make other plans, we would not leave each other with negative feelings. The impact of this brief exchange is likely to carry over too. If I do not acknowledge my ungraciousness or apologize for the pressure I put on you, you are likely to be cautious the next time you see me. You may even avoid me for fear of a conversation with me that begins with friendly Small Talk but ends up like the last one.

To help you be more sensitive to your own impact as reflected in other's nonverbals, here are some important points to remember:

1. Sight is faster than sound. Nonverbals usually precede words. For example, a subtle nod of the head usually precedes a verbal "yes" or "no."

2. Nonverbals either match and confirm the words spoken or mismatch (to some degree) and discount them. When nonverbals discount words, they raise questions and doubts.

   Betty: "How are you today?"

   Jay: (no smile, eyes turned down) "Fine."

3. Words can be more easily censored than immediate unconscious, subtle nonverbal responses.

4. Nonwords punctuate a dance. Attend to nonverbals as you would punctuation marks — ? ! : " " , . They signal beginnings and endings; what is certain, questionable, or a joke; when to shift the focus, and so forth. They also give you clues for recognizing styles and determining if a communicyle is complete.

5. Try to take a "before" picture in your mind's eye of the other person as your begin an exchange: look for body tension, posture, face. This will help you to notice any changes (new pictures) along the way so you can better judge your own effectiveness — whether the impact of your actions matches your intentions. If your dance goes well, the "after" picture will look different than the "before."

Where Do Words Fit In?

With all this attention to nonverbal communication you might be wondering, "How important are words?" They are very important. Words confirm or disconfirm nonverbals. If they confirm what you see, you tend to believe the words. If they do not, you doubt, question, and distrust them. For example, if a fellow says, "I'm sorry," but he does not really feel sorry, some part of his face, voice, or body will communicate his real feeling — 30 percent sorry, 70 percent not sorry.

Nonverbals are powerful but they are not precise; while they suggest or imply meaning, they do not explicitly define meaning. Words enable us to define, describe, examine, clarify, and even anticipate future actions. When words are neither too few or too many, but right on target, they are wonderful tools. Language is a uniquely human characteristic.

In CONNECTING we focus a great deal on words which are involved in specific communication skills for sending and receiving messages more accurately and effectively (see Chapters 9, 10 and 11). At this point however, we want to emphasize the importance of nonverbals as a critical source of information.

Intuitive Sensations

Another important kind of data are intuitive sensations — "data" that do not come from your immediate, external, physical world but rather from your *internal world* of memories, associations, insights, knowings, dreams, hunches, and so forth. When one of these intuitive sensations occurs, it may be difficult to document your perceptions with physical data. This is true in part because intuitive sensations often draw on bits or fragments of both internal and external data. However, when pressed to describe the source of their information, most people can describe specific internal or external sensations — memories, dreams, fantasies, and observations. These data probably represent a blend of sensations and thoughts. (See the next section.)

Tips

1. Notice individual patterns. Everybody has a "body signature." Like fingerprints, every person you observe has a unique pattern of body movements which recycle frequently. If you see a person in a number of situations you get to know his or her signature quite well; *small* changes in nonverbals then take on special meaning.

2. Let yourself see and hear all the data. Do not deny or avoid what you perceive. This is part of "what is," and it is important information. While it may be disappointing or inconvenient, acknowledge, accept, and act on it.

3. Pay particular attention to conflicting data — when someone says one thing, but looks like or does something different — and comment on it if you need to be sure what is meant.

THOUGHTS — The Meaning You Make

Thoughts are the meanings you make out of sensory data. Although all thoughts are certainly not organized and coherent, this zone of the Awareness Wheel emphasizes the logical, analytical, and rational process of weighing data to arrive at an interpretation or conclusion. Here are some words that reflect this aspect of your awareness:

beliefs	conclusions
interpretations	reasons
expectations	possibilities
impressions	analyses
ideas	objections
opinions	predictions
theories	explanations
assumptions	benefits
evaluations	principles
judgments	risks or odds

Thoughts are influenced by your past, present and anticipated experience. They draw on the *memories and beliefs* you bring to a situation, the *interpretations you make* of immediate and recollected sensory data, and your *expectations and anticipation* of the future. Thoughts are categories for organizing meaning.

Beliefs

The beliefs you bring from past experience either limit or expand what can grow out of the circumstance. Beliefs are powerful. They influence your perceptions — what you actually see and hear — as well as other parts of your Awareness Wheel.

For example, your self-esteem is a distillation of your beliefs and judgments about yourself in different circumstances across time. If you judge yourself to be innovative, competent, and responsible, you will carry confidence into different situations. Likewise, if you have doubts about your abilities, you will broadcast this self-evaluation as well. In this way, beliefs often become self-fulfilling prophesies.

Beliefs set parameters for what you think is possible, how you feel, and what you want. This is why faith can be such a powerful force; it expands your expectations beyond what is normal or what past experience suggests is possible.

Certain beliefs are a source of wisdom which provide stability in times of turmoil or rapid change. However, not all beliefs are rational or true. They can trap you, causing you to follow the same behaviors even though their consequences are negative. Although we often behave according to what we believe is in our best interest, we are sometimes mistaken. Be willing to challenge your own beliefs; they can work for or against you.

A Note of Caution About Beliefs.

Watch out for "hardening of the categories." It is the biggest obstacle to processing fresh information. The more expert and experienced you are in any area, the more vulnerable you are to your own belief system and this cognitive disorder. Hardening of the categories often implies the attitude, "Don't confuse me with the facts; my mind is already made up," and takes many forms:

- jumping to conclusions on limited data
- making assumptions that others share your perspective without checking it out
- stereotyping others — failing to distinguish individuals
- projecting — assigning your own thoughts, feelings, or wants to someone else, and then treating that person as though he or she had these thoughts
- disregarding your biases — failing to recognize that you bring experiences to a situation which color your thoughts
- obligating with "shoulds," "oughts," and "have to's" and making others salute your opinions

Interpretations

Whereas beliefs represent what you bring to a situation, *interpretations are the meanings you make out of sensory data.* We use this term to include the logical analysis of facts.

Interpretations are affected by your beliefs, but they are also influenced by what you are feeling and wanting at that point in time.

Thoughts are subjective. They are not objective truths. Your interpretations are not "the way things are." Rather, they represent *the way you put your world together* — the way you make sense out of data. This does not devalue your thinking, but instead it trumpets your uniqueness and your right to think for yourself. What is real for you counts; however, others may see and hear the same data and come to very different conclusions.

For example, if you do not see the smile (sensory data) which accompanies your partner's, "You nut!" you may conclude that you have just been put down (interpretation). This is more likely to happen if you do not see the smile and are feeling insecure and uncertain about yourself. If you are feeling good, see the smile and hear the words, you may conclude that your partner is joking.

Your intentions are involved here too. If you want to have a serious discussion at that time, you may conclude that your partner is joking in order to avoid the conversation. But if you simply want to have a good time, you may conclude that your partner's joking indicates he or she wants to have fun too. The interpretations you make depend upon which sensory data you take in, how you are feeling, and what you want or desire.

Your beliefs may have an impact too. If you believe that partners should not call each other names, even as a joke, then you may interpret your partner's remark as offensive. But if you assume that partners can affectionately call each other names now and then, you interpret the remark as a sign of affection.

Expectations

Expectations are how you organize your future. You expect to meet a client at two o'clock.. Following a conversation about table manners, you expect a more relaxing dinner with the kids. Expectations are future beliefs waiting to happen.

As with beliefs and interpretations, expectations become "self-fulfilling prophecies"; we consciously or unconsciously select data and actions that fulfill our expectations. Anticipated experience can be as real as past experience. If you imagine yourself doing well on an exam, based on thorough preparation and a feeling of confidence, you wield a potent force.

In the process of forming thoughts, it is easy to filter (delete) or imagine (add) data. In addition, other people's actions (your sensory data) can have multiple meanings. Because so many aspects influence your thoughts, it is very important to understand yourself: to be able to recognize how your own beliefs, interpretations, and expectations are formed.

Take a couple of minutes and think about what you believe about yourself and one other significant person in your life. How do these beliefs influence your perceptions and actions toward that person? Are your beliefs limiting or supportive? Do they get you into good or bad situations?

Tips

1. Treat your beliefs and interpretations as working hypotheses.

2. Consider the possibilities. Several interpretations are usually possible from the same set of data. If you find yourself thinking "either/or," look for more alternatives as well.

3. Recognize different interpretations. People tend to choose an interpretation that fits their preconceived beliefs. For example, I think I am teaching responsibility by having my son help with the dishes. He thinks I am picking on him when I ask him to do the dishes.

4. Be aware of your beliefs and expectations as you approach a new situation. Thoughts color perceptions. They can interfere with fresh data and the gaining of new understanding.

5. Prepare to switch. To close a communicycle, sometimes it helps to alter your beliefs, reframe your interpretations, or change your expectations.

6. Question when necessary. What you see and hear can conflict with what you think and expect. Rather than force a conclusion, check out the differences.

7. Recognize that performance rises or falls to meet expectations.

8. Understand how stress has an impact on sensory data and thoughts. Under stress, thinking tends to become more rigid and sensory data are often ignored, denied, or imagined.

9. Consider all the data before coming to a conclusion.

10. Ask yourself, "How are my thoughts influencing — perhaps limiting — what can happen in this situation?"

FEELINGS — Your Emotional Responses

Dealing with your own and other people's feelings, especially in tough situations, is the greatest challenge to relationships, and being able to connect with feelings is central to effective communication.

Feelings are your spontaneous internal physical response to the comparison between your expectations and what you experience in a situation. Whether you are aware of them or not, you have *thoughts about what will or should happen* during most of your waking hours. Your senses are constantly scanning the environment for signs of fulfilled or unfulfilled expectations. And depending on how well the external input matches your internal anticipation, positive or negative feelings fire off constantly.

For example, if you run out to buy a newspaper, and unexpectedly bump into an old friend whom you have not seen for years, suddenly you feel surprised and thrilled. On the other hand, if you are expecting to receive a particular job offer, and it goes to someone else, you might feel angry, jealous, and maybe a little relieved, too, if part of you believed the job might be over your head.

Your internal physical-emotional response registers on the outside of your body as well. Anger can be seen in tight muscles and flushed skin, and it is heard in loud, strident speech. When you feel sad, tears may appear. When you are happy, others see smiling, laughing, or joking. Unless you have learned to mask your feelings completely, clues to what is going on emotionally inside are shown nonverbally on your outside.

As a result of their thorough analysis of mood studies, Watson and Tellegen constructed the following model which summarizes various types of emotional or mood states that people experience.

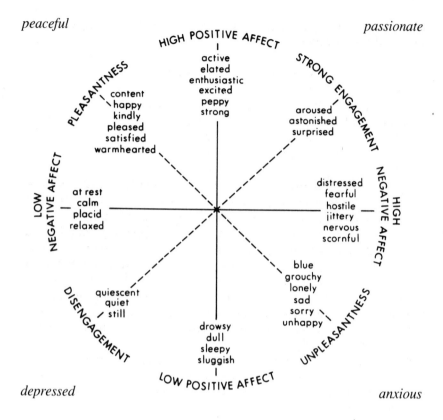

Figure 5.1. The Two-Factor Structure of Affect.[*]

As you can see in Figure 5.1, Watson and Tellegen found that words representing emotions can basically be depicted in two-dimensional affective space. The two major dimensions are represented by the solid lines in the diagram labeled, High and Low Positive Affect, and High and Low Negative Affect. The other two dimensions — Strong Engagement to Disengagement, and Pleasantness to Unpleasantness — represent a mixture of the two major positive and negative axes.

[*] Figure 5.1 is reprinted with permission of authors, D. Watson and A. Tellegen, "Toward a Consensual Structure of Mood," *Psychological Bulletin*, 1985, Vol. 98. No.2., page 221. (The italicized words outside the circle were added by us.)

Here are some additional feeling words. Place them where you think they would fall within the circle.

proud	cautious	disappointed
trusting	angry	eager
confident	comfortable	disinterested
frustrated	uneasy	irritated
excited	fascinated	bored
hesitant	agitated	

What you feel moment to moment — its valence and intensity — depends on the circumstance. The match or mismatch between your experience (what you see, hear, taste, touch, and smell) and your expectations (what you think will or should happen) gives rise to a corresponding positive or negative feeling. The greater your expectations, the stronger the resulting feeling. The more that your positive expectations and desires are being fulfilled in your life, the more positive feelings you have. The more that you do not know what to expect, the more uncertain and anxious you feel. Uncertainty is a major cause of stress disorders. And repeated expectations or desires without fulfillment leads to depression.

When things are going well, feelings are generally positive from step to step and dance to dance. When you get caught in an impasse, your feelings can swing wildly and widely, or become negative and static.

Take a few moments and think about your own life events, issues, and relationships. What feelings come to mind? Do your feelings spread around the circle or do they cluster in one or two locations? What do your feelings tell you about your life at this point in time?

Risk and Irrationality

Some people consider feelings to be risky, irrational, and dangerous. But feelings are actually very predictable and rational. They come from *somewhere.* and they will be positive or negative depending on the outcome of a situation — feelings are part of the payoff. In a sense, you risk feeling good or bad. However the real focus should be on the expectations and desires which you have for yourself and others, and how realistic they really are.

We recall a fellow in a Couple Communication group who told the following sad story. He was being considered for promotion to manager in his company, but he found himself unable to tell his wife of fifteen years about the possibility until he had successfully received the promotion. For two months he withheld the news for fear of what she might think of him if he was not promoted. When the promotion came and he told her, she was thrilled with the outcome.

At the same time, she was disappointed that he had not told her earlier about the possible promotion. She would have liked to have shared the process with him, experiencing the uncertainty of his high hopes and encouraging and supporting his quest. Had he not been promoted, he would have suffered the pain of his loss alone. She would have seen his sadness but might never have really known the cause. If the promotion had not come, would he have ever shared his disappointment with her?

Feelings Are Information

As you can see, feelings are remarkably rational. Unless they are distorted by a chemical deficiency or imbalance in your body or by drug abuse, they do not just suddenly appear out of a vacuum. Your feelings, whatever they are, reflect other parts of your Awareness Wheel. They are information about you at that moment, important in their own right. They do not have to be justified, denied or avoided. They are a part of "what is."

When you consider your feelings, it is common to think of having just one feeling. More often however, several feelings operate at the same time, such as frustration, disappointment, and irritation. But feelings are not always all negative or positive. Frequently they are mixed. For example, it is possible to feel frustrated, disappointed, and hopeful at the same time. Usually each specific feeling is associated with a particular thought or fragment of a cluster of expectations.

Manage Yourself by Being Aware of Your Feelings

Feelings cannot be successfully controlled by ignoring them, nor can you do away with them by denying them. Sooner or later they come back to haunt you physically, mentally, interpersonally, or spiritually. Unrecognized and unresolved negative feelings can block the flow of your energy, dampen wellness, and undermine productivity.

Feelings do not change by just wishing or willing them to to be different. They change when you *choose* to believe, interpret, or expect differently or when something else affects your thinking, intentions, or actions. Feelings respond to other parts of your Awareness Wheel; they reflect rather than initiate. For example, you are unhappy with the way your boss treats you, but you believe you cannot say anything to him about your dissatisfaction because he is busy and would not be interested in what you would have to say anyway. Besides, he might use

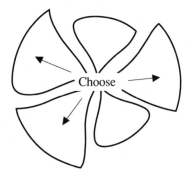

what you would say against you. Your beliefs, not your feelings, are keeping you trapped. Your feelings will change when you risk your beliefs.

Rather than disregard your feelings — negative as well as positive ones — use them as internal cues to "what's happening." They are like a barometer and thermometer: they take readings on your external and internal world; they tell you pressure and temperature; they alert you to check out what is going on in other parts of your Awareness Wheel. Negative feelings tell you that parts of your Wheel are out of sync, do not fit together congruently, and are in need of attention. Genuine positive feelings also tell you when things are going well. You can trust your feelings.

Acknowledging your feelings puts you more in control of your life. When you accept what you discover, and use the information about feelings to successfully act on the current issue by realigning the other parts of your wheel, your feelings do you a service. And, as other parts of your Wheel come into balance, your feelings will become more peaceful, reflecting your new, more centered state.

Some people try to control their feelings by stifling them. This blocks catharsis and connecting. Often it is useful just "to go with" what you feel, as long as you do not endanger yourself or others. Be in charge of your feelings by letting them be. Let yourself feel what you feel: really experience your emotions.

If you are sad, feel the loss and grief; do not fight it by trying to alter it right away. Likewise, if you are delighted about someone or something, take it higher, celebrate; do not hold back. Life has its own natural course of ups and downs. Our bodies will right themselves if we allow them to. As Solomon wrote, everything has its season; there is "a time to weep and a time to laugh; a time for mourning and a time for dancing" (Ecclesiastes 3:4, *The New English Bible*).

How Do You Feel About Your Feelings?

Most of us have feelings about feelings. For example, we feel embarrassed about fear of closeness; guilt about anger or pride; shame about envy and jealousy. In effect, these are *rules* which we have learned about our feelings. Without arguing what you should feel about your feelings, be aware that your *rules about feelings* can interfere with how you actually feel at any point in time.

In summary, your emotions are not irrational and uncontrollable. They do not just come "out of the blue." When you see them as helpful cues to "what is," they become guides to other parts of your Awareness Wheel. Feelings do not change by themselves; they shift when your thinking, desires, or actions change.

Tips

1. Attend to your feelings. Most of us have had the experience of becoming aware later — sometimes days later — of how we really felt about something. We recall, regretfully, how differently we might have acted if we had been aware of just what we were feeling at the time. Experiences like this highlight the value of attending to your feelings on the spot by asking yourself, "What am I feeling right now?" Consciously becoming aware of your feelings can help you to understand how they link up with sensory data, beliefs, and wants, and help you direct your actions better.

2. Attune to your body. Your body has its own language if you can understand it. What do your recurring physical sensations — tension in your jaw or neck muscles, shallow breathing, sweating, or queasy stomach — say to you?

3. Learn about your responses. How you respond to others — your communication style, eye contact, posture, rate of speech, and quality of listening — can also tell you much about how you are feeling. How do you typically recognize what you are feeling? Stop and think about it for a moment.

4. Go ahead and feel. When your feelings are unpleasant, do not try to deny, avoid or repress them. Ignoring feelings will not make them disappear. In fact, they only become stronger and more difficult to handle later.

5. Change your activity to change your feelings. One effective way to change your negative feelings is to dramatically change your posture or activity. Stand, walk, run, swim. A break in state like this gets oxygen to your brain which can temporarily shift your mood

and enhance your thinking. Longer-term changes typically require changes in your situation and in other parts of your Awareness Wheel. Strong feelings tell you to look to other parts of your Wheel for answers.

WANTS — Your Intentions

Wants are your intentions, desires and wishes for yourself, for others, and for your relationship together. As such they reflect your core values. They are the attributes you hope to be, the activities you hope to accomplish, the things you wish to acquire and even the direction you turn to be energized. Wants can be small or large, short-term or long-term. They often start as a dream or fantasy and are translated into specific goals and objectives.

Wants can be tentative hopes and "iffy" dreams or deep desires of the heart. They generally imply a moving towards or moving away from something or someone. When you are processing an issue, they give tentative direction to future action.

Here are some common words associated with wants:

goals	drives	desires
objectives	intentions	wishes
motives	interests	needs
hopes	values	targets

Intentions Are Organizers

Think of your intentions as mini-plans — your priorities. They give direction to your awareness, yet remain flexible and tentative until you put them into action. They can be shuffled about and reordered as you consider alternatives.

When you connect with what you really want, you focus your energy and release a strong force. However, the tentativeness of intentions —

could, might, perhaps, maybe — can be problematic. The lack of commitment, even with the "the best of intentions" can leave other people confused and frustrated if your wants are not clearly defined and put into consistent action.

Wants Are Motivators

Everybody wants something! Wants are energizers. If you ask someone what he or she wants, usually you will see and hear the person light up nonverbally and toss out a desire or two. Basically there are three types of wants:

1. *To be:* honest, respected, liked, appreciated, successful, healthy, helpful.

2. *To do:* general — compete, win, collaborate, get even, ignore, clarify, destroy, demand, listen, persuade, understand, undermine, support; specific — finish a project, read the newspaper, cook supper, talk to parents, increase income, change job.

3. *To have:* a good education, a stimulating job, good friends, a happy family, a nice car, money in savings.

Like feelings, you rarely have just one want at a time. Typically you have *multiple intentions* which vary in level (to be, to do, or to have) and in intensity. For example:

I want to be healthy,	(to be)
lose 10 pounds,	(to do)
and get a health club membership.	(to have)

This cluster of wants converges on all three levels. Whether or not they are put into action depends on their *intensity* (how strongly they are valued) and how much they *compete or conflict* with other intentions.

Intentions do not always run smoothly down the same track. Sometimes they conflict, competing for *time* and *other resources*. For example:

I want to be relaxed,	(to be)
make three phone calls,	(to do)
catch the 10 o'clock news,	(to do)
exercise,	(to do)
study,	(to do)
balance the check book,	(to do)

get a good night's sleep,   (to have)

and be prepared for tomorrow's presentation. (to be)

And these are only one person's wants for the night. Toss in three other family members' desires and you can have a fractured evening. If people's wants are not shared and negotiated, confusing and stressful behavior will result from the multiple, conflicting and competing wants.

For example, when a pair or family take a vacation, almost invariably an argument breaks out sometime during the first few days. The reason is that before the trip began everyone had private wishes and fantasies about what he or she would do on the vacation. These desires can become strong expectations. As the holiday progresses, if each person's wishes have not been shared, negotiated, and built into their time together, members become increasingly anxious as their wants go unfulfilled. Eventually feelings of disappointment erupt.

Some family members slide into Fight Talk to get what they want, while others retreat to Spite Talk or withdraw into excessive sleep. In any event, energy is dispersed and dissipated. The antidote to this syndrome is to start the trip, perhaps every day as well, with a brief discussion of everyone's wants and build them into plans as much as possible. When this is done successfully, group energy is directed, sustained, and even generated by the activities of the day.

As you can see, wants motivate and energize you and others from moment-to-moment. However, multiple and conflicting wants can work against you, scattering energy, which results in incongruent and confusing messages. This is why it is important to be aware of and talk about wants, both your own and others.

Why Are Wants So Important?

Your wants are very important for two reasons: (1) over the long term, they demonstrate your real (not just stated) values; (2) they impact action. Much can be inferred about your intentions *to be* and *to do* from the different communication styles you use in a situation. (See Chapters 3 and 4, for the characteristics of each style.) Intentions are a powerful force behind actions.

In the short-run, behaviors can be faked, keeping real intentions covered as hidden agenda. But over the long term, we become what we really want and value. For example, if someone really wants an education, he or she takes full advantage of the best learning opportunities available. The person does not just say, "I want to get a degree," and then lay around on a couch watching TV all day long. If he or she lays around day after day, getting an education is not a primary value. Watch a person's actions over time and you will see his or her real values. We have observed that people basically do what they value, whether they admit it or not.

The Interpersonal Ecology — Wants For Self, Other, and Us

The benefactors of our wants fall into three categories — *me, you, and us.*

Wants For Self

Most of the the time when we think of wants, we think of ourselves: what I want *for* myself. Surprisingly, some people have difficulty identifying what their wants are. They are usually people who have been socialized to care primarily for others or individuals who have been taught that it is selfish to want something for self. As we mentioned earlier, however, most people do not have this difficulty.

Wants For Other

When it comes to thinking about others, many of us think about what it is we want *from* others — not *for* others. The difference between *from* and *for* is rather subtle, but it has enormous implications for how you relate to people.

When you think about what you want *from* others, you are still really thinking about what you want *for yourself.* Your attention is focused on what they can do to help you achieve your own desires. The things or actions you want from other people can easily become something you demand of them.

When you think about what you want positively *for* others, with no strings attached, you are truly in their court, thinking about their interests instead of your own. Wants *for* others are like a gift to them based on what you know about them and their own wants. Thinking about what you truly want for others is a powerful bridge-building activity. In effect you are helping them attend to and achieve their own wants. This is a critical element in any successful negotiation.

For example, suppose you are a person who is not particularly punctual, but being on time is important to your partner. Making a special effort to arrive at events or appointments on schedule is something you can do *for* your partner. You may not experience any immediate personal benefits from your action; nevertheless, out of respect or love for your partner, you transcend your own interests and do it for him or her. The narcissist or person who is preoccupied with self to the exclusion of everyone else is unable to freely do things *for* others (Lowen, 1985).

Wants For Us

The third frame of reference you can adopt in thinking about wants is, "What's in it *for us* — as a pair, group, family, team, or organization?" Here you think of yourself and others as members of a larger unit, focusing on wants for the bigger entity. Usually wants at this level are to build trust, increase esprit de corps, enhance our working or loving together, and succeed in our joint project.

Hidden Agenda

When wants are unknown, or are known but left unstated, they can affect interaction adversely. Others have to guess what your intentions are. If your behavior is seen as strange, uncooperative, or manipulative, others may think you are operating out of a private or "hidden agenda." This can happen in the following situations:

1. You are *unaware* of what you really desire.

2. You are aware of what you want, but *fail* to be clear with others about what you desire. Perhaps you genuinely forget or think your wants are not important enough to disclose.

3. You *choose* to keep your wants unstated for one reason or another.

Hidden agenda occur most often when we think other people would not like our wants or "buy into" them. So, rather than disclose them directly, we try to work around others to get what we want. We also usually try to hide our intentions when they are ornery, mean, or embarrassing:

"I want to get even with you."

"I want to take advantage of you."

"I want you to admire me."

Likewise, we typically assign intentions to other people's behavior based on how it affects us. If we are hurt or disadvantaged by their actions, we are likely to attribute malicious intentions to the other person.

When communication becomes confusing, hidden agenda and conflicting intentions are often at work. Tuning into wants and intentions is central for understanding what is really going on in yourself and in others. Your intentions have dramatic impact on your communication, because what you want, consciously or unconsciously, comes out directly or indirectly in your actions, the next part of the Awareness Wheel.

Tips

1. Ask yourself from time to time, "What do I really want?" Setting priorities for your wants will help you focus energy, enabling you to set goals and follow through with congruent action.

2. Discover the wants of other people. If you want to motivate and connect with others, find out what they want and work with them to fulfill their wants. Figure out "what's in it *for* them."

3. Clarify wants — your own and others — when a conversation (or meeting) is confusing.

4. Check your wants when you are feeling desperate. Are they keeping you stuck?

5. Think about your hidden intentions. How are the intentions which you are willing to admit to yourself privately, but are unwilling to disclose to others, influencing your actions toward them?

6. Acknowledge your own behavior rather than deny it, because your behavior can give you clues to your real intentions and values.

7. Use awareness of your intentions to help you send clearer messages, using an appropriate style of communication.

Feelings and Wants Supply "Juice"

Up to this point we have talked about four parts of the Awareness Wheel — sensory data, thoughts, feelings, and wants. The first two parts are the "rational" parts of the wheel, focusing on perception and analysis, the cognitive work done by your head. Notice, however, where the line in the diagram below cuts through the Wheel. Some of our thoughts fall below the line representing the portion of our thinking and believing that is "irrational" from time to time.

The third and fourth parts represent the "affective" or more emotional dimensions of the Wheel. Think of your feelings as coming from your stomach and wants as coming from your heart. These affective parts provide the energy and drive — the juice if you will — for your actions. They are also the parts where energy is most often blocked or diffused.

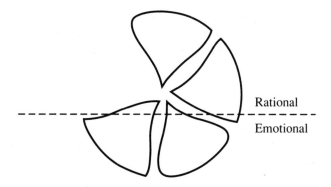

Rational

Emotional

Often people, projects, and programs get stuck because of irrational thoughts, negative feelings, and conflicting wants below the line. Beliefs of low worth and vulnerability or feelings of anger, fear, and frustration surface in the outbursts and pot shots of Fight Talk and Spite Talk. Actions are thwarted when wants are not known or when they are in conflict.

The first step in dealing with an impasse is to attend to the *hot, sore, or soft spot* below the line. Getting this information out in the open will lead you to other parts of the Wheel and eventually enable you to get your energy flowing again into future action.

ACTIONS — Your Behavior

The action zone of the Awareness Wheel includes:

Past Action: what you have done or were doing earlier (yesterday, last week or year).

Present Action: what you are currently doing.

Future Action: what specifically you will do later (next hour, tomorrow, or next week); the commitments you make.

Actions are your behavioral output; they are the results of how you process sensory data, thoughts, and your feelings and wants; they are the visible signs of what you are experiencing in various parts of your Awareness Wheel. It is here that you make *choices and commitments* — to do or not to do; to say or not to say. Choosing and exercising options requires the conscious act of your *will*. (That may be why the secret of self-control is self- and other-awareness.)

Think of actions as:

behaviors	promises
activities	achievements
action plans	accomplishments
solutions	

Most of us are conscious of these broader categories of actions, but we are often unaware of the little things we do that punctuate our conversation: the pauses, foot-tappings, frowning, finger pointing, laughing. These are the small steps in a dance — forwards, backwards, sideways. All of this output becomes sensory data that influences how others perceive us. We tend to be aware chiefly of what we say, while ignoring the accompanying gestures and expressions. But our listeners take in far more than our words. They note the tone of our voices, the way we hold our bodies, and the look on our faces. And these body signs may say as much or more than our words. In short, both our verbal and nonverbal actions send messages, and unless we are conscious of both, we cannot accurately assess the impact we have on others.

Think about some of your small patterns of behavior. Can you identify some of them? For example, do you lean forward and point your finger when you really want to make a point? Do you break eye contact, step back, and start to move away when you have lost interest in a conversation or don't have time to talk?

Future Actions

Future actions can be confused with intentions. The difference is that here we are talking about what you *will* do. As you move from intentions to future actions, you cross an invisible line called *commitment*. Intentions do not carry a definite commitment to act; future actions do.

When you commit yourself to specific actions, and announce them to others, you create expectations — beliefs about what will happen in the future. Your actions will become others' sensory data. Their thoughts and feelings about you will depend on the expected match between what you say you will do and what they actually see or hear you do.

Participant and Observer

Although it is hard to be both a participant and an observer at the same time, it is very useful to become aware of your repetitive behavior patterns, especially the ones that work for and against you. Being aware of the actions which you repeat in certain kinds of situations will help you change them if you wish. For example, one of the co-authors drops his voice to a near whisper at the end of a sentence when he is not confident about what he is saying. Another used to have a tendency to say "no" to any request before really thinking about it. What are your own behavior patterns?

We are not suggesting that you constantly monitor yourself. This would rob you of much spontaneity. However, being aware of your own verbal and nonverbal actions is vital to understanding the reactions that others have to you.

SELF-TALK

The next time you anticipate a difficult situation, or find yourself in the middle of one, talk to yourself. Use this map to increase your awareness by asking yourself, "What's going on right now?" Communicating honestly with yourself is central to communicating effectively with others.

When we talk about increasing "self-awareness," we are talking about *connecting with yourself* by becoming more aware of these five dimensions. Awareness is a resource; it is information about "what is."

Tips

1. Ask yourself, when you get a *positive* response from someone, "What did I do, verbally and nonverbally, that brought about that response?"

2. Ask yourself when you get a *negative* response from someone, "What did I do, verbally and nonverbally, that brought about that response?" Then do something different; do not keep repeating the same action that is not working for you.

6

INDIVIDUAL SIMILARITIES
AND DIFFERENCES:
Conflict or Collaboration

Reflect for a moment about what you really liked about your partner when you first began to know one another. Was as it the way that person seemed to be on just the same wave length as you? Or did you find somehow that, because your partner was different and interesting, he or she brought new energy and life to you? Did your partner enjoy you just the way you were?

The similarities and differences we gravitate to in other people affect our relationships in several ways. First they attract us. They bind us together. But they may also bring boredom, cause stress, tear us apart, or give us strength. In short, their influences are profound.

We are similar or different in fundamental ways: in how we view the world and in what we perceive or tune out. We may march to the same or a different drummer in how we think, how we feel, and in what brings energy and motivates us from deep within. Often we take the similarities in our relationship for granted and fail to appreciate the foundations they provide.

Mostly, we are all too aware of the differences between us. We seem to know that after a time two people in a relationship will experience differences intensely. The differences that at first intrigued us become amusing or maybe simply annoying. Sometimes they lead to a resigned or, perhaps, bitter acceptance, and when these differences lead to parting, we are not surprised. Seldom do we recognize, however, that differences between partners can actually build a stronger and more satisfying relationship system.

Through the ages philosophers, poets, and artists have portrayed basic clusters of similarities and differences between people. In more recent times psychologists have categorized the clusters. Now brain scientists have even found physiological and neurological bases for them. Today a number of maps describing these clusters of similarities and differences show us that these phenomena are not random or due to chance.

This chapter presents one map that corresponds closely with the Awareness Wheel. It can help you:

1. See how the similarities between you and your partner give strength to your relationship.

2. Learn how the differences between you and your partner create issues and recognize how misunderstandings and miscommunications arise.

3. Discover how the ways you and your partner differ can balance your relationship system and provide a resource for the system.

4. Find renewed appreciation for yourself and for your partner.

PSYCHOLOGICAL TYPES

This major map for understanding similarities and differences among people originated in the work of the Swiss psychologist Carl Jung, who developed a theory of psychological types. Others, such as Isabel Briggs Myers and Katherine Briggs, have built upon Jung's foundation of types. The basic framework gives insight into ourselves and others as individuals. Jung's map of psychological types contains four complementary ways of being and of experiencing the world.

Taking in Information by Sensing or Intuiting

Jung formulated that people use one of two different ways of taking in information — of perceiving: *sensing or intuiting*. People focus on one of the two streams of impressions and all but tune out the other stream. Note that how you perceive may differ substantially from — or be quite similar to — how your partner perceives.

People who prefer *sensing* attend most acutely to the five senses. They often are more detail-oriented and see the pieces of a situation. (Recall the sensation part of the Awareness Wheel.) The concreteness of sensory data makes the strongest impression on them. They also emphasize and trust past actions. (Again, recall the Awareness Wheel.)

On the other hand, those types of people who prefer *intuiting* use sensations as a starting point for perceiving. However, they also tune into seemingly unconscious associations and mix them together with the sensory data to form a general picture. They cannot document their perceptions well because some of what they perceive may not be apparent to the senses. Yet, they connect various impressions and trust their hunches about future actions. (Also recall the "Intuitive Sensations" discussion regarding the Awareness Wheel.)

For example, imagine a "sensor" and an "intuitor" who live together getting ready to move their household. The sensor looks around and sees all the specific items which need to be packed and thinks about all the separate jobs to accomplish. Remembering past moves, the sensor recalls who did specific activities and what a huge undertaking a move entails.

The intuitor, on the other hand, anticipates the upcoming location and figures that everything involved with the move will all come together. The intuitor looks around and makes a quick estimate about boxes and truck size. Confident that any difficulties will be overcome, the intuitor imagines the whole thing being accomplished.

In this example both people view the moving scene from entirely different perspectives. Without understanding and accepting the differences in their viewpoints, the partners probably find that making the move brings possibilities for much miscommunication.

Coming to Conclusions by Thinking or Feeling

The framework of psychological types also shows that people come to conclusions (make judgments, to use Jung's word) about their perceptions from differing but preferred bases. Some people base judgments on their *thinking,* and others make them as a result of *feelings* or value orientations (their intentions).

Those who prefer to use thinking base their conclusions most heavily on analysis and a logical process. They organize the facts and ideas and see principles. In making decisions, they are less comfortable factoring in personal values or feelings. As as result, their conclusions can be more impersonal.

Other people prefer to use feelings as a basis for making judgments or coming to conclusions. (According to Jung's framework, the word "feeling" goes beyond referring to an emotional response to include a value orientation also.) Those who base conclusions to a large degree on feelings do so by judging the impact on themselves or others. They put weight on what they like or dislike, on what they prize, and on what seems to bring harmony. They find appeals to emotions compelling. As a result, they are comfortable coming to conclusions that may or may not seem logical.

For example, consider how a "thinker" and a "feeler" would decide about an unplanned, emergency appeal for donations to feed the hungry in another country. The thinker might do an analysis of how much money has been designated in the budget for various charitable categories, and determine if the appeal fits into what is available in the specific category. The thinker might also consider what this means in terms of their policy of providing the largest percent of funds for local organizations. This person also will want to know about the track record of the organization soliciting the donations.

The feeler may instead be moved by the human suffering and determine immediately that regardless of categories or policies, this is a special situation. Feeling sympathetic and fairly helpless to stop the pain, the feeler wants to give as quickly and as generously as possible. While this person would be angry if the organization were not reputable, the feeler would consider the emergency situation to be worth the risk of some misappropriated funds.

When partners come to conclusions from these two fundamentally different standpoints, they must be self-aware and genuinely respectful of the other person. Otherwise their decision-making about a current issue can turn into a struggle in the relationship.

Dealing with the World by Perceiving or Judging:
Openness versus Closure

According to Jung's map of psychological types, people prefer to deal with the world using one or the other process: *perceiving or judging.* That means either you would rather *continue taking in information,* or you would rather *come to a conclusion* about your impressions. Your actions reflect your orientation.

"Perceivers" prefer to deal with the world by continually becoming aware; they desire *open-endedness.* They like to live life for the experience, the process. Because it appears that all of the evidence is not yet in, they may back away from making a decision or coming to a conclusion. They often hold out for more data and feel restless after a decision — and then they may change their mind.

Those who prefer to deal with the world by judging, by coming to conclusions, want *closure.* They want order in their life and are outcome-oriented. They push for decisions and feel at ease afterward shutting off more information once they have reached a decision.

Consider how a "perceiver" and a "judger" would go about purchasing a desk for a home office. The perceiver goes to a store to see options and possibilities. After ordering a desk, the perceiver then returns home and wonders if the desk actually will look right in the corner of the room where it will stand. Once the desk is delivered, the perceiver moves it around to various spots and decides to try it for awhile. However, because the desk may be returned, the perceiver keeps the packing materials. Also, to see other ideas, the perceiver arranges to have office and home furniture catalogs sent.

The judger, on the other hand, goes to the store to make a choice. The judger knows the dimensions of the space and takes time to measure the fit before ordering. Once the desk is delivered, the judger makes sure it is set up in the determined spot and is ready to use the desk immediately.

Because their basic comfort levels with openness differ so much, perceivers and judgers can be difficult for one another. It takes understanding and respect, as well as good communication, to determine how to deal with particular situations in which the two perspectives are at odds with each other.

Being Oriented to the Outer World or to the Inner World

Jung's map explains that people find their source of energy in either the outer world or the inner world. In drawing energy, you either prefer an *extroverted* experience or its complement, an *introverted* one. Either one can mold your intentions and serves as a motivating force for your actions. (Again, consider the Awareness Wheel.)

Extroverted people turn outward to energize themselves. Talk, work, and play with others stimulate them. They move quickly towards action and like to expend energy. Outside interests fascinate them, and external conditions provide decisive elements for their choices. Too much aloneness makes them uncomfortable so they desire and seek others.

On the other hand, people with an introverted attitude turn inward to renew energy. They find the inner world of ideas and imagination most important and rewarding. They experience contentment in reading, working quietly, or doing activities alone or with only a few people. They look for depth rather than breadth in their relationships. Since too much interaction can be draining, after a time they may feel lonely in a crowd. To recover, they desire and seek solitude.

Reflect on how an "introvert" and an "extrovert" enjoy getting away to relax for a weekend at a lake. The introvert wants some peacefulness and a rest, perhaps a walk in the woods, and dinner at a quiet restaurant. The introvert may see the weekend as a chance to have some time alone together with a partner.

The extrovert, however, will suggest that some friends come along or make an effort to meet others who live near the lake. Because more people provide more chance for fun, the extrovert will invite others to join in and even make a party atmosphere. Moving around and identifying available activities, especially those that involve others, is important to this action-oriented person.

Again, partners who differ on this dimension need to clarify what they each want and expect in a situation. It may take real effort to take account of both their desires.

Combining the Complements

The various combinations of these four complementary sets of preferences form 16 distinctly different personality types. (Additional readings and survey instruments are available to help you learn more about your type. See the appendix.)

Because these preferences or characteristics run very deep within us, people in relationships who represent different types may easily experience profound misunderstandings and miscommunications. Realize, however, that people do not operate only according to a single personality type, yet they do have preferred ways of operating. The theory suggests that people should first fully develop their unique, individual way of being — their type. Acceptance and support, as well as awareness, aid this development. Once a person's comfort with his or her own type is in place, that person can more easily expand to incorporate aspects of other personality types in a satisfying manner.

The framework above is not the only one available. If you are interested, other frameworks such as those based on brain dominance or behavioral styles also provide insights about similarities and differences between people. (See the appendix for instruments growing out of those frameworks too.)

CONCLUSIONS AND PRINCIPLES

Theory and research on psychological types propose that people have strongly developed preferences and activity patterns. First your natural inclinations and then your life pathway work together to make you more adept and comfortable with certain ways of being and behaving.

You can truly value what comes naturally and also see where those tendencies help your relationship or get you into trouble with your partner. You can also learn to recognize the validity of, as well as appreciate more fully, areas where your partner differs from you. This framework of similarities and differences suggests several principles to keep in mind regarding relationships:

- There is no *one* best way to be — no right or wrong, but simply similar or different. Each aspect by itself offers both advantages and disadvantages.
- People who are similar to you in how they function will probably be easiest for you to understand. A faster bonding (connecting) may occur early in your relationship with them because you both take for granted the same ways of doing things and the same areas of importance. The similarities give your relationship strength.

- As time passes in a relationship with a person similar to you, so much sameness may not bring enough renewing, balancing, or synergistic energy.

- People who differ from you, though more difficult to understand, may at first be fascinating and appealing. As time passes and issues arise in a relationship with a person who differs, the two of you may each come from opposite directions in how you approach the issues. Without understanding and genuine acceptance, the opposition can put a real strain on your relationship.

- Typically people do not trust different ways of viewing and dealing with the world. Often during times of stress, without awareness and, in some cases, without a strategy for handling conflict, we each revert to our most comfortable way of operating. If you and your partner differ, you may try to change one another to be more like yourself. With real and deep differences, attempts to change the other never succeed.

- If differences are communicated, accepted, and accounted for, they can bring freshness to the relationship. They can also provide more resources for resolving the issues and potential problems of daily living.

- The areas of differences are complementary to one another. Having a range of possibilities in a relationship system, each with its own strengths, provides balance for the system and helps it function well.

Tips

1. Understand as fully as possible your own preferred mode of operating — your own psychological type (or your brain dominance or behavioral style). Know how that mode influences the way you respond to situations and what that means about your most comfortable communication patterns. Learn the advantages of that pattern as well as your blind spots.

2. Understand your partner as well.

3. Once again, think about what attracted you to your partner in the first place. Was it more your similarities or your differences? If you have been in your relationship for some time, think about how those similarities or differences affect you now.

4. Build your own and your partner's esteem by truly appreciating the way each of you are. Express this attitude of appreciation with clear communication, using the "speaking skills" discussed in Chapter 9.

5. When you are in conflict with someone, try to experience the situation from the other person's perspective as well. Make presentations and offer solutions that "speak" to the other person's type, but do not discount your own orientation-strengths in the process.

6. Recognize where similarities between you and your partner overlap. Consider how these ways of being or behaving strengthen or weaken your relationship.

7. Figure out where you and your partner differ. Think about what the areas of difference potentially provide for your system.

8. Consider another person's psychological type (not your own) to really be on target when you think about what you want for him or her. When you do things for others — give loving behaviors or gifts — do so in terms of what "fits" for the other person instead of for yourself.

9. Determine which complementary dimensions your relationship system seems to lack. What does this void imply for your system? Think about how you and your partner might compensate for the missing part.

Your personality type influences the way you connect with yourself and others around the five zones described in the Awareness Wheel. Learn how you limit yourself from tuning into all the zones and how you may experience partial awareness. The next chapter shows you how limited or partial awareness occurs.

7

PARTIAL AWARENESS

Try the following experiment.

Place the open palm of your hand comfortably in front of you at arms length. Now look at your hand for about 10 seconds, observing the color and texture as well as the length and the shape of lines on your hand. We will refer to this position as your "foreground."

Now keeping your hand in the same position, focus your eyes beyond your hand at the wall, carpet, or whatever is beyond. Again for about 10 seconds notice the color, texture, and shape of the object(s) beyond your hand. We will call this position your "background."

Now again bring your eyes back to focus on your hand for 10 seconds.

Next move your focus back and forth several times between the background and foreground. Notice how your eyes shift from foreground to background.

Finally try to focus your eyes equally on the foreground and background at the same time. You will discover it is impossible. Our eyes are designed to focus clearly on one spot at a time. They can, however, move from spot to spot very rapidly.

Your Mind Brings Your Experience Into Focus

Conscious self-awareness works a lot like your eyes, lifting different aspects of your experience from your unconscious background to your conscious foreground. Your conscious mind moves from one part of your Awareness Wheel to another as it monitors *inputted* sensory data, *computed* thoughts, feelings, and wants, and *outputted* actions.

Think back to the experiment with your hand. When your focus was on the foreground (your hand), the background (wall, floor, etc.) did not disappear; it just went out of focus or consciousness for the moment. Likewise, when your attention was directed to the background, your hand did not disappear. Your awareness operates much the same way. While you are actively thinking, your feelings are in the background, but they do not disappear. When you shift attention to your feelings for a moment, your thoughts move to the background, but they do not evaporate. At one instant you may be aware of what you *want,* then *act* to achieve it. Suddenly a *feeling* looms up and you begin to *think* about what is causing the feeling.

The Awareness Wheel is a map for helping you become more aware of yourself and others in any situation by turning unconscious background information, from any zone of the Wheel, into conscious foreground awareness. Remember, in any situation, the background is composed of five different types of information.

Your Comfort Zones

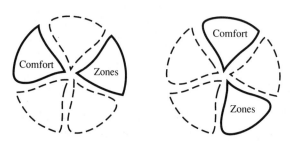

As we discussed in Chapter 6, Individual Similarities and Differences, people tend to perceive and understand situations from the perspective of their personality type. You can think of your personality type in terms of your *informational comfort zone,* the information you really trust in your Awareness Wheel. As you tune in to a situation, often one or two areas dominate or regularly come to mind first. As a result, you might be particularly attuned to your thoughts while your partner is first and foremost aware of feelings.

> George often wants and acts. "I *want* to wind this discussion up and *move* to the next point."

Fred is different. He typically feels situations and studies decisions, "I'm *concerned* that a decision will be made prematurely. Let's be *confident* about what we do."

Judy on the other hand says, "We don't have enough *data,* I doubt that our *analysis* is accurate." She relies primarily on data and thoughts.

Each person processes information differently and uses the Awareness Wheel in a distinctive way; consequently, different people have different patterns. This is both an advantage and a disadvantage. The advantage is that by collectively pooling information about a situation, you and others are potentially able to create a more complete picture of the situation. Your action plans can be based on better information.

The disadvantage of having different information processing patterns is that each individual tends to have only a partial picture of the situation. Since most of us believe our orientation is the best, discussions of issues can easily turn into struggles about whose view is "right" instead of drawing on each person's information to resolve an issue. Under pressure we tend to lock into our comfort zones even more, seeing only parts rather than the whole. Since not everyone's zones are the same, the potential for conflict is considerable.

Different patterns add variety to relationships. Recognize, however, that because each person brings different talents or resources to a situation and only sees a partial picture based on a distinctive pattern of using the Awareness Wheel, no one has the full story. If you know something about your own pattern, and are quick to discover and draw on others' orientations as well, you are ahead of most people in interpersonal competence. The key here is to appreciate these differences and capitalize on everyone's strength to develop more complete information.

When we speak of "complete" awareness, we are talking about being able to "tune into" all five dimensions of your Awareness Wheel, in any order within a situation or around an issue. And when we refer to "congruent"awareness, we mean the information in all parts of your Wheel "fits" together. Congruence is a state of internal harmony rather than dissonance, even in a tough situation. Internal congruence (or incongruence) is signaled externally — particularly in your nonverbal behavior. Communicycles thrive on complete and congruent information.

What is your pattern in using the Awareness Wheel? Can you identify one? How about your partner's pattern? How does it differ from your own?

PARTIAL AWARENESS

Recall a recent experience of leaving a conversation with your partner, a friend, or someone at work with an unfinished communicycle? You walked into the next room or drove home unaware of anything along the way, or began some other activity, but your conscious mind and feelings did not shift with you to the next activity. They were stuck behind, churning over and replaying the incomplete conversation.

Your experience is typical of situations involving only *partial awareness*. Your mind has difficulty closing the communicycle because something was missing in the situation. Some key part of your Wheel or something operating in the other players' Wheel, was being ignored. Either one or both of you were operating out of partial awareness, or perhaps you did not have the communication skills to disclose crucial information yourself to help the other person put key information on the table.

As you relive the experience, your mind tries to find the missing part so it can bring the situation to closure and allow you to move on to the next situation. If the missing information is outside of your typical informational comfort zone — for instance, you are primarily a thinker and the critical information is a feeling — you are at a disadvantage in that situation.

Have you also been in the opposite situation where you leave a conversation feeling energized and enthused about what just happened? If you use your Awareness Wheel to recall and process this situation, you will find you were probably operating out of a state of heightened awareness with all parts of the Wheel covered in the situation. You just had the experience of a complete and congruent exchange that led to a pleasing outcome.

Unfortunately, when people want to grasp a situation, they often look everywhere but in the most logical place: inside themselves. They watch what others are doing and listen to what others are saying. They pull in global generalities to spring into action with no forethought at all, or they freeze and do nothing.

Too often the key information for understanding and improving a situation is overlooked because it is inside yourself! *Knowing what you are experiencing, completely and congruently, is the foundation for clear and effective communication.*

Following are the three most common sources of partial awareness: *incomplete, incongruent, and blocked* awareness.

INCOMPLETE AWARENESS

While you cannot expect to be constantly aware of your senses, thoughts, feelings, wants, and actions — the very idea is exhausting — you may have an approach that habitually ignores some parts of your Awareness Wheel.

Blind Spots

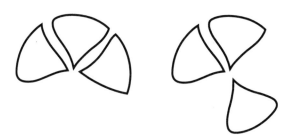

When you operate primarily from your strength, but disregard one or two of the other information zones, you lose information and *blind spots* develop. Perhaps you live in your head and ignore your gut (feelings). Or you barrel into action and disregard your heart (real desires). The one part you bypass may throw a whole situation out of kilter. In the short run, incomplete awareness may seem to work. But in the long run, it takes a toll: poor decisions, increased stress, and troubled relationships.

Blind spots occur when you *overlook, ignore, or disregard* information in any zone of your Wheel. The result is having only *partial information* on which to act.

Here, for example, is a situation in which leaving out intentions resulted in doing and saying something that John really did not want.

> John's teenage son, Mike, was telling him about trying out for the basketball team at the high school. As he listened to Mike talk about making the team, John saw how happy Mike was and began to remember with pleasure his own high school days playing on the football team. Pretty soon he interrupted Mike and started telling some stories about games he had played in. After a while, Mike excused himself and walked out of the room with his shoulders drooping.

> John took in sensory data (Mike's description of the tryouts), made an interpretation (Mike is really happy), but when John began to talk, he missed the sensory data (Mike's loss of energy) as indicated by his drooping shoulders. He was blind to his pride in Mike, while he delighted in his own memories.

Because John was not clear about his own intention — to really listen to Mike and enjoy his enthusiasm — he acted largely on the basis of his own feelings, cutting himself off from Mike. Imagine what Mike is thinking: "Every time I tell Dad about something good that happens to me, he has to brag about himself."

Your Mind and Closure

In addition to focusing your awareness, your mind brings things to closure. It fills in blanks, gives meaning to experience, and facilitates decisions which enable you to resolve issues and move ahead. This is the basic force at work in a communicycle. After you send a message, your mind looks for an acceptable response. If it receives one, the communicycle is complete; business is finished and your mind moves to the next exchange. If it does not gain closure, the cycle may stay open for days, months, or even years.

As we saw in Chapter 6, people vary in regard to their need for closure (they go to action or stop taking in data). Some people strive for quick closure and become impatient if it is delayed. Others are uncomfortable with immediate closure. They must mull over and consider alternatives before they can bring things to closure.

Most of the time your mind operates on automatic in your own style, moving from situation to situation, bringing issues to closure or delaying closure. Whether you are a person who jumps to action without much reflection, or someone who labors to make a decision, you can benefit from increased awareness. This is where the Awareness Wheel is particularly useful.

The Awareness Wheel can be used as a mental map to help you make better use of your self and other information. As you bring parts of the Wheel to consciousness, it helps you recognize what is there, fill in the missing information, and make more confident and competent decisions.

Pre-closure

When you move to *action* too fast, failing to consider all parts of your Awareness Wheel in situations which require careful consideration, you pre-close on an issue. This short circuits the information process. You do this by:

- missing sensory data
- jumping to conclusions
- disregarding feelings

- ignoring wants
- acting on impulse

Shortcuts end up taking more effort in the long run. Eventually the issue, product, or project comes back to haunt you. Look back on issues you have attempted to shortcut. More often than not, the information available inside yourself, which you overlooked, was central to the best solution. If you pay attention to others' reactions, you will immediately see in their nonverbal response the unsatisfactory results of a premature move to establish closure.

The antidote to pre-closure is being aware of all parts of your Awareness Wheel in order to find an action that really fits.

Slow to Reach Closure

Some people simply need more time than others to think about things and make decisions. To hurry this person only creates frustration and stress. In general, they fear the consequences of overlooking or missing information. They must mull over issues and sleep on the big ones before they can act confidently, and often have difficulty committing themselves to a course of action until all alternatives are considered. Then, for some, once they see several alternatives, they have difficulty deciding which one to take. They prefer to keep their options open rather than to risk a mistake. Rushing a person like this into closure overloads his or her circuits and blocks workable outcomes.

If you are "wired" this way, here is how the Awareness Wheel can help you. By knowing that there are only five different types of information to consider in a situation, you can learn to fill in your awareness faster and with more confidence, realizing that you are not overlooking key information. Also, as you put your awareness into action, you have a tool for monitoring the results better.

INCONGRUENT AWARENESS

As you become more in touch with yourself, you may find yourself in situations where what you do (or what others tell you that you do) does not match with what is going on inside of you. As a result, *your verbal messages are not congruent with your nonverbal messages — there is a mismatch between them.*

The mismatch of your verbal and nonverbal behaviors reflects the dissonance and incongruence between the parts of your Awareness Wheel. Several of the parts of your Wheel are out of sync, twisted, so to speak, and in conflict. For example, what you see does not fit your beliefs; what you feel is out of alignment with your intentions; or what you do does not match your feelings or. wants. In short, one or two dimensions of your awareness do not fit with the others.

The major problem with incongruence is that you are working against yourself by dissipating energy and creating stress in yourself and other.

> Dad is helping Jimmy with his homework and has just explained how to work a problem in arithmetic. Jimmy indicates he does not understand and begins to sob. Dad demands to know why Jimmy is crying. "Because you're mad at me," Jimmy sobs. "I am not mad at you," Dad exclaims. Jimmy continues to cry and leaves the room. Dad throws down his pencil and paper. "That kid," he groans.

Dad is not in touch with his feelings of frustration and irritation, which Jimmy picks up from Dad's subtle behavior (breathing, voice tension, posture). When he denies being mad at Jimmy, this leaves Jimmy with a perplexing situation: which message should he believe, his Dad's verbal message — "I'm not mad" — or the behavioral message — "I am mad at you?"

A mismatch can occur between any of the parts of the Awareness Wheel. Here is an example of incongruence between *thoughts* and *feelings:*

"I expected (thought) I would be happy about Jean's promotion, but I'm sad (feeling). I guess I hadn't allowed myself to recognize (think) that her promotion would mean we'd have much less time together."

As we see here, feelings cannot be programmed. They spontaneously arise out of our experience to tell us "what is." That is why you can trust your feelings. When there is a misfit between what you are "supposed" to feel and what you actually do feel, attempting to deny or force a change in your feelings will result in your behaving incongruently.

If you will allow yourself to do so, you can recognize the "misfit" inside yourself. When you acknowledge internal mismatches, *incongruence* can be a turning point. It can alert you to adjust the parts of your Wheel that do not fit together. The earlier you recognize dissonance, the sooner you can take steps to align yourself to act more effectively. If you remain unaware of or deny dissonance, it too will take its toll in stressful and confusing communication. The greatest impact of dissonant and incongruent awareness on others is that they begin to distrust you.

Congruent actions have a subjective "fit" inside you and others!

Stop for a moment and think about yourself. Do you have a chronic pattern of incomplete or incongruent awareness? With your partner? With other people? What parts do you typically leave out? Does your pattern become self defeating?

BLOCKED AWARENESS

When your awareness is blocked, you do not overlook information — you get stuck on one part of your Awareness Wheel. This can happen when you are:

- stunned by what you see or hear
- plagued by a recurring thought

- scared of the consequences (so you feel vulnerable)
- torn by conflicting desires
- burned by past actions

Sometimes you can become preoccupied with something you see, hear, or want. Most often, however, you become stuck and are unable to act effectively when there is a powerful belief that you cannot get past or reconcile with the rest of your Wheel. As a result, you lose flexibility and become immobilized. Rather than *pre-closing* on an issue, you *do not close*. You freeze, unable to move with confidence.

A blockage occurs when a belief coalesces with a fear of an anticipated consequence. As long as you maintain your belief, you will stay stuck. Many beliefs which keep us stuck are basically irrational if we examine them closely. They serve only to inhibit us from expanding our experience and comfort zone. Many beliefs maintain low self- or other-esteem.

Here are some sample blockages:

You know an upcoming report is critical. Furthermore, you *believe* it has to be perfect. You procrastinate and possibly have an anxiety attack. (Feared consequence: poor grade or being passed over for promotion at work.)

You do not ask someone for a date because you *think* you would be rejected. (Feared consequence: embarrassment, tarnished self-image.)

You dodge intimacy because you *believe* it would limit your freedom. (Feared consequence: being smothered, trapped.)

You avoid saying something because you *assume* it would hurt the other person. (Feared consequence: loss of relationship.)

When your energy is blocked, you do not see alternatives and are convinced you cannot risk the consequences. Blockages can be very disabling and painful experiences. The solution to a blockage is to do something — almost anything — except to simply repeat what you are currently doing that is not working for you. Here are some suggestions for things to do to unblock yourself:

- gather more sensory data
- reprogram or reframe your thinking
- revise your expectation
- work through your fears
- reorder your priorities

- expand your comfort zone
- test alternative actions
- let go of the irrational wants or beliefs you are desperately hanging onto — your "false security blanket"

When the Blockage Becomes the Issue

Occasionally, as you begin to process an issue, you may find that you are blocked. In this case, you may discover that the real issue is not the situation confronting you, but rather your disabling belief itself which is creating the blockage.

The test for determining the real issue is this: do you find yourself becoming blocked across several issues as a result of the same underlying belief? If so, the real issue is not the surface concern, but rather a deeper problem associated with the underlying belief.

For example: suppose you *want* to do the following but are having difficulty doing so:

- go back to school
- meet new friends
- take on more challenging responsibilities at work

These sound like three different issues, but when you examine the point at which you are blocked on each one, you find a common, powerful and disabling belief at the base of each issue — you do not think you are very smart. The real issue is your low self-esteem; your chronic negative self-evaluation keeps you stuck.

To resolve the three surface issues, you will first have to do something about your esteem. When your self-esteem is altered, energy will begin flowing in new ways which will resolve the smaller issues.

If you will examine your blockages, they can guide you to deeper levels of self-awareness and your core issues!

Moving Beyond Incomplete, Incongruent, or Blocked Awareness

Partial self-awareness means you have incomplete access to the richness of your own inner experience. Since you can only choose to act upon the parts of your experience of which you are aware, partial self-awareness means limited choices about what to do and about what you can choose to communicate to others.

The process of expanding your awareness may involve risk and sometimes even pain because you may discover an incongruence or blockage which requires action. For example, you may need to change some behavior or value, realign your beliefs or expectations for yourself, or make things right with another person.

So there are risks. But there are great risks in partial awareness too. Partial awareness often leads to a behavior pattern which causes personal and relationship difficulties. Depression, for example, is often a symptom of serious blockage. If you could look inside the body of someone suffering with incomplete or incongruent awareness, you would find muscular tension, headaches, chest pain, elevated blood pressure, upset stomach, disturbed sleep patterns, and very often an extra amount of fatigue. This is the price of partial awareness. It takes energy to limit your awareness and maintain incongruities and a struggle within yourself. And that internal struggle, that stress, reaches out to your relationships too.

You do not have to pay this price, however. You can use your expanded awareness as a resource for growth; you can use it to make modifications in yourself or in your relationships to bring dissonant dimensions into alignment. We think you will find that working toward complete and congruent awareness will enrich your life. Besides the obvious benefit of increasing your knowledge of yourself and keeping you more in contact with who you are, you will find other substantial benefits: greater spontaneity in your actions, feelings of self-acceptance and calm, and a greater sense of purpose and direction as life's energy flows freely through you.

Tips

Partial awareness limits your options. When you want to expand your awareness to increase your options, ask yourself:

1. What information am I missing, avoiding, or denying?
2. What communication style am I in?
3. What are my real intentions?
4. What is actually behind my blockage?
5. Does my action really "fit" with the rest of my Wheel?

8

MAPPING ISSUES

Much of modern living revolves around processing internal and external information. But in a world where information processing has become a top-level industry, most of us have no systematic organized way to sort out the vital information that connects us with ourselves and others. The Awareness Wheel fills that void. It breaks issues and situations into manageable pieces and realigns them in more complete and, sometimes, new shapes. And if you choose to do so, it provides a tool for making changes.

Good solutions to topical, personal, and relational issues grow out of the rich soil of complete and congruent awareness of self and other(s). Poor solutions are the result of partial awareness and incongruent "fixes" which are superimposed on situations. Our goal, then, is to help you learn how to generate complete and congruent solutions.

MAPPING ISSUES:
A PROCESS FOR MAKING DECISIONS,
SOLVING PROBLEMS, AND RESOLVING CONFLICTS

Do you have a tough situation to handle? Here is a process that takes into account all five key pieces of information to produce a concrete action plan.

Mapping an issue involves these eight steps:

Step 1. Identifying and defining the issue.

Step 2. Contracting to work through the issue.

Step 3. Understanding the issue completely.

Step 4. Identifying wants.

Step 5. Generating Options.

Step 6. Choosing actions.

Step 7. Testing the action plan.

Step 8. Evaluating the outcome.

When to Map an Issue

As you can see, this process for mapping an issue is quite thorough. Obviously, you do not use it for every issue and every situation. But once you are familiar with the map, you will find that it is an invaluable guide in many different situations.

Mapping issues, the term we use for proceeding through the eight steps, is an effective process for working on an issue when:

- the issue is important or complicated
- considerable tension and conflict exist
- you want maximum input from other people involved with the issue.
- you are seeking the best solution in the situation.

Map Issues by Yourself or With Others

The same tool can be applied in a number of different situations. Use the mapping process to:

- think through and resolve an issue for yourself.
- help someone else work through an issue.
- resolve an issue you have together with someone else.
- assist a group of people who have a common issue.
- help groups who interface to effectively express their awareness with each other in order to discover mutually satisfying options.

In this chapter we will use an example of an individual mapping an issue to illustrate how you can use the process by yourself to think through a situation. When you map an issue with other people, each person fills out his or her Awareness Wheel privately and then shares this information with the other(s) at each step. When you do this with a group of people, it is useful to develop a group Awareness Wheel by recording everyone's input on a blackboard or flip chart.

STEP 1. IDENTIFYING AND DEFINING THE ISSUE

Issues often arise when there is some disruption in expectations — when there is a gap between what is *anticipated* and what is actually *experienced*. The gap can register in any awareness zone — sensing, thinking, feeling, wanting, or doing. The gap usually stirs concern and requires that you deal with the matter. Occasionally someone else spots an issue first and brings it to your attention. In any event, in Step 1, you ask:

1. What is the issue?
   - a topic or task
   - a personal concern
   - a relational matter
2. Who is involved and likely to be affected?
3. Whose issue is it?
   - mine
   - yours
   - ours

When you have identified the issue and have a clear and agreed upon definition of it, proceed to the next step.

STEP 2. CONTRACTING TO WORK THROUGH THE ISSUE

This step mainly applies to mapping issues with other people. Before processing an issue with others, establish an informal "contract" to work together on the issue. (See Chapter 11, "Meta Talk," for the section about Pre-Talk and Contracting.)

Have you ever wanted to talk with someone about something but found the other person unreceptive? When this happens, it is easy to feel resentment and assume he or she is not interested in your concern. Often it is not the issue, but rather it is a bad time for the other person to talk about your concern; at another time, he or she may be very willing to talk.

Contracting means getting a clear verbal or nonverbal "go ahead" from everyone involved to discuss an issue. Without this commitment, the discussion may be hurried, flat, or guarded, if it occurs at all.

So in Step 2, make sure all of you have the "rules straight" (have clearly defined the issue you want to work on) and have established a solid contract with all the relevant parties to work through the issue. Then write the issue in the center of the Awareness Wheel and go to the third step.

Illustration

Here is how one fellow used this process to think through an issue for himself:

> Tim was a partner in a consulting firm. The company was five years old, and its growth had created a heavy load of

administrative work that he found oppressive. He was a person quick with ideas and great with people, but paperwork and administrative detail left him cold.

Over a period of several months Tim began to feel increasingly dissatisfied with his life. He was thirty-eight and, like many men his age, felt a need for change, but he was not sure in what direction. His sixteen-year marriage was solid and interesting, and his two children were a responsibility he welcomed. Taking them out on weekends to a farm they owned, teaching the eight-year-old how to ride horseback and the three-year-old to plant seeds was often the high point of his week. But it was not enough. One rainy afternoon, Tim sat down and made a list of the aspects of his life that seemed troubling:

- my role in the company
- time with my family
- meeting my financial commitments
- time for reading, gardening, and photography

His role in the company stood out as the most prickly thorn among his issues. He had the time and interest to "have a look," so Tim "contracted" with himself to work through this issue by writing it in the hub of the Awareness Wheel, and moving on to Step 3.

STEP 3. UNDERSTANDING THE ISSUE COMPLETELY

The purpose of Step 3 is to develop complete understanding of the issue before taking action. This prevents pre-closure — jumping quickly to solutions which do not fit.

To understand the issue, answer these four questions about the issue:

1. What have I done, or what am I currently doing, that is working and not working?
2. What have I seen and heard?
3. What do I think is going on?
4. How am I feeling?

In Step 3, Tim wrote the following in his Awareness Wheel:

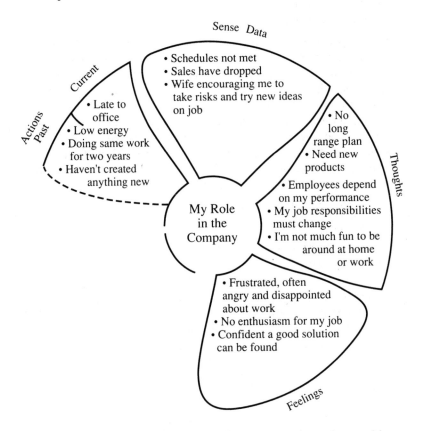

When you have answered each of these questions thoroughly, you will have a good information base on which to build in Step 4.

Understanding as the Solution

Occasionally you will discover that it is not necessary to go beyond Step 3 because the very process of understanding the issue has become the solution in itself. When this occurs your external and internal information will all fit together peacefully. You will experience a shift where understanding and knowing, not action, is the only solution necessary.

STEP 4. IDENTIFYING WANTS

After a solid base for understanding the issue is developed (and discussed with others mapping the issue with you), Step 4 moves you around the Awareness Wheel to identify all the wants that surround the issue. Here you focus on your general wants: your wishes, desires, goals, objectives, and intentions. At this point, do *not* think about specific actions. Consider things you want to *be,* to *do,* and to *have.* You might also identify things you do not want, if that is relevant. This step is a way to clarify your goals before considering actions.

If other people are involved in the issue, think about the wants they may have for themselves — what their wishes, desires, goals, objectives, and intentions might be. Consider what you *want for others* based on your understanding of their desires. Then imagine yourself giving a nonmaterial gift to them. Be careful not to confuse what you want *for* others, with what you want *from* others. Put what you want *from* others under your wants for self.

When you attend to others' wants, you raise the level of consciousness beyond your own self-interest to other- and relationship-interests. This system perspective increases good will and creates a collaborative spirit which builds trust and strengthens relationships.

To identify wants, answer these three questions:

1. What do I want *for me* regarding the issue?

2. What do I want (positive) *for other* individual(s) involved?

3. What do I want *for us* — our relationship?

Here is what Tim wrote in Step 4 as he mapped his own individual issue:

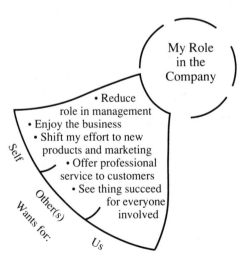

STEP 5. GENERATING OPTIONS

In Step 5, you brainstorm options which you could consider to resolve the issue, or at least move it ahead. The question to ask here is:

1. What *can I do* about the issue?

   • For me

   • For other(s)

   • For us

When considering this question, imagine what a successful outcome would actually look, sound, or feel like, based on the diagnostic information gathered in Steps 3 and 4. Think "expansively," "small," and "positively." Rather than trying to visualize one big solution, brainstorm (no censoring) a diverse list of small positive actions you could actually take as a next step. Sometimes it is useful to set your expectations for improvement in terms of a percentage figure. For example, if you could achieve 20 percent improvement in a situation as a next step, would that be satisfactory? Without ever really thinking about it, we often unconsciously set unrealistic (100 percent) expectations and then feel overwhelmed or discouraged trying to bring about a gigantic solution. Consider every option possible. Be sure to include both new possibilities which you have not done, and actions you have taken in the past which have been helpful.

Here is the list Tim developed:

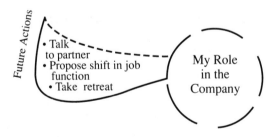

STEP 6. CHOOSING ACTIONS

When you have your list of possibilities, consider the worst and best things that could happen with each action. Also determine which options are the most workable. Synthesize and combine actions if you wish. The primary question at this point is:

1. What *will* I commit to doing?

Select one or two actions you *will* actually do. If you are mapping an issue with others, gain a solid agreement about what each person will do.

Here is what Tim wrote:

ACTION PLAN

What I Will Do	*By When*
Talk to partner	One week from today
Propose shifts in job function	One week from today
Consider taking a two-week retreat	One month from today

STEP 7. TESTING THE ACTION PLAN

After you have chosen your action plan, test it. Pause for a moment and visualize yourself actually carrying out each action at a specific time and place. If you see, hear, and experience yourself following through with each step effectively, great! Your plan "fits."

However, if you cannot see yourself carrying out your action plan, what is blocking you? (See the section on, "When The Blockage Becomes The Issue" in Chapter 7, "Partial Awareness.") Is it something you think, feel, or really do not want to do that prevents action? The zone of your Awareness Wheel in which you find yourself "stuck" becomes a new issue: your belief, fear, or intention. This new issue may be the real issue that is blocking you so shift your attention to it.

If you are mapping an issue with others, watch nonverbal responses indicating agreement or a lack of commitment to take action. If you see or hear a mixed message, 60 percent "yes" and 40 percent "no," for example, pick up on the "no." Ask others to indicate what does not fit for them. Keep processing the issue until you gain as much commitment as possible. If 100 percent commitment is not reached, acknowledge that as part of the action plan. Without belaboring, you may want to explore how the "no" could sabotage the plan. Does the "no" really represent a blockage and "a bigger issue" that is not being faced?

When Tim visualized himself carrying out these actions (talking to partner, proposing shifts in job functions, and taking a two-week retreat), he found that the first two fit well for him. In his imaging, his conversation with his partner — sharing his thoughts and feelings and proposing shifts in job duties — was very comfortable and was well received by his partner. However, visualizing his two-week retreat did not have the same result. He saw himself as being very restless, not wanting to be there. Tim decided not to think further about the retreat now, but to consider the possibility in a couple of months after the changes in his job were well in place.

STEP 8. EVALUATING THE OUTCOME

The moment you act on your plan, you move from "future" to "current" action. As you act, others observe your actions and respond in some fashion. As you see and hear (sense) their responses, you begin evaluating (thinking) whether or not your action is effective. If it is effective, you will feel something positive. If not, you may experience a range of negative feelings — disappointment, frustration, embarrassment. If the outcome is pleasing, celebrate! If the outcome is not satisfactory, revolve around your Awareness Wheel again, and come up with a different action plan. Do not keep repeating actions that do not work.

What happened in Tim's situation?

No longer mired in uncertainty, Tim did discuss these ideas with his partner three days later. Within a short time, both of them made major changes in their roles in the company that helped both themselves and the company.

What Mapping Issues Does For You

In a way, we all use the Awareness Wheel unconsciously to think through issues in our lives. But most of us tend to operate in our comfort zones and ignore our blind spots; we tend to make decisions based on partial information. Short circuits and blockages prevent us from mapping issues effectively.

Mapping Issues is a way for you to slow down and become more conscious of the different parts of your experience, so you can use them in resolving issues. This process enables you to base your decisions on more complete information. It also will help you to understand yourself better so you can avoid being intimidated or manipulated by others and keep from putting yourself down.

ALTERNATIVE MAPPING STRATEGIES

There are occasions when altering the eight steps described above would serve you best. After you identify and define the issue (Step 1), consider developing a modified strategy for processing the issue, by reducing the number of steps. This is an aspect of contracting (Step 2).

Setting Goals and Taking Action

For example, sometimes issues are pretty well understood while wants and future actions are the "hot" spots. If this is the case, focus your energy and discussion on identifying wants and brainstorming actions. Here is a suggested strategy:

Step 1.   Identify and define the issue.

Step 2.   Contract to work through the issue.

Skip step 3. Understand the issue completely.

Step 4.   Identify wants.

Step 5.   Generate options.

Step 6.   Choose action.

Step 7.   Test the action plan.

> As you test your plan, look for any relevant information in the zones you skipped — past and current actions, sensory data, thoughts, or feelings — which must be considered to assure the success of your action plan.

Step 8.   Evaluate the outcome.

Think about a particular strategy that would help you and another person best tackle a current issue together.

SELF TALK

The Awareness Wheel can be used informally to huddle with yourself before, during, or after a situation to understand yourself and others better. Do not let the map burden you. Rather use it as a quick guide which you can call on to help you answer these personal or interpersonal questions:

1.   What is happening right now?

2.   Where am I stuck?

3.   Where is the other person?

4.   What can I do next?

Using the Awareness Wheel to "diagnose and treat" situations will help you go to the core of confusing and difficult matters faster, creating insights and options for action.

When You Feel a Pinch . . .

Tune in to your Awareness Wheel when you feel a *pinch — an internal or external, verbal or nonverbal cue that an issue exists.* Start with any dimension of your Wheel.

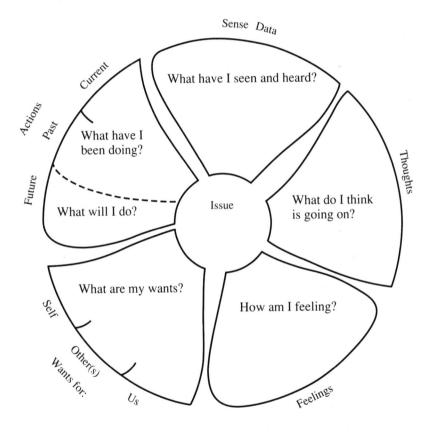

Mentally put your issue at the center of the Wheel and begin with any dimension that pops into your consciousness. Then proceed to the goal of creating a complete and congruent solution by:

1. Filling in the rest of your Awareness Wheel, especially any incomplete information.

2. Ironing out incongruencies.

3. Working through blockages.

While it can go quickly, this process does not always happen in a few minutes. Often it takes time spread across hours, days, or even months. As your awareness unfolds, you will find the Awareness Wheel useful for reflecting, talking with others, testing actions, and seeking counsel on occasion. Following are some specific situations in which your Awareness Wheel can help you.

Sizing Up Situations on the Spot

It may seem awkward to huddle with yourself mentally in the middle of a situation and ask: "What am I seeing and hearing? What do I think? How do I feel? What are my wants for self and others? What action can I take?" But football teams huddle after every play and call "time out" to do something of this sort several times in a game.

You may even think you are not capable of such a rational approach. Do not underestimate yourself. At first, these time-outs will require some extra concentration, but the more you use the Wheel, the more natural the process will become. Eventually, it will be second nature to hopscotch mentally around the Wheel whenever you sense a need for more information or clarification.

For example, you are walking out the front door with your partner on the way to a movie.

You *hear* Sue say: "Just a second," and see her turn back and go into the house.

You *think:* We'll be late and miss the beginning of the film.

You *feel:* Annoyed, confused, tense.

You *think:* What is she going back for? She's always forgetting something.

You scan your *intentions:* I don't want to be late. I don't like guessing what I've missed in a movie. I want to leave now. I don't want to irritate Sue.

You *think:* Maybe I should follow her into the house and holler so she'll hurry.

You *pause,* tuning into your *feelings* and *expectations:* I feel frustrated. I've been annoyed and pressured all day and I was looking forward to a fun and relaxing night with Sue.

You *ask* yourself: What do I want to do? What action do I want to take?

You *think:* If I go in and yell, it will increase my own tension and cause some strain between us. Is missing the start of the movie worth the increased tension? I could start relaxing while I wait.

You choose an *action:* You sit down on the front step, take a couple of deep breaths, center yourself, and begin to unwind and take in the beauty of the early evening.

You *notice* your tension subside.

You *see* Sue come bounding out of the house five minutes later carrying a sweater.

You *decide* to remain calm and silent, walk to the car, and get on with the evening in a relaxed frame of mind.

You *think* to yourself: I will talk to Sue about her habit of running back at a more appropriate time.

Most daily activities do not require this kind of quick self-inspection, but it is important to have a map to use if and when you need it. However, in certain kinds of situations, a look at your Awareness Wheel is always productive.

Handling Intense Feelings

When strong feelings well up inside you and you are not sure what is causing them or what to do about them turn to your Wheel. Gaining understanding can focus your energy and expand your choices.

As Jack was leaving for work, he asked his ten-year-old son, Mark, to shovel the snow in the driveway. When he returned home that night, the driveway was still full of snow. He felt anger well up inside so he pulled into the garage and sat for a minute before going into the house.

Jack *thought* that his was another example of Mark's pattern of ignoring Jack's requests for help.

Jack also remembered exploding at Mark on other occasions, berating him for being lazy and neglecting chores. Mark would become sullen and withdraw from him. Clearly these *actions* were not having the desired impact on Mark and hurt their relationship.

Jack *decided* to wait a few minutes for his anger to cool before going into the house. Then later, he would talk calmly with Mark about why he needed Mark's help with these kinds of chores and lay out his expectations very clearly.

Clearing Up Confusion

Occasionally, you may be receiving different messages from the same person or from different members of your family or sources within your company or organization. You find yourself confused, pulled off balance by the multiple signals. Use your wheel to find your center and develop a plan for clearing up the confusion.

> Barb was asked by her boss to compile sales figures from the last quarter for a report he was preparing for the Division Manager. He said he needed the figures right away. When she went to Bill to get some of the figures, he told her that he was supposed to provide the figures and, in fact, was just about ready to give them to the boss.
>
> Barb *wondered* whether her boss forgot that he had given this assignment to Bill or whether this indicated he did not trust Bill.
>
> Barb *felt* uneasy, caught in the middle between Bill and her boss.
>
> Barb *wanted* to get out of the bind of being caught in the middle if there was tension between Bill and her boss.
>
> Barb decided to *talk* with her boss, tell him what Bill had said, and ask him whether she should continue with the assignment. She was not certain whether to raise the issue of being caught in the middle, but she decided to raise it if her boss' response gave her an opening for raising this issue.

Identifying Patterns

Something happens once. You feel it, but dismiss it. Later it happens again. It has the same impact on your feelings. You think, "It's probably just a coincidence," but still it registers in your memory bank. The third time it gets to you. You realize, "Hey, this is a pattern. I'm not crazy. I'm getting thumped. I've got to do something about this."

You ask your teenage daughter a question and your spouse, who had discussed the same topic with your teen earlier, answers your question. You feel some irritation.

Sometime later you scold your daughter for using all the gas in the car. Before she can respond, your mate jumps in with an excuse. You feel more irritation.

The very next day you ask your teenager about her homework and your spouse replies for her. You recognize a pattern so you resolve to discuss it with your spouse before it happens again and you explode.

An event really has to happen three times before it becomes a pattern. By attending to your Awareness Wheel, you will recognize recurring sensory data and negative feelings which are usually the first clues to an unpleasant or destructive pattern. If you are not attuned, or if you repeatedly deny what you see and feel, a pattern may recycle ten, twenty, or more times before you catch on and decide to do something about it.

Curbing Impulsiveness

Have you been in a situation where you say to yourself, "Here I go again, I really don't need to be doing this again." Impulsiveness is a pattern fostered by your personality type. Your Awareness Wheel can help you get in contact with your longer-range intentions and values by anticipating consequences which will help you curb the impulsiveness that gets you into trouble.

Jack's handling of his anger with Mark in the snow-shoveling incident illustrates this situation. Previously when Jack allowed his anger to explode, Mark's withdrawal showed that Jack's outburst caused some damage to their relationship. Taking the time to reflect on prior incidents enabled Jack to overcome his impulsiveness and, instead, to choose a different way of responding.

Bolstering Confidence

At other times, you may lack sufficient confidence to take any action. Mired in "what-ifs" and "yes-buts," you cannot meet the challenge. Turn to your Awareness Wheel; then attend to your feelings: how strongly do you want to take on the challenge? Do you have powerful beliefs which are holding you back about your competence or the risks?

Joan was a new graduate student taking her first seminar. She developed an idea for her seminar project that she thought represented a new approach to a key topic in the seminar. When she explained it to Hal, a second year student in the department, he told her it was too risky. If it worked, she would get a good grade, but if it did not work, she would probably flunk, he said.

Then Hal added, "I don't think the odds are in your favor to bring it off. If I were you, I wouldn't do it."

When Joan looked at her Awareness Wheel, this is what she found:

I *think* I understand the material and I'm convinced my approach is a new one. I've read most of the articles about the topic so I'm pretty certain no one else has taken this approach.

I *hope* that trying new approaches is what graduate education is all about.

I *feel* pretty confident that I will be able to explain my approach adequately.

I *think* Hal is overstating the risk of failure. To check on this, however, I *will talk* with my professor about the idea before getting too far into the project.

Assurance When You Have to Act Fast

Occasionally we have to make a quick decision. As a way both to bolster your confidence in the decision you do make and to identify any important dissonant information which could come back to bite you later, quickly connect with each part of your Wheel. See if you get a red (Stop!) or green (Go!) light from each zone.

Reality is such that not all our experiences fit into neat little packages of issues to consider or situations to resolve immediately. Many experiences develop over time; therefore, all the relevant information cannot be gathered at once.

When you have processed a good deal of information but not quite enough to act from full awareness, or when you are unsure of the right path to follow, leave the future action dimension of your Awareness Wheel open-ended for awhile. Live with the awareness of your feelings, thoughts, and intentions for a period of time. See if they change at all. You may even want to jot down some notes on your awareness as it progresses or changes. Formulate your action plan when your Wheel is complete.

Advantages of the Mapping Process

The Awareness Wheel is a dynamic guide to help you center and balance yourself as you move through stressful situations. Mapping Issues is a process which:

1. *Organizes* "soft" interpersonal data around a *rational* approach.
2. Allows you to start anywhere and go anywhere on the map to find a solution; in this way it is non-linear.
3. Includes both *objective* and *subjective* information.
4. Builds on the *five areas of critical* personal or interpersonal *information* in any situation.
5. Attends to *process* and *outcome.*
6. Reduces *partial* awareness.
7. Helps each player identify his or her own *contribution* (past action) and *response* (current action) to a situation.
8. Incorporates *others'* concerns and wants.
9. Maintains your *focus* on the central issue rather than on tangents.
10. Is *action oriented,* while restraining tendencies to pre-close on issues.

11. Encourages *full participation and collaboration* among stake-holders.

12. Assumes that each person holds pieces to the puzzle.

Tips

Use the Awareness Wheel to:

1. Help you understand yourself better and use your awareness more effectively.

2. Help you tune into and understand others more accurately so you can relate in modes that connect best with them.

3. Assist in clarifying confusion and reducing misunderstandings.

4. Help you prepare for and work through difficult situations by increasing your choices.

5. Enhance your decision-making, problem-solving, and conflict-resolving skills.

6. Serve as a basis for your communication (see Chapter 9, "Speaking Skills").

COMMUNICATION SKILLS

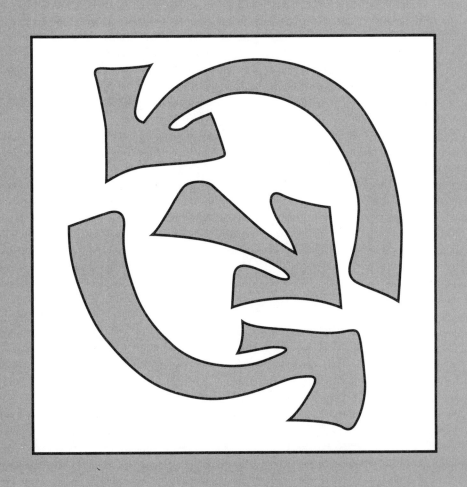

9

SPEAKING SKILLS
For Sending Clear Messages

Whether you want to connect with the most important person in your life or an interesting stranger, you cannot assume that someone will know what is happening inside you unless you tell him or her. The Awareness Wheel can aid that process. In addition to being a map for helping you connect better with yourself, the Awareness Wheel is a communication skills map for helping you connect better with others by sending clearer and more accurate messages. The map creates understanding by reducing guesswork, a major roadblock to connecting.

As we have discussed before, relationships are primarily nonverbal dances. Partners choreograph their dance around different issues and events over time. Words clarify and enhance the dance steps, but the basic experience of the dance, including change, precedes words. Connecting with yourself during a dance stimulates awareness. And communication skills help you speak your awareness accurately. Both awareness and skill increase your repertoire, the choice of dance steps available to you.

In this chapter we present a set of speaking skills based on the Awareness Wheel. The behaviors we discuss are *skills* because they can be *practiced and learned* to increase your chances of producing certain useful outcomes. Think of them as small communication tools to help you build meaningful relationships.

Like any tool, these communication skills have an appropriate time and place for their use; this decision is left up to the judgment of the user; we recommend that you use wisdom and tact in *choosing* what, where, when, and how you communicate your awareness.

SPEAKING SKILLS

If you decide to share your "self-information," here are six basic talking skills that will help you state your awareness more clearly. These are skills that let other people know what is going on inside you at a given point in time. They are:

1. Speaking For Self
2. Giving Sensory Data
3. Expressing Thoughts
4. Reporting Feelings
5. Disclosing Wants
6. Stating Actions

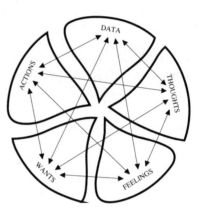

SKILL NO. 1: SPEAKING FOR SELF

"I'd like more time to think about it."

"Your decision really pleases me."

"I feel sad about Bob's illness."

"Here's my idea."

"I'll get the assignment completed by Thursday."

This first skill, speaking for self, is prerequisite to all other speaking skills. The other speaking skills combine with speaking for self to accurately express your awareness in the five parts of your Awareness Wheel. In speaking for self, you attach a personal pronoun — "I," "me," "my," or "mine" — to a part of your Wheel. You claim ownership of your experience: "I see/hear..."; "My thoughts are..."; "I feel..."; "I want..."; "I will...."

You may be saying to yourself, "Aren't people who frequently refer to themselves self-centered and selfish?" The answer is "yes" if the content of their conversation focuses primarily on themselves. However, there is a distinction between talking *about* yourself, and speaking *for* yourself.

As we discussed in Chapter 2, four areas of content include: a topic, yourself, your partner, or your relationship. If you talk mainly about yourself, it is self-centered and does become tiring for others because you rarely tune into their activities, interests, and concerns. Think about yourself for a moment. If you are a person who talks about yourself too much, we strongly encourage you to practice tuning into others, using the listening skills described in Chapter 10.

Speaking for yourself, on the other hand, clearly *identifies* you as the source and originator of your message: you take responsibility for your awareness and actions; you are accountable. In this sense, you alone are the authority on what is happening inside yourself, nobody else is. This differentiates your experience from other people's experience. Furthermore, speaking for self does not mean you focus only on your own activities, interests, and concerns. You may express your awareness about any kind of content: "I'm puzzled by the intricacies of opera" (focus-topic); "I cracked my tooth today" (focus-yourself); "I'm fascinated by your story. Tell me more" (focus-other); "I want our relationship to be satisfying for both of us" (focus-relationship).

Speaking For Others Produces Resistance

The opposite of speaking for self is *speaking for others:*

"You know that's not right." (Rather than, "I see it differently.")

"We don't really believe that." (Rather than, "I don't really believe that.")

"Don't feel hurt. Jack didn't mean anything by his remark." Here the person is speaking for you and Jack. (Rather, "I hope you won't feel hurt. I don't think Jack was trying to be mean.")

"Everyone has to face up to it sooner or later." (Rather, "It's my belief that everyone will have to face up to it sooner or later.")

Over-Responsible "You-Statements"

When you speak for other people, you use words like "you," "we," or "everyone." This hems others in and cuts off their choices; they feel trapped and pressured, and it kindles unnecessary resistance and negative challenge to your messages. (Do you remember the last time someone spoke for you: how did it feel?)

Most people do not like someone else running their lives, no matter how small the attempt. They find it invasive and pushy. They recoil and resist in subtle — or not so subtle — ways to what is being said, even if what is said is true or is something they might normally accept.

When you speak for others, you work against your own objective because few people want someone else to speak for them. Their normal response is to defend and protect themselves against invasion. Your statements come off like rigid pronouncements or facts, rather than flexible considerations with room for negotiation. Others almost have to disagree with you to protect themselves. On the other hand, when you speak for yourself, statements are more negotiable.

People who speak for others are often unaware that they do so. They often do not know of an effective alternative — *speaking for self about the other.*

Do a little experiment the next time you have a conversation. Speak for the other person. For example, with a male friend, tell him what *to* think or feel, or what he *should* want. As you speak, watch his subtle nonverbal responses. You will see his head twisting "no." He may physically back away and withdraw, or he may match your assertions with Control Talk or even Fight Talk and a pointed finger. Notice how the way you talk backs him into a corner, and discounts him. Most people do not like to be around a spouse, friend, parent, colleague, doctor, or boss who does this. Afterwards you might tell him it was just an experiment and explain what you were doing.

How you say what you say makes a big difference. Speaking only for yourself encourages others to speak for themselves, eliminating needless interference with the real messages to be exchanged.

Many people are completely unaware that they create resistance in others when they speak for them. If you were to ask those doing the speaking how they experienced the conversation, they will usually tell you the "other guy" was acting impossible, when in fact their own actions caused the other person's reaction. As they unconsciously saw themselves getting a negative response, they pushed harder and spoke more for the other person.

People who speak for others are usually seen as being mildly to strongly abrasive. Their dominant communication style is Control Talk, which easily slides into Fight Talk. They fail to recognize that they create many of their own interpersonal troubles by the way they approach others.

Think back to a Fight Talk conversation you have had and recall how much speaking for the other went on. You were probably acting out a power struggle — who would be in charge of whom — by speaking for each other. The skill of speaking for yourself will help you avoid useless power struggles and express your real message.

When you speak for yourself, you are not forcing your perspective on others; you are not saying that you are an expert on *their* inner awareness, only on your own. While you may be interested in or concerned about them, you are not in charge of their experience — they are. By speaking for self, you respect others and give them room to be themselves to report what is in their own Awareness Wheels. This skill affirms and differentiates each of you.

Under-Responsible, "No-One Statements"

"It might be good for us to be more open with each other."

"One could get upset about this."

These statements have no juice. They leave you wondering who is talking and what is meant. These are examples of what we call *under-responsible statements*. They speak for no one by substituting "it," "some people," "they," or "one" for "I." Or, they include no pronoun or referent at all. As a result, the ownership of the statement is left in question. You can only guess at the opinions, intentions, or feelings of the under-responsible speaker because they are voiced in such an indirect, cautious, uncommitted way. The speaker does not appear to value them enough to claim them directly. In time, if you continually talk in an under-responsible way, you will succeed in getting others to devalue your opinions, intentions, and feelings too.

"Poor Me" Statements

In Spite Talk, the speaker avoids taking responsibility for his experience. These statements often seethe with cynicism:

"It's nice to know somebody is interested."

"No one ever listens to anyone around here."

"They never let you know what's going on."

Phrases like these cloak angry powerlessness. Vague references to "it," "somebody," "one," or "they" are substituted for clear Straight Talk messages in which the speaker clearly speaks for himself.

There are times when it is necessary to be *direct* and times when it is appropriate to be *indirect*. But most of the time you will get the best results by being direct, which starts with speaking for yourself.

SKILL NO. 2: GIVING SENSORY DATA

Giving sensory data is the skill of describing what you specifically see, hear, touch, taste, and smell — your input from the external world. When you give sensory data, you provide concrete examples of what you perceive or have observed at a *particular time* or *place*. These descriptions can be of past events, observations of current behavior, or graphic images about what you would like to see and hear in the future. Sensory data also includes facts, figures, and information from printed material.

In interpersonal situations, giving sensory data mainly means describing other people's actions, their specific verbal and nonverbal behaviors.

"Tonight I made a gourmet veal dish, but you didn't eat much or comment on it."

"I hear a lilt in your voice right now."

"I noticed everyone became very quiet after you proposed the budget cuts at our operations meeting this morning."

Most people look for large pieces of data and overlook significant small pieces, such as changes in breathing, tone, eye contact, and skin color. Nonverbals, like those just mentioned, can alert you to others' communication styles and can cue you to make appropriate shifts in your own style as well.

Documenting — Linking Observations to Interpretations

Documenting simply means providing specific sensory data with your thoughts. Although sensory statements may seem like an unnecessary comment on the obvious, they are quite important in providing a frame of reference so that others can understand how you arrived at an interpretation. Compare these two statements:

"You look tired." (This speaking for other interpretation may spark a sharp retort like, "Well I'm not.")

"I see dark circles under your eyes this morning. You look tired to me. I notice you've been putting in twelve- and fourteen-hour days for the last six weeks." (Speaking for self and and giving sensory data makes this message much clearer and easier to hear.)

Just adding data to an interpretation does not necessarily mean you have effectively documented your point. Some data are irrelevant, vague, overly general, distorted, exaggerated, fabricated, biased, or inaccurate. To provide good documentation, sensory data must be:

- pertinent
- observable
- specific
- comprehensive
- honest
- verifiable

Describing your specific data base orients others and gives them a chance to tell you how they are interpreting the same input. Giving sensory data also supplies information for "what," "where," "when," "how," and "who" questions. Data sometimes explain "why" (certain statistics, for example), but more often "why" takes you into reasons and interpretations, not to more data.

Sensory data can be used in Fight Talk to try to prove a point, or they can be used in Straight Talk to help create understanding. How you use sensory data all depends on your intentions.

Like any part of your Awareness Wheel, you are free to choose whether or not to say anything about your sensory input. You may simply notice a certain nonverbal expression and without commenting on it, use it as a "marker" to monitor change in another person's response to your action.

For example, Warren noticed the two lines on his wife's brow which typically appear when she is under a lot of pressure. Rather than telling her to relax — pointing out the two lines to document his inter-pretation — Warren marks the two lines in his mind and asks,"Is there anything I can do to help you?" If she suggests something he can do such as pick up the kids or start supper, he watches to see whether the two marker lines lessen or disappear. If they do, the sensory data tell him he has been effective in helping her relax; he helped create a positive effect without having to comment.

Besides letting others know how you arrive at your conclusions, documenting:

1. Cuts through vagueness and generalities.
2. Gives your comments more objectivity by providing a common behavioral reference point.
3. Forces you to clarify and focus your thinking.

Tips

1. Realize that two or more different and valid interpretations can often be made from the same data.
2. Use questions which fit. "Who, what, where, when, and how" questions ask for sensory data. "Why" questions call for reasons.
3. Do not disregard conflicting verbal and nonverbal data; talk about what you see or hear that does not match.
4. Consider the value of data for making interpretations. People are more apt to listen to and accept interpretations accompanied by data. They resist ungrounded conclusions.
5. Document positive and negative feedback as well as requests for change in behavior.
6. Be as specific as possible, when giving instructions or coaching, about the behavior you would like to see in the future.

SKILL NO. 3: EXPRESSING THOUGHTS

Expressing your thoughts is simply the skill of saying *what it is* you are thinking, believing, assuming, or expecting. Since saying what you think is rather common, its importance can be overlooked. Thoughts need not be vague, general, or illusive. Rather, they can be clear, concise, and focused if you experience them this way.

"I believe Dr. Watts is the best chemistry professor I have ever had."

"You're crazy to let Bart out of your life." (Notice the speaking for other.)

"I expect to be on time."

"I think the salesman knows that his product isn't competitive. Did you see him flinch when I said we had already had an impressive demonstration by his competitor?" (Interpretation with data.)

Expressing your thoughts is important for two basic reasons: first your beliefs about yourself, others, and situations determine to a large extent what can happen; they often become self-fulfilling prophecies. Second, interpreting is an ongoing process — something you are creating, perpetuating, modifying, or destroying over time. You are constantly constructing your own meaning in every situation. Expressing your ongoing thoughts lets others know where you are cognitively and helps others to assist you in shaping issues and the future.

Tips

1. Do not confuse thoughts with sensory data. Sometimes people think that they are supplying more data for their point of view when, in fact, they are only supplying more interpretations. You can always check by asking "Is this fact or opinion?" Sometimes reasons for doing something are treated as data if they describe how you arrived at a particular point. Reasons are more likely to be other thoughts or intentions, not sensory data.

2. Watch out for "hardening of the categories" — carving your thoughts in stone. Rather, treat your thoughts as working hypotheses about "what is." This is especially important in interpersonal situations. Be ready to express changes in your thinking as new information becomes available.

3. Express assumptions, evaluations, and expectations; they are powerful beliefs. They strongly influence your understanding of what is happening or what should happen. Expressing these kinds of thoughts to others will help them better understand you and will help you check your thoughts against their assumptions and expectations. This can prevent serious misunderstandings.

SKILL NO. 4: REPORTING FEELINGS

Reporting feelings means stating your emotions directly. Feelings are like salt and pepper — they add seasoning to your communication. Most of the time you can report your feelings without using the phrase, "I feel":

"I'm surprised."

"My disappointment will die down, but it's strong right now."

"I sure am relieved hearing that from you!"

"I'm concerned about you. "

"I'm anxious about the exam."

"I'm proud of you and really thrilled by your success."

Feelings are commonly expressed through nonverbal behavior, either indirectly and symbolically (buying a gift; staying away) or directly (kissing; laughing; crying; slamming doors; storming around). Nonverbal expressions of feelings often have high impact. In some situations actions do "speak louder than words," demonstrating that something is going on inside of you. But these are are not necessarily "clear" expressions for feelings.

Take crying, for example. Do the tears communicate sadness, disappointment, anger, joy, relief, or some combination of these? Does the gift mean affection or guilt? "Can't others know how I feel by the way I act?" you might ask. Not always, especially with subtle and less intense feelings. The fact is, nonverbal behavior may be convincing (actions speak louder . . .), but words may be needed to clarify exactly what it is you are feeling.

Acting out feelings occurs when you express them nonverbally, often without being conscious of how you feel. Conversely, *acting on* feelings occurs when you are aware of how you feel and put those feelings into words. Friendly feelings are indirectly expressed in Small Talk. Angry and hurt feelings are acted out in Fight and Spite Talk. All feelings, positive and negative, can be acted on and disclosed in Straight Talk. On occasion a metaphor can be a very effective way to let others know your emotions: "I have butterflies"; "I feel like I was just 'shot out of the saddle' "; "I feel like an eagle, floating on air."

Feelings are only moment-to-moment bits of information that tell others directly how you are experiencing a situation. They let others know what the temperature and barometric pressure is. And usually they are not big secrets about your personal life. When you withhold your feelings, or only express them indirectly, you are withholding significant information — one of the five key pieces of information central to most issues.

There are many reasons all of us give for not reporting our feelings:

1. We do not know what we feel. (Men have been given much credit for this.)

2. We have "meta-feelings" or *feelings about how we feel* which prevent us from stating our emotions directly. This is particularly true when we have strong emotions — either negative or positive. For example, if you feel envious, greedy, or jealous (to name a few feelings that people frequently disown), you might also feel guilty or ashamed about feeling this way, so you keep all of these feelings to yourself. Likewise, you may feel deep affection, admiration, or sexy, at one level, but also feel too embarrassed, awkward, or silly to share the positive emotion.

3. Our *culture* at home, work, or school places high priority on controlling emotions. Ironically, the best way to manage our emotions is to *acknowledge, accept, and report* them, rather than to fight ("control") their expression.

4. There is risk involved when we let others know who we really are. But the risk does not just involve feelings; we can be rejected or thwarted if we disclose any other part of our Awareness Wheel too — senses, thoughts, wants and actions. Frequently it is these other parts that are in fact rejected, and so we feel badly. The bigger risk of reporting feelings, then, is that if you actually are feeling badly, saying so will lead others to discover what your real expectations, intentions, and behaviors are — and you would rather have these remain hidden because they are too risky.

5. Some people habitually substitute opinions, evaluations, and questions for feelings. Thoughts and feelings are not interchangeable. People think they are reporting their feelings (because they do feel something) when they make strong statements (usually in Control, Fight, or Spite Talk):

"You have no right to say that!" when you mean, "I feel angry when you say that."

"How could you forget my birthday?" when you mean, "I felt very disappointed and hurt that you forgot my birthday."

"We have good times together," when you mean, "I love you. I enjoy being with you."

As you can see in these examples, failure to express feelings directly often increases pressure, confusion, and misunderstanding.

Many men, in particular, see danger in stating their feelings. They do not like to stir up something they cannot control. A lot of men associate feelings with either explosiveness or weakness; they do not know how to use the wealth of different emotions in between these two extremes.

When you deny your feelings or avoid reporting them, you reduce your personal power. Feeling statements have impact, especially immediate, uncensored, "now" feelings. People generally perk up and respond to clear and authentic feeling statements. Unlike ideas, it is hard to argue about feelings. If people really feel something, they feel it.

Some people are afraid that emotions contaminate good thinking. It is true that emotions affect thinking. But that is why it is better to express them — everyone can then understand how feelings are influencing thinking. It is what you do not know that can really hurt you!

When unspoken negative feelings build up, people become cautious — tension mounts, trust drops, and the dance slows. Energy for decision-making is diverted to second-guessing others and protecting yourself. When strong feelings can be expressed constructively, differences can be brought into focus and issues dealt with effectively.

Take a moment and recall a tough situation where you and someone else were able to relax and clear up accumulated misunderstandings as you each filled in this piece of missing information.

When you want to be clear, report your feelings directly. Reporting feelings is a way to reduce stress, build morale, clarify thoughts and actions, and increase understanding.

Tips

1. Do not confuse, "what you think" with, "how you feel." People often use the word "feel" when they mean "think," and, because they have used the word "feel," they believe they are telling their feelings. For example,"I feel that we made a good decision," is a

thought, not a feeling. "I'm confident we made a good decision," is a feeling statement. Usually, the phrase, "I feel that..." is a clue that a thought is coming instead of a feeling.

2. Know the value of reporting feelings and realize that rational arguments waste time when important feelings are being ignored.

3. Put words to your feelings. Feelings are always there whether or not you report them. Strong feelings are reflected in your actions even when you do not verbalize them. If you want others to be clear about what you are feeling, a direct report communicates emotion more effectively than nonverbal expressions.

4. Report all the emotional ingredients when your feelings are mixed or contradictory.

5. Bring strong emotions — fears, sadness, anger — to your awareness and share them with a significant and trusted person. This can help you release them and gain new perspective.

6. Do not forget to tell the positive feelings you have too. Saying "I'm pleased," "I'm excited," or "I'm thrilled" adds a positive tone to a situation, builds morale, and helps people connect.

SKILL NO. 5: DISCLOSING WANTS

Disclosing wants and intentions lets others know in a direct way what you desire *to be, to do, or to have*. When you make intention statements, you use words such as, "I want...," "I don't want...," "I'd like...," "I intend...." Here are some examples:

"I want to be honest with you."

"I intend to climb as many peaks over 14,000 feet this summer as I can."

"I 'd like to have a faster computer with more memory."

Wants also identify "what's in it for whom": (1) *for* me; (2) *for* you; and (3) *for* us.

"I don't want to take the time to consider several alternatives."

"I'd like you to pick me up tonight about 7 p.m."

"I want to help you get the promotion."

"I'd like to give you the space you need."

"My objective is to have a good time together."

"I would like for the two of us to really be able to count on each other."

Saying What's in it For Whom

Verbally expressing your wants, not only *for* yourself, but also for the other(s) and your relationship, is a bonding force. It transcends self interests and affirms interest in others when your wants for them are translated into positive action.

Experiment by ending conversations with the phrase, "What can I do for you?" Often you win a friend. This is so because few people really think about others' interests. It is also a small gesture of love to say to your spouse, child, colleague, friend, or enemy, "Is there anything I can do to help you?"

Wants are Influential

Your intentions influence your actions. Wants are motivators of yourself and others and color your decisions and actions. The wants you express often affect others' decisions and actions as well.

Disclosing your intentions helps others understand what motivates you, what you value, and what you desire. When you express your wants, you eliminate "hidden agenda." This takes the pressure off others by cutting through the guesswork. As we have said before, whether or not you acknowledge your intentions, you have them and they are bound to surface.

Disclosing wants also cuts through wishy-washy communication like "maybe I can...," "possibly we could...," "if perhaps we might...." These messages usually signal a hidden agenda that someone is afraid to state in an effort not to offend, disappoint or cross someone else. After awhile, the inability to express wants and develop an action plan drives others nuts at home or at work.

Wants and intentions are least likely to be revealed when:

1. You believe that what you want does not match what your partner wants.

2. There is ill will toward the other person and you want to get even, reject, ignore, snub, disregard, or hurt that person.

3. You are in a competitive situation and think it is best to withhold as much information about yourself as possible. Beware — some people put out false information about their intentions to catch their opponent off base.

Wants as Demands

Wants are often stated as commands and demands, using "should," "ought," "have to," and leading questions:

"You should go camping with us this weekend," (Speaking for other); "Don't you want to get away from your work once in a while?" (Closed leading question). Stated as a want rather than a demand, it becomes, "I would really like you to go camping with us this weekend. What chance is there that you can come along?" (Speaking for self and an open question).

"You shouldn't spend all that money," when you mean, "I think that's too expensive. I'd like to see if we can find the same thing for less money."

When wants are stated as demands, they sound non-negotiable. The control aspect of the communication overrides the content of the message and control becomes the message which sets up needless resistance in others. These types of messages are often intended to make the others feel guilty as well.

"Need" is a tricky word too. "I need to have you..." is often used to express a want. But too often it has a manipulating, desperate quality that tends to overstate most intentions and puts others off. Furthermore, the phrase "I need" is arguable. Wants are not arguable since each of us is the final authority on our own wants. If you really do *need* something, it is a good idea to give your reasons and explain what might happen if your need is not met. Otherwise use "I need" sparingly as an intention statement. Do not misuse its power.

The attainment of most wants and desires can be negotiated. By stating them, you invite your partner's help in making them a reality. Being direct about what you want or like does not guarantee that you will get it, but it certainly improves your chances and minimizes the possibility of unpleasant surprises when hidden agenda emerge from the shadows.

Tips

1. Know the value of disclosing your wants. Simply telling others what you want does not mean that you will automatically get it. However, it puts things out in the open so others can respond more directly.

2. Ask yourself, if fear prevents you from saying what you want more directly, "What's the worst thing that can happen if I really say what I want?" Visualizing the worst and thinking it through may put your fear in a different perspective, enabling you to be direct about your want.

3. Check how you communicate your wants. When you phrase your wants and desires as demands, others usually resist. Remember that *the meaning of a message is mainly in its impact.* If others are resisting your wants, check to see if you are speaking for yourself and disclosing your wants in a non-demanding, negotiable fashion.

4. State your wants directly rather than act them out. As with feelings, intentions can be in conflict. Putting them all on the table makes it easier to sort them out rather than keeping one or two hidden under the table.

5. Notice what happens to your communication when you hide your real intentions. It is possible to fake your intentions, but they usually come out as mixed messages.

6. Think about what you can do *for* your partner, in contrast to what you can get *from* your partner.

SKILL NO. 6: STATING ACTIONS

Action statements describe your behavior — what you *have* done, *are* doing, or *will* do. They refer to your *own* past, current, or future actions, and are often expressed using "being" verbs — was, am, will.

"I called you yesterday about 2:30 in the afternoon, but didn't get an answer."

"I'm listening."

"I was thinking about some stuff at the office. I didn't really hear what you said."

"I got the computer I've been dreaming about."

"I believe you."

"I will make the decision tomorrow."

"I'm going to be more affectionate."

Are these statements really necessary? Is your behavior not obvious to everyone? No, not always. Consider this action statement, "I'm thinking about what you just said." All that my partner may be able to see is that I am staring off in space and frowning. He or she may or may not be able to guess that I am attending to the comments and may think I am disinterested. Consider the statement, "I tried to call you earlier." The other person could not see that I tried to do this; the action took place out of sight or hearing. Or "I will call you tomorrow." Now my partner knows what to expect. These statements provide information not otherwise available.

There is still another reason why action statements have value: they let other people know that *you* are aware of your behavior. Consider the statement, "I interrupted you." My partner probably noticed the interruption; the information which I provide by my action statement is that I noticed it too. Expressing this awareness can indicate that I care about the impact my behavior has on you. It is a way of commenting on our communicycle so that we can get back to the original content, if it is important.

Stating your actions also lets others know the meaning behind your behavior (what your intention was or your interpretation of your own behavior.)

Stating Actions Builds Trust and Confidence

Your actions (output) become other people's sensory data (input) about you. When you *acknowledge* and *accept responsibility* for your past and current actions — both for what was useful and for what was not useful — you let others know that you are *accountable*. Likewise, when you state your future actions — what you will do — and then follow through with the action you announced, others notice that you keep commitments; they learn to trust and have confidence in your words.

Congruence is the key, the fit or match between the nonverbal and the verbal, between "what is" and "what is said." Do you say one thing, "I'm doing fine," and look like you are? Or are your action statements incongruent with your behavior? For example, do you say, "I never did that," but the other person saw you do it? Do you commit to future action, but seldom follow through?

Stating your actions is a critical speaking skill. It involves risk because your actions have consequences — they become visible for others to praise or condemn. Consider the difference between saying, "I might," "I could," or "I want to," and clearly committing yourself to action by saying "I will." *Commitment* distinguishes Skill No. 6 (Stating Actions) from Skill No. 5 (Disclosing Wants). Taking responsibility for your actions and committing yourself to future actions are key ingredients that keep you in Straight Talk.

Tips

1. Watch other's nonverbal responses to your honest statements about your past, current, or future actions. People usually reduce their defensiveness when you focus on yourself and do not blame or attack them.

2. Check your own behavior first when a conversation is not working.

3. State your actions — accept your own behavior — to demonstrate positive self-esteem.

4. Make leadership statements by making future action statements.

5. Be aware of your own "body signature" — your characteristic pattern of nonverbals — when you are speaking. Notice the small things you do that get positive and negative responses — tone, facial expressions, posture. Stop repeating actions that bring a negative response. Keep doing those things that get a positive response.

6. Ask yourself occasionally, "Is my behavior congruent with the other parts of my Awareness Wheel?"

MULTIPLE-PART STATEMENTS

Getting into the habit of speaking for yourself to reveal what is in your Awareness Wheel is a major step in connecting. The key to completeness and clarity in disclosing your experience is to put all the skills together during a conversation so that you express all parts of your Wheel. This makes for richness and depth in your communication.

A conversation does not need to be lengthy. As you make your statements combine two or more parts of the Wheel. Documented interpretations (sensory data and thoughts) are one kind of two-part message you are familiar with already. Other types of two-part messages are a combination of any two dimensions of the Awareness Wheel:

"I'm excited about my new job *(feeling)*, and I'd like to start as soon as possible *(want)*."

"I wasn't sure I wanted to go *(want)*, so I haven't said anything about it since the first time you mentioned it *(action)*."

Three-or-more-part messages are even more complete and, if they are stated well, can be clear:

"I'm excited about my new job *(feeling)*, and I'd like to start as soon as possible *(want)*. I think it will open new career opportunities for me *(thought)*."

"I wasn't sure I wanted to go *(want)* so I haven't said anything about it since the first time you mentioned it *(action)*. Also I've been afraid *(feeling)* to turn you down, because I think I might offend you *(thought)*."

Notice how each part of the message adds new information. Are you a person who typically expresses only one or two dimensions such as facts and ideas, or feelings and wants? If so, try sending messages in "25 words or less" that cover three or more parts.

Self-awareness, self-disclosure, and choice are dynamically interrelated. Awareness provides you with choice. You can *choose* to disclose to others only what you are aware of. Limited awareness thwarts disclosure. In turn, disclosing can increase your self-awareness and overcome limited awareness.

SKILLS AND STYLES

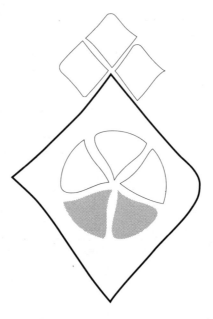

Each of the styles draws on some of the skills we have described. Control Talk centers on action. Fight Talk and Spite Talk draw heavily on Over-Responsible You-Statements and Under-Responsible Poor Me-Statements, respectively. Search talk mainly explores and generates thoughts.

Straight Talk uses all six skills. In Straight Talk, you speak for yourself, give significant data, express relevant and powerful thoughts, report deep feelings, identify the "ecology" of wants and state your own past and current actions as well as commit to future actions. Straight Talk is the only style that fully integrates the *affective and cognitive* aspects of communication to disclose a complete picture of the personal and interpersonal dynamics surrounding an issue or situation.

We close this chapter with a longer dialogue to illustrate how two people express all parts of their Awareness Wheels as they use Straight Talk to discuss an issue:

Dialogue	Dimension of Speaker's Awareness Wheel
Jean: "I get really *frustrated* when I have a day off or a weekend when I'm not working and I *want* to spend time with you. I *want* to do something, go outside, run, ride a bike, anything. But it *seems* you just want to sit home and watch television all afternoon."	feeling want want interpretation
Joe: "Well, I *think* we've got a problem. You know, I just *don't like* to get up and meet your schedule when you've got a day off to run and play through the woods. I might *want* to do something else."	interpretation want (preference) want
Jean: "Well, I *interpret* that as you don't want to do it with me.	interpretation
Joe: "Now, is that what I said?"	
Jean: "No, but that's what it *looks like* to me because when I invite you to do it, you usually say, 'No, I'd rather watch TV.' "	interpretation sensing (documenting)
Joe: "Well, wouldn't you like to sit here and watch TV with me?"	
Jean: "I don't *want* to watch TV; I get *antsy*. When I come home and on weekends I *like* to get exercise so that I can fell good about going back to work on Monday."	want feeling want (preference)

Joe: "What kind of exercise are you talking about?"

Jean: "It usually *doesn't matter*. Anything that's active. I could skate in the winter or ski or go for a walk or run or bike ride or . . . "

thought
action

Joe: "A *walk* sounds possible. Yeah. *It's not* a matter of the time, you know. If you're talking about spending time with me, there are different ways we can spend time with each other and maybe different times that we can spend away from each other. Do you want to spend the whole weekend with me? I mean I've got some other things I *want* to do too. I've got some things for school, I've got a paper due for American Studies. So there are a lot of those things that are happening with me too. But *let me try to tell* you what I think I'm hearing you say."

action
thought

want

action

Jean: "I *don't think* you understand what I'm saying."

interpretation

Joe: "Okay, well, let me see if I *can* identify. I *heard* you say you like to do things active when you've got some time and you get antsy sitting around here and you get frustrated when I don't want to get up and get going at the crack of dawn, which is one of the things you like to do. And you know me, I really *like* to sleep."

action
sensing

want (preference)

Jean: "Yeah, *you've got it*. But how would you *feel* if I did that?"

interpretation
feeling

Joe: "Fine, I like you to go out and exercise; you can exercise for me."

want

Jean: "I *enjoy* doing it by myself, but I don't *want* you to feel bad and think that I don't want you along And yet when you don't do it I *wonder* whether we're this together family 'cause we don't do stuff together."

feelinng
want

interpretation

Joe: "I don't *know* where you're getting that because you know. . . One of the things that I *like* doing with you is doing things where we can go someplace and talk, and sometimes we can talk while we walk, but I don't like jogging. . . And skiing you know, I *will go* cross country skiing but getting up early to go downhill skiing or something like that is not where it's at." — thought / want / action (future)

Jean: "But you're *not* saying that you don't want me to do it." — interpretation

Joe: "No. I *want* you to because I think that's something you enjoy. It is obvious. . ." — want

Jean: "That's really hard for me to *believe* that you really want me to do it but I *believe* you. Because *last Friday* when I did it and came back, I was really excited and *saw* you smiling and you seemed to get some excitement from my enjoyment. And *it seemed* like it was better the rest of the day. Even though you watched TV, I *watched* you watching TV, and I felt better because I did my own thing." — action* / sensing (documenting) / thought / action / feeling

Joe: "Yeah, when I *watch* TV I'm doin' my own thing." — action

Jean: "I know. But it's really hard for me to *think* that everybody doesn't want to exercise as I do." — action*

---

* Words which report the speaker's active cognitive action (e.g., thinking, assuming, trusting, believing — being verbs) are included as action statements.

10

LISTENING SKILLS
For Understanding Others
And Building Relationships

Recall for a moment a time recently when you had something important to say and the other person really put some effort into understanding your point of view. You left the situation feeling good.

Now recall another situation when you were talking to your partner, parent, boss, friend, teacher, or doctor, and you had something important to say but you left feeling frustrated and discouraged. Chances are no one really understood what you had to say.

Everyone likes to be understood. That is why much of our communication is aimed at getting others to see the world as we see it. The real crunch comes when it is time to understand others — to reach out and attentively listen to what another person is experiencing — especially when it does not match your experience.

If you are going to deal effectively with others and the issues you face together, then each of you must understand the other person and be understood by him or her.

Self-awareness is one thing, but awareness of others is another. When you are self-aware, you know what is going on in your own Awareness Wheel. *Awareness of others* means tuning into their immediate experience, their Awareness Wheels. When you are accurately aware of someone else's sensations, thoughts, feelings, wants, and the meaning of their actions, you are truly aware of that person. But just as it is not easy to become completely aware of yourself in a situation, it takes effort to be aware of another person too.

In the previous chapter, we provided tools to help you disclose yourself more completely to others; disclosing helps others understand you. In this chapter, we will introduce tools to help you understand others better. Using these two sets of tools can reduce misunderstandings in most situations.

LISTENING IS THE KEY
TO BUILDING RELATIONSHIPS

We all know people who are fun to be with, the "life of the party," but if they cannot also be good listeners, chances are they wear thin over time and probably have no long-term intimate relationships. If they always have to be in charge, leading and absorbing attention, and cannot follow your lead by listening to your jokes, dreams, and fears, the relationship becomes exhausting and unfulfilling.

Before we present a practical and powerful set of interpersonal listening skills, we want to alert you to three dynamics at work in every relationship dance, whether it is a short or extended exchange.

Rapport, Control, and Trust

Whether we are talking about a husband-wife, stock broker-client, parent-child, teacher-student, doctor-patient or any other relationship, how effectively two people relate and work together depends largely on these three underlying and ever-present forces: rapport, control, and trust. These dynamics are captured in three ongoing questions:

1. How do we fit together?

   This is a question about *rapport*. How much basic similarity, harmony, and alignment is there between us? How comfortable am I with you? How approachable are we to each other? How in sync are we in terms of energy, interests, values, beliefs, and behavior? To what degree do we grate on each other? How much respect do we have for each other? What is the "chemistry" between us?

   "How do we fit together?" is often the first unconsciously-asked question that you answer in deciding whether you will encourage a relationship with another person or not. Most of us gravitate toward people with whom we have natural rapport. We typically avoid or experience difficulty with people with whom we have little affinity. This is why it is so difficult to live or work with someone you do not like. You are mainly out of sync with them. Unless you do something to reduce the dissonance and build rapport, you cannot be together or work together well.

2. Who is in charge?

   This is the question of how *control* will be distributed and exercised. Will control be shared, rotated, differentiated, or hoarded by you or by the other person?

   Formally, control is determined in part by the nature of the relationship — the symmetry or asymmetry of positions and roles in an organization, for example. Informally, control is more subtle. Control is expressed by who takes the lead in getting together, initiating a conversation, suggesting ideas, switching topics, ending a discussion, and so forth.

3. How much do we trust each other?

    How much confidence do I have in the other person? How much concern do I have for the other person's well-being, and how much concern does he or she have for my well-being?

    As a relationship develops, these questions are usually answered in the order we have listed them — first rapport, then control, and finally trust. Over time, the questions are asked and answered again and again. And as we change our answer to one of the questions, answers to the others may change as well.

    As you will see, how you deal with these three dynamics — rapport, control, and trust — is heavily influenced by the quality and effectiveness of your listening skills.

THREE TYPES OF LISTENING

Is Your Listening Goal to Control or Connect?

Think of listening as *the process of developing a full understanding of another person's "story"* (situation, concern, point of view). To be an effective listener, it is important to be aware of and make a choice about how much you will attempt to control (direct and influence) the speaker as he or she tells his or her story.

Here your intentions are paramount. As you listen, you may have one of three basic intentions:

1. To *lead* by persuading

2. To *clarify* by directing

3. To *discover* by attending

Control is the central consideration with each listening mode. The question is, are you going to *follow the leader*, allowing others to relate their stories in their own way? Or are you going to *be the leader* — getting speakers to tell their stories in the way you want to hear them? As you can see, the answer to this question has enormous implications for the quality and integrity of information exchanged and for the health of the relationship.

The diagram shows how your influence or control varies as you alter your listening intentions. Notice how you can increase the quality of information, reduce resistance, and build a stronger relationship as you move toward Attentive Listening.

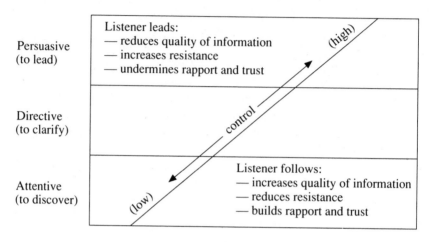

Figure 10.1 Three Types of Listening

PERSUASIVE LISTENING: WANTING TO LEAD

Persuasive Listening can hardly be called listening at all. You listen just long enough to get an idea about what others are saying, jump to a conclusion, and then interrupt to disagree, give advice, and attempt to superimpose your perspective or solution on the other person's ideas. You anticipate their next statement and mentally rehearse what you are going to say, and in doing so, you miss or disregard their significant nonverbal reactions. This type of listening does not have to be flamboyant or dramatic. The pattern can be played out subtly and quietly with equal power.

Bob: "How's the project going, Joan?"

Joan: "Okay, I guess, but I've got a problem. Can I tell you about it?"

Bob: "Sure, go ahead."

Joan: "It's about Phil. Last week I asked him when he would be done with the initial design..."

Bob: (interrupting) "and he isn't finished yet?"

Joan: "Well, no, he told me he would be done yesterday, and he gave me the design as he promised. But the design is too complex, and..."

Bob: (interrupting) "You know Phil always makes designs too complicated. What you need to do is tell him straight out that the design has to be simple. Did you do that?"

Joan: "I told him to try to keep it simple, but when he gave me the design, he said he added features to make it more efficient."

Bob: "Well that's the problem. Go back to Phil and tell him he's got to make it simple, period. No frills, no added features. Make it simple. That will take care of it."

The basic intention is to get others to see the world the way you do as fast as possible. This listening style is used most often in pressure and conflict situations — when you just want to get others to comply with your resolution of their story.

Recall that these are the intentions of Style II communication. Other people seldom comply freely and quickly, however. In your rush to action you stir up their frustration and resistance. Their responses usually take the form of objections to your ideas. If you increase the pressure, your Control Talk may turn into Fight Talk.

Other people's reactions to Persuasive Listening come more from the way you are listening than from the content of your questions and comments. This type of listening discounts others. People experience you as taking over their story, and they feel as if they never really had a chance to complete their communicycle satisfactorily. In turn, the resistance created by your listening style prevents your ideas from being heard as well.

When Persuasive Listening is used, both the speaker and the listener lose. Both walk away feeling negative about the other. Productivity and morale drop.

DIRECTIVE LISTENING: WANTING TO CLARIFY

The intention behind Directive Listening is to lead others as efficiently as possible into telling you what you (the listener) judge to be the most important aspects of their story or situation. To do this you ask a lot of questions and generally lead them to clarify your areas of interest, which may not necessarily be the same as theirs.

Questions are useful; in fact, studies show that an excellent salesperson asks four times the number of questions an average salesperson asks. But *questions control the direction of the conversations.* If the listener asks many questions, all of a sudden he or she is directing the story. The problem is that even with the best of intentions, the listener may lead the speaker away from key information. The listener is attending to his or her own agenda — not to the speaker's. Unless the speaker is rather assertive about making sure his or her story gets told in full, the speaker usually leaves the situation with incomplete communicycles — frustrated that the story really was not heard.

"Experts" — parents, doctors, managers, teachers, ministers, counselors, consultants, salespeople — use Directive Listening all the time. The "contract" is, "I'll ask the right questions, and if you give good answers, we can handle this issue fast." From their background knowledge and experience, experts decide which direction the inquiry will take. However, although inordinate pressure is placed on experts to be smart and right, they can miss the target.

Directive Listening builds on Search Talk. There are times when it is the most effective and efficient mode of listening. But be aware of its control. You may lead someone in the wrong direction by asking the wrong questions. Here is a replay of Bob and Joan's earlier conversation with Bob using Directive Listening to guide the conversation:

Bob: "How's the project going, Joan?"

Joan: "Okay, I guess, but I've got a problem. Can I tell you about it?"

Bob: "Sure, go ahead."

Joan: "It's about Phil. Last week I asked him when he would be done with the initial design, and he told me he would be finished yesterday. He gave me the design as he promised, but the design is too complex."

Bob: "Well, did you tell him initially that the design had to be simple?"

Joan: "Yes, I did."

Bob: "Why didn't he keep it simple, then?"

Joan: "He said he added some features to make the design more efficient."

Bob: "Will his design be more efficient?"

Joan: "It might be, but I think it will cause some real production problems."

Bob: "What kind of production problems?"

Five Different Kinds of Directive Questions

Directive Listening relies on questions, and the type of questions you ask influences the responses you get. Here are five different kinds of questions, ranging from *least to most effective* for gaining understanding:

1. "Why" Questions

   Pause for a moment and recall the last time someone asked you a "why" question. For example,

   > "Why did you do that?" or "Why do you think that?"

   Do you recall feeling tense or on the spot? If so, this is a typical reaction to "why" questions. They have the impact of challenging, blaming, and calling upon you to justify or defend your actions or position. Furthermore, you can seldom give a satisfactory answer to a why question because the intent of most why questions is not to gain information but to impute stupidity or wrong-doing.

   Avoid Asking "Why" Questions

   When you find yourself about to ask a "why" question, restate it as a "who," "what," "where," "when," or "how" type question. These questions can be answered with a description instead of a justification (reason). This will help you get useful information instead of just a reaction.

Avoid:	Ask instead:
"Why do you think that?"	"How did you come to that conclusion?"
"Why did you close the account?"	"What went into your decision to close the account?"

   If you really just want information, and do not wish to tie on the extra baggage of challenge and blame, limit your use of the word "why"as a question. Most "why" questions can be rephrased in the form of an "open question" discussed later.

2. Leading Questions

   Leading questions disguise statements. You use a question format to really make a personal statement. For example, you ask,

   > "Don't you think it would be better to call first, rather than just drop in?" instead of simply saying, "I'd like to call first, rather than just drop in."

3. Closed Questions

   Closed questions give the other person a choice, but it is usually between two limited alternatives. This severely narrows the amount of information exchanged. For example,

   > "Do you want to start today or tomorrow?" (instead of "When do you want to start?")

"Did George say 'yes' or 'no'?" (instead of "What did George say?")

4. Multiple Questions

Multiple questions ask for two or more answers at once. For example,

"What do you think the reason is that we weren't invited? How do you feel about it? Who did get invited?"

The problem with multiple questions is that they flood the respondent. When you use multiple questions, you dilute your effectiveness as an information gatherer. Typically the respondent only answers one part of the question. Unless you ask the other part of the question again, that particular information gets lost.

5. Open Questions

Open questions are the most effective ones. They give others more choice in how they answer. If you do not use a challenging tone, others will feel free to answer open questions by describing their experience in their own words.

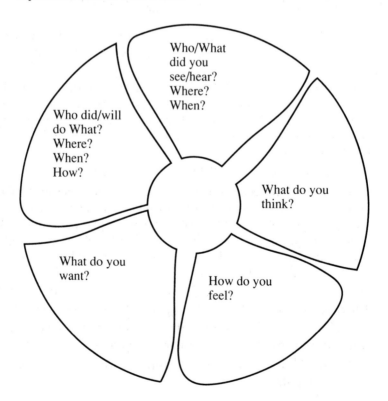

Open questions usually begin with a W-word: Who, What, Where, When, How, but not Why.

When you want to direct a conversation, the Awareness Wheel and open questions give you a map and the tools to fill out a situation. Put any issue at the hub of the Wheel and ask open questions about each zone.

The Advantages and Disadvantages of Directive Listening

Directive Listening provides these advantages:

1. It quickly focuses a conversation.

2. It allows you to take charge of a conversation, assuming the other person cooperates with you by freely responding to your questions.

Directive Listening has a major disadvantage, however. In your quest for efficiency, you can easily misdirect and stifle crucial information. Your line of questioning can lead the other person away from the most important information.

ATTENTIVE LISTENING: WANTING TO DISCOVER

The idea behind Attentive Listening is quite simple: let others tell their story spontaneously. Don't direct it, just encourage it. Follow the leader!

Doing this is not so easy. In fact, you are probably saying to yourself, "You've got to be kidding, I don't have time for that." Actually, Attentive Listening takes less time and is more productive, especially in pressure situations, than either Persuasive or Directive Listening. Is this surprising? Here are the reasons:

1. Most people can freely tell their story in *two to four minutes.*

2. When people talk about an issue in their own way, you get fresher, better quality, uncontaminated information. The spontaneity of the content, sequence, nonverbal pace, and so forth all communicate. Besides leading you to their "hot" spot, "sore" spot, or "soft" spot, others will often tell you things they might not think to say if you were doing all the questioning.

3. When you get the full story the first time, you do not have to waste time later going back for more information, clarifying misinformation, or mopping up after poor decisions.

4. The quickest way to cut through defensiveness — your own and others' — is to listen.

5. When you let other people freely tell their full story without influencing it, you help complete their communicycles. This increases the chances of having others take your story seriously too.

6. Letting people speak their truth reduces fear and resistance, and it generates trust. Quality listening puts a deposit in the relationship bank for resolving future issues.

ATTENTIVE LISTENING SKILLS

Attentive Listening carries out the intentions of Search Talk and Straight Talk: to gain an overview, understand, deal with "what is," count both self and other, and to *connect* with others rather than control them. Attentive Listening skills help you get the full story efficiently, the first time. The secret of Attentive Listening is to go into the speaker's world and experience the situation or issue as he or she does.

Attentive Listening does not come naturally. Often your own emotions interfere with good listening. The more involved and invested you are in a particular situation or outcome, the more difficult it is to set aside your own reaction. Here it is important to *be self-aware and manage yourself* as you follow the speaker's lead. Wrapped up in your own thoughts, feelings, and wants, it is difficult to listen to the thoughts, feelings, and wants of others. It is much easier to act out your anxiety by advising, directing, judging. When you listen attentively, however, you rein in these tendencies and let the speaker lead.

Here are five skills that can dramatically improve your listening ability (These five skills continue on from the six speaking skills introduced in Chapter 9):

7. Looking, Listening, Matching, and Tracking

8. Acknowledging Messages

9. Inviting More Information

10. Checking Out/Clarifying Information

11. Summarizing — To Ensure Accuracy Of Understanding

SKILL NO. 7: LOOKING, LISTENING, MATCHING, AND TRACKING

Interpersonal communication is a series of sensory (visual, auditory, tactile) feedback loops. *Observing* nonverbals and *listening* to other people's tone, pace, and words provides you with your data base for understanding others. If you are not alert both to what (content) is being said, and how (style) it is being said, you cannot begin to understand others accurately. Many aspects of communication are at work in this skill. The next few pages will give you more detail.

Establishing Rapport

In order to connect effectively with another person you must establish rapport — harmony, accord, alignment — with that person. Rapport is the chemistry that leads to cooperation and trust.

> In moments of great rapport, a remarkable pattern of nonverbal communication can develop. Two people will mirror each other's movements — dropping a hand, shifting their bodies at exactly the same time. This happens so quickly that without videotape or film replay one is unlikely to notice the mirroring. But managers can learn to watch for disruptions in this mirroring because they are dramatically obvious when they occur. Instead of smooth mirroring, there will be a burst of movement, almost as if both are losing balance. Arms and legs may be thrust out and the whole body posture changed in order to regain balance. (McCaskey, 1979, page 179.)

Think for a moment about someone whose company you enjoy. What is it you like about that person? Chances are the person is someone with whom you spontaneously get into "step." You understand, feel comfortable with, and accept each other.

Now recall someone you find it difficult to be around — an antagonistic competitor, for instance. When the two of you are together, you feel awkward, uncertain, uncomfortable, "out of step," and on a different "wave length."

Everyone encounters difficult people — people with whom we do not unconsciously and inadvertently fall into nonverbal and verbal synchronization. They are folks we do not dance with easily. In fact, we each send off grating, dissonant nonverbals, if not actual words,which say we are unapproachable to one another.

Rapport is hardest to establish with people most unlike yourself. But it also develops quite naturally with people who are like you. Sometimes, however, the people you must connect with are the people with whom you have the least rapport.

Matching to Create Rapport

When rapport is absent, gaining it becomes the top priority to communicate effectively. The quickest way to connect with another person in any situation is to attend consciously to the other person and match (mirror, reflect, but not mimic) his or her activities and experience. It involves getting into alignment with the other person so that your behavior says unconsciously, "We're alike," "You can trust me," "We're on the same side." This creates a powerful connection that reduces interpersonal resistance and encourages cooperation.

When you match other people, you follow their lead and match their activities and experiences as much as possible. *The key is that you start where the other person is; do not run ahead or drag behind.* You fall into the same rhythm and tempo.

There are a number of ways to do this. The more aspects you match, the stronger your connection with others.

- energy level/mood
- posture
- facial/body movements
- style of communication
- topic of discussion
- zone of awareness wheel
- words/images/metaphors
- speech tone/rate/loudness
- breathing
- space (closeness/distance)

Matching is powerful because it quickly puts you in an area of commonality — nonverbal synchronization — with another person. It communicates alikeness and acceptance of the other person. You do not jar the other person, subliminally challenging him or her or creating conflict. Instead, your actions affirm the other person and unconsciously say "you're okay."

A big part of Small Talk is rapport building. It gives people a chance to discuss and enjoy something in common. Watch two people meet for the first time as they engage in Small Talk. If they like each other, they soon begin to match each other nonverbally.

Conversations in any style are more productive when both partners join in the same style and get into sync. When people are not in the same style, they are generally out of immediate rapport, in transition to a new topic using different styles more appropriate to the moment, or perhaps signaling conflict by refusing to settle into a mutually agreeable productive style of communication. Style is also a way of both signaling and negotiating rapport, control, and trust.

In the high-pressure, fast-paced, busy world in which we live, partners often go for considerable lengths of time out of sync. Finally a fight breaks out. If they match each other's energy and style in the fight, they regain rapport, albeit with a negative tone. And if they both shift to a more productive style of communication, soon they are back in rapport dancing. Likewise, love-making can be done in or out of sync. An unhurried meal, conversation, and caressing often help partners synchronize.

Matching is particularly useful when you are dealing with someone who is very different professionally or personally from you. Here you must expand your typical behavior pattern to incorporate the other person's. Matching must be done skillfully with the sincere intention of connecting constructively. If it is done to mock, belittle, or take advantage of the other, it will backfire.

Matching accomplishes a number of things:

- prevents you from sending off negative nonverbal messages that say, "I don't like you."

- takes attention off yourself

- helps you share the other person's experience

- avoids overpowering or underpowering the other

- reduces interpersonal conflict and resistance

- prepares the other person to be led more easily

Tips

1. Look for and build on similarities with others. If you focus primarily on differences, you will communicate rejection nonverbally.

2. Match body language. In a meeting, if you want to connect with or influence someone, match their body language — posture, rate of movement, breathing, and perhaps even specific motions such as crossing your legs.

3. Build on the words and metaphors a person uses. Everyone has his or her own vocabulary.

4. Match others to get into a group if you are feeling excluded. You may have been excluded because you were out of sync.

5. Match subtle actions. You do not have to compromise your integrity to match another person. Just match subtle actions — ones that have no moral or ethical value for you.

6. Look, listen, and mirror the other person's posture, energy, and pace. This signals acceptance and availability and will help you connect faster so you can get to the heart of the exchange.

Tracking

It is amazing how much information is lost because people do not use the Awareness Wheel as a "Listening Wheel" to *track* the content of a speaker's story. If you listen in terms of the Wheel, you will be able to:

1. Hear messages more fully.

2. Remember parts of the story that represent different zones of the Wheel.

3. Recognize that information is missing.

4. Be more conscious of your choice of the next steps to gain more information or to take action.

Listen for these kinds of statements and information:

Look and Listen for the Hot Spot in Others' Awareness Wheels

"Hot" spots tell you where the positive energy is. You can see people "light up" while talking about something they are doing (action), have seen or heard (sensory data), a new idea (thought), something exciting (feeling), or a special desire (want).

A quick way to strengthen your relationship with another person is to be aware of where the other person's positive energy is and build on that energy.

Listen For Information "Below The Line" — Sore Spots and Soft Spots

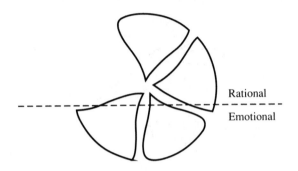

Most conversations focus on cognitively-based information above the line — events, facts, ideas, analyses, and proposals (future actions) — that are thought to be rational and manageable. What is often avoided or handled poorly is the information below the line — feelings and wants. These are viewed as irrational and unmanageable, but, in fact, they are quite understandable and manageable when they are treated as an integral part of any situation.

Unclear, confusing, and indirect messages usually have two parts: a "rational" piece and an "emotional" piece. Unless someone is using Straight Talk to share his or her feelings and wants directly, you have to listen very carefully for the information below the line and then respond directly to that part of the message. This is the pay dirt! No amount of "reasonable" talk above the line will satisfy a festering communicycle below the line.

"Sore" spots (pain, disappointment, and anger) and "soft" spots (fear and vulnerability) are part of the negative emotional piece of any message. To be an effective listener, you need to be alert for these "cloudy" messages.

Other people's emotions can control the interaction unless you know how to deal with emotions; one way is to acknowledge the feelings and then pursue them to their source — the sore spot or soft spot.

Watch The Dance

As you carry on a conversation, a dance is going on whether you are sitting or standing up. You and your partner are literally moving back and forth. (You could see it on a speeded-up video replay of the conversation.) One person leans forward to make a point, and the other leans backward to gain space to consider it. As we have seen, many different dances occur in life: one person leads, the other follows; both try to lead, neither follows; neither leads, both try to follow; and of course, two partners' dance may change from issue to issue.

Effective listeners watch the dance as they listen. The dance tells you much about what is going on at that moment, especially about how effective you are being. It gives you clues to shift what you are doing — change from speaking to listening, shift styles, open or close physical space, lead or follow, and when to Now-Talk (talk about what you see going on at that moment).

Ineffective listeners miss the dance but experience its impact, often to their wonderment or chagrin. Unaware that they are crowding others, their proposals and ideas are rejected. Inattentive to subtle shifts, they miss significant turning points in sales, conflict, decision-making, and negotiation situations.

Watch for Incongruence

Words and nonverbals do not always match. For example, people may say they are interested in doing something, but their nonverbal response (tone and body) do not completely agree with what is being said — this is incongruence.

Believe the nonverbals over the words! Sometimes it is not only useful, but also necessary to comment on the difference you see.

When incongruence occurs, a person is working against himself or herself. The person is not fully aware or is not being honest with himself or herself. People lose credibility when their actions are not consistent with their words. You can help others overcome incongruence by commenting on it and by asking for clarification.

Tips

1. Look and listen for the "sore" spot or "soft" spot in a message. Listen for content, emotion, and intent.

2. When you hear an indirect feeling, replace it with a direct statement.

3. As you listen, let your eyes soften their focus so that you can see more nonverbal information — small facial, hand, posture, and muscle movements throughout the speaker's body. This will help you pick up on incomplete communicycles, shifts in the dance, and other important nonverbal signals.

4. Listen for other people's figures of speech, metaphors, and imagery. Then when you speak, build on their language. This builds rapport by demonstrating that you have been attentively listening and understanding.

5. Keep a pleasant, relaxed look on your face, or let your facial expressions match the speaker's when you are listening carefully to someone. Some people unconsciously drift into a somber or stern look which works against them as they listen.

6. Match the nonverbals in other people because this creates comfort in them, freeing them to tell their story.

SKILL NO. 8: ACKNOWLEDGING MESSAGES

Acknowledging other people's messages lets them know verbally and nonverbally that they are leading and you are following what they are saying. Acknowledging ranges from a nod of your head or an "uh-huh" to brief interpretations like, "That sounds important"; "I can see you're really concerned"; or "That must have been exciting."

Acknowledging helps you connect by demonstrating that you are:

1. Following their train of thought and not sidetracking them.

2. Trying to understand their situation by standing inside their shoes.

3. Respecting what they are saying as their "truth," even though you may not fully agree with it.

Acknowledging builds bridges by conveying your acceptance of the speaker's right to say what he or she is experiencing at that moment. In effect, you are "going with" the speaker instead of blocking or reacting.

Often just acknowledging what the other person is experiencing is all that is necessary to connect and create understanding.

Joining Others in Their Zone of the Awareness Wheel

In listening, the key information at any moment is where other people's energy is, not where yours is. Join them in the zone of the Awareness Wheel they are emphasizing. For example, if they are talking about an idea, acknowledge the idea. If they are talking about wants, acknowledge wants.

Acknowledge, pick up, and build on positive *hot* spots, their positive energy. Acknowledge and let yourself be energized by their excitement. Go with their enthusiasm; do not squash it with a limiting or negative comment. Help them extend their communicycle.

Acknowledge and pick up on their *sore* or *soft* spot, and work to understand it. When your partner recognizes that you understand "where he or she is," you will see it in the nonverbal response.

In any event, join the hot, sore, or soft spot on the person's Awareness Wheel — the idea, feeling, want, or action on which he or she is focusing. Be there. Let the other person lead. Amplify the focus. Do not shift away until the communicycle is complete.

Tips

1. Use brief acknowledgments to show the speaker you are tracking.

2. Use nods, uh-huhs, and short comments to show you are following. Longer comments and questions move you toward leading.

3. Acknowledge messages "below the line." When you hear a "pressure" message, acknowledge the feeling part of the message. Do not treat the message rationally by giving the other person reasons why he or she should not be upset. Accept what is below the line so you can proceed above the line.

SKILL NO. 9: INVITING MORE INFORMATION

Here you simply say or do something which encourages others to continue spontaneously talking about their story:

"Tell me about it."

"I'd like to hear more about what you are saying."

"What else can you tell me?"

"Is there anything more you want me to know?"

"I'd like to hear anything else you think I should know."

Inviting as a Response

When others tell you their story, they often pause looking for your response. Many people take the pause as a cue to jump in and start directing the conversation by giving advice or asking questions. Do not do this. Rather, let them lead you to more useful information by inviting them to tell you more.

Invite (time #1)

"Tell me more."

Invite again (time #2, time #3)

"Is there anything more you can tell me?"

"Is there anything else you want me to know?"

Continue inviting until the speaker says something to the effect: "I don't think there's anything more I can say about the situation," and in fact has nothing more to add.

Most people unconsciously test listeners with brief pauses to see if it is okay to continue talking. They do not tell what they are really thinking, feeling, and wanting unless they are sure the listener wants to know what is going on inside of them. An invitation to continue is a very powerful message. It says two things to the speaker:

1. What you are saying is important to me.

2. I have time to listen. Keep talking.

Did You Get to the Core? — The Real Pay-Off

Often at the third or forth invitation, people will say to you, "I don't know if this has anything to do with the situation or not, *but...*" What follows the "but" is usually gold! This is because you have demonstrated enough interest that they now have the trust and courage to say what is really on their minds. At this point, they give you their core information.

Do not assume that others have told you the whole story. Test by saying: "tell me more." If there is more to the story, people will usually give you more information. If the story is complete, they will say, "That's all I can tell you." (And you will see congruent nonverbals indicating that is all.) Then is a good time to begin directing with open questions like: "What do you want to do about it?" "Who else knows about this?"

Tips

1. Stop when you feel the urge to begin directing a conversation. Instead, invite and see what happens next. You will be amazed at the important information you might have missed.

2. Invite when someone asks you a question and you are not sure you understand exactly what he or she is asking. Ask the person to say more about his or her question. Often the person will save both of you time by telling you what he or she really wants to know — the real intent behind the question.

3. Invite again. Inviting two or three times will help people reach the core of their story, objection, or feeling.

4. Invite after a pause. Sometimes a comfortable, silent pause before an invitation will add to its effectiveness.

SKILL NO. 10: CHECKING OUT/CLARIFYING INFORMATION

As you listen to others talk about an issue, parts of their story will naturally fall into different zones of the Awareness Wheel. But even after you have looked and listened carefully, acknowledged, and invited them to say more, you may still want more specific information. At that point, it is time to actively *fill in and clarify missing or confusing information*. You can do this by using the skill of *checking out* which involves asking questions that seek specific kinds of information.

Use The Awareness Wheel and Ask Open Questions

Use the Awareness Wheel and ask open questions to help you fill in missing information and clarify confusing data. As noted earlier, the Awareness Wheel and open questions give a map and tools to organize and gain good information. (See the section entitled "Five Different Kinds of Directive Questions" earlier in this chapter for details on asking effective questions.) While open questions are focused, they give the other person room to answer. For example:

"Who was there?"

"What was decided?"

"How did you feel after the meeting?"

Checking Out Your Interpretations

Even when you know someone well enough to interpret certain private signs — a frown, a shrug of the shoulders, a particular facial expression — judging nonverbal behavior is risky business. You may be way off base in what you think it means. Check it out:

"I notice you are frowning." *(Sensory Data).* "What's up?" *(Checking Out).*

Checking out is also useful when you have made an interpretation and want to see how accurate it is:

"You look confident to me. How are you feeling?"

"I know you agreed to go sailing with me on Friday, but I have the impression your heart isn't in it. Am I accurate?"

Checking Out a Speaker's Sore and Soft Spots

As you look and listen, you will observe hot spots, sore spots, and soft spots. Sometimes the speaker will share them directly. Often you must move beyond the actual words spoken to try to capture what the speaker is not saying directly. To do this effectively, you must look and listen for signals between the lines and pick up on indirect or mixed messages.

Speaker: "Sometimes I want to walk out and never come back."

Listener: "You sound really angry with me. Is that the way you feel?"

This can be a very powerful way to connect with another person. It can capture masked expressions of thoughts, feelings, and wants which the speaker is too cautious to disclose directly. It can also help a speaker become aware of hidden parts of his or her Awareness Wheel.

Reading between the lines is tricky, however, because you are interpreting what the person is *not* saying from body language, tone, pace, and other nonverbals. *Make these types of interpretations cautiously.* The intention behind another person's behavior can be quite different than your interpretation.

Do not get stymied by whether your interpretation is right or wrong; this will make you fail to understand what the other person is really experiencing. Forcing your interpretations on others creates defensiveness.

It is best to keep your interpretations tentative, subject to change by the speaker if they do not fit. Pressing for agreement does not work. Rather than directing the other person with your interpretations, use the previous skill — inviting — to learn what he or she is experiencing.

Tips

1. Stop to check.If you see or hear anything that suggests to you that a communicycle is incomplete, check it out.

2. Check out what someone wants. Often the most crucial missing information relates to intentions. Asking others what they really want will clarify objectives and expectations at the core of an issue.

3. Treat feelings as seriously as facts.

4. Comment cautiously on incongruence between what you see and what you hear.

SKILL NO. 11: SUMMARIZING — TO ENSURE ACCURACY OF UNDERSTANDING

Have you ever found yourself in a situation where you and your partner sincerely agreed to something only to learn later that what you had agreed to was not the same as what he or she had? Or have you ever been in a tense discussion only to discover finally that the two of you were talking past each other? In each instance, you were victims of "unshared meanings."

Sharing Meaning — A Process for Guaranteeing Understanding

Many misunderstandings have nothing to do with limited intelligence or lack of good will. Communication is complex and many factors contribute to misunderstandings. You say something, and your partner internally embellishes the message a bit, putting more into your message than you mean or intend:

Or the reverse happens: you say something to your partner and he or she internally reduces your message to less than you mean or intend:

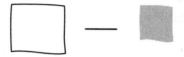

When what you say to your partner is understood exactly as you mean or intend, the two of you have a shared meaning:

A shared meaning occurs when the message sent by one person is the same as the message received by the other. You can also think of this as completing a communicycle. *A shared meaning summarizes the essence of a message.*

Summarizing When Accuracy or Understanding is Important

Much of the time it does not matter if there is a little slippage and the message sent is not *exactly* the same as the message received. But in some routine situations, such as giving directions, making appointments, or transferring account numbers, accuracy is obviously needed, and replaying a summary is useful.

In non-routine, complex and uncertain situations, summarizing is even more important. But the urge to "playback" comes less naturally. Think of summarizing when you want to:

- guarantee that an important message is heard
- minimize guesswork

- demonstrate respect for others by showing an interest in understanding them
- help yourself to hear others accurately
- track a difficult or mixed messages
- send a positive, intimate message and minimize its being discounted
- confirm a contract (see Chapter 11, Meta-Talk)
- set priorities on issues
- clarify perspectives
- take a positive step toward resolving a conflict
- confirm action plans

In short, summarize when misunderstandings would be costly or when misunderstandings seem to be occurring.

Either the Listener or the Speaker Can Summarize

Summarizing as the *listener* involves:

Stopping for a moment and repeating back (in your own words) what you have just heard as the speaker's points (Step 1), and asking the speaker for confirmation or clarification of your summary (Step 2).

Summarizing as the *speaker* involves:

1. Making a statement and asking the listener for a summary of what you have just said using his or her own words (Step 1).

2. After the listener has summarized your message (Step 2), confirm the accuracy of the summary (Step 3).

3. Restating missing points or clarifying points which are summarized inaccurately.

Speaker: "I'd like to know what you think I'm saying because this is important to me."

Listener: (Describes meaning received.)

Speaker: "You got most of it, but let me clarify one thing. What I would like to have happen is..."

Summarizing serves two major functions:

1. It *demonstrates* understanding by showing the speaker what the listener has understood. When you are the listener, an accurate summary shows that you listen well. This increases the speaker's confidence and trust in you. If your summary is inaccurate, you have given the speaker a clear opportunity to clarify your misunderstanding.

2. Summarizing can occur at any point; it *punctuates* a conversation. It signals that the first chapter of the story is finished and you are now ready to move on to the next chapter in the conversation. One communicycle is completed and the next is about to start.

   When you have thoroughly heard a speaker's story and wish to *shift from following to leading,* a summary provides a nice bridge that assures the speaker that you have accurately understood him or her. Because you have "earned the right to be heard" by listening to the speaker first, he or she will usually follow as you begin to lead in the next part of the conversation.

Tips

1. Learn to summarize well. The trick to summarizing is to be complete, yet not add to or subtract from the original message.

2. Recycle if necessary. Sometimes it is important to recycle a summary more than once until both parties are satisfied that the message sent equals the message received.

3. Pay attention to the nonverbals. Nonverbals are the most convincing evidence that a speaker and listener share a meaning. If either party has any question about the accuracy of a summary, it will show in hesitant head and body movements, as well as in the tone of voice. Watch out for false agreements — words that say "yes," but bodies that say "no." If you spot any nonverbal hesitation, check it out and recycle the summary.

4. Avoid using the phrase, "I understand what you mean." It is often used insincerely, as a ploy to recapture the lead in a conversation. Instead, *demonstrate* your understanding by summarizing in your own words what you hear the other person saying.

5. Recognize the value of Attentive Listening. It is the most effective way to connect up, across, and down any organization.

Attentive Listening Illustrated

In Attentive Listening, you use the skills Nos. 7-11 — in the general order in which they have been presented — when someone approaches you with an issue. Notice that Skill No. 10, Checking Out/Clarifying Information, which involves asking specific questions, does not occur until the speaker has spontaneously told as much as possible of his or her story. This minimizes the listener's influence on and contamination of the story. Here are the skills in action as Bob and Joan again replay their conversation from earlier in the chapter, this time with Bob using Attentive Listening:

Bob: "How's the project going, Joan?"

Joan: "Okay, I guess, but I've got a problem. Can I tell you about it?"

Bob: "Sure, go ahead." (Inviting)

Joan: "It's about Phil. Last week I asked him when he would be done with the initial design, and he told me he would be finished yesterday. He gave me the design as he promised, but the design is too complex."

Bob: "Uh-huh." (Acknowledging)

Joan: "I had told him to try to keep it simple, but when he gave me the design, he said he added features to make it more efficient. I'm concerned because I know how hard Phil worked on the design, but I think the extra features will cause real production problems."

Bob: "That sounds like a serious problem. Is there anything else?" (Acknowledging and Inviting)

Joan: "Well, Phil is a bit of a problem generally. He works hard and has good ideas, but too often he runs off on his own. He seems to be very ambitious, and I think he believes that he'll get ahead quicker by doing this. I've told him a couple of times that we value team work here, but he doesn't seem to accept that. That's been frustrating."

Bob: "What do you want to happen?" (Checking Out Wants)

Joan: "I'd like Phil to keep his enthusiasm and continue to contribute his ideas. But I can't have him go off in a different direction like he has been doing. I've thought about talking to him about this again, but that didn't work before. Another idea I had was to have the two of us talk to him about the problems with the design he just turned in and, at the same time, stress the importance of team work. What do you think about that?"

Bob: "Well, before I answer your question, let me make sure I've got everything. It sounds like you've got two problems here. The short-run problem is that the design is not adequate. The long-run problem is that Phil is not really acting as a team member. You are frustrated about this because it's been going on for some time and your attempts to correct it have not been successful. You want to get Phil on the team without losing energy. You think that both problems can be dealt with at the same time, and you think I could be some help in this." (Summarizing)

Joan: "Yeah, that's it."

Bob: "Is there anything else?" (Inviting)

Joan: "No, you've got it. One thing, though. It's really been frustrating, and I'm starting to think I'm incompetent as the project manager 'cause I haven't been able to turn Phil around. I really need some help."

Bob: "Well, I'll try. Tell me more about your attempts to talk to Phil about the teamwork issue...."

We would like to point out several things about this conversation.

1. Joan filled in most parts of the Awareness Wheel naturally as she told her story. Starting at the top, she talked about her past actions

and Phil's action (her sensory data), then added a thought about Phil, before sharing her feeling of frustration. With some encouragement from Bob, she expressed her wants and also indicated the future actions she was considering.

You can use the Awareness Wheel as a map to keep track of the other person's stories. Most people will spontaneously fill out the Wheel as they tell their story, if you let them. You may need to ask for missing parts, but keep this to a minimum until they have had an opportunity to complete their story.

2. Acknowledgments that you are with the speaker and invitations to say more are about all the encouragement most people need to tell their story. Notice how much information Joan gave in response to Bob's "Uh-huh" and "Is there anything else?" Notice also the effect of summarizing and then testing the completeness of Bob's understanding of her story with a final invitation after Joan confirmed his accuracy. This brought Bob to the core of Joan's story — that she was experiencing self-doubt and needed help from him. This last disclosure probably would not have been made without Bob's final invitation.

3. Think of using the skills in the order listed as a *listening strategy*. You unobtrusively encourage the speaker to do all the talking until he or she has completed the story. Then, if necessary, you intervene with specific questions to fill in missing information. Finally, you summarize to test the accuracy of your understanding in preparation for moving onward in the conversation — possibly to future action.

4. There is quite a difference between Bob's behavior here and his actions in the two earlier examples. Two big differences are the quality of information generated and the relationship satisfaction between Joan and Bob.

5. Finally, you can put more stock in information spontaneously reported by others than you can in information "artifically" stimulated by your questions.

Quality Listening

Quality listening means getting the whole story accurately, the first time. As a listener you can do a great deal either to hinder or help the speaker make his or her point. Consciously creating rapport (getting into sync) and letting go of control (by following the leader) will make you a better listener. To a large extent, trust is the product of your skill in creating rapport and following.

The three different types of listening — Persuasive, Directive, and Attentive — reflect the three underlying dynamics of rapport, control, and trust. As you move from Persuasive to Attentive Listening, rapport increases, controlling behavior subsides, and trust grows. This is the stuff out of which strong, enduring, and viable relationships develop.

11

META TALK:
Talk About Talk

In this chapter we will introduce another level of communication skill: Meta Talk — "talk about talk." But first we want to summarize briefly how the communication maps and skills introduced so far fit together as a basis for understanding the importance of Meta Talk.

Focus, Style, and Awareness

In Chapter 2 we explained that the "focus" of a conversation can be about:

Topics — events, tasks, and people not present

Other — person(s) present

Self — me personally

Relationship — you *and* me, us

In Chapters 3 and 4 we presented various "styles" of communication — *how* people talk about *what* they talk about. They can chit chat in Small Talk, get up to speed in Shop Talk, give directions in Control Talk, argue in Fight Talk, communicate hurt in Spite Talk, explore possibilities in Search Talk, or go to the core of their experience in Straight Talk.

In Chapter 5 we explained that the specific content of what you talk about depends on what is happening in your Awareness Wheel — your sensory data, thoughts, feelings, wants, and actions. Chapters 6 and 7 showed that the kind of information you communicate is influenced by your personality type and how complete or limited your awareness is.

Speaking and Listening Skills

Assuming you have full awareness of your experience on a particular issue, you have a *choice: to disclose or withhold your information.* If you choose to tell your partner what it is you are experiencing, Chapter 9 detailed six Speaking Skills for sending complete and clear messages:

1. Speaking For Self
2. Giving Sensory Data
3. Expressing Thoughts
4. Reporting Feelings
5. Disclosing Wants
6. Stating Actions

Chapter 10 presented the other side of the communication equation — listening — and explained five specific skills for helping you hear your partner's full story. The five Attentive Listening skills are:

7. Looking, Listening, Matching, and Tracking
8. Acknowledging Messages
9. Inviting More Information
10. Checking Out/Clarifying Information
11. Summarizing — To Ensure Accuracy of Understanding

Plain Talk

When you discuss an issue with another person — using the talking and listening skills to communicate — you are doing what may be termed Plain Talk. The graphic below represents two people Plain Talking — acting, reacting, and interacting around an issue — as they exchange messages about their life or work together.

META TALK

There are occasions, however, when Plain Talk is not enough. Sometimes it is necessary or useful to *shift from talking about an issue or situation* to *talking about the process of your interaction* — the pattern or way in which you and the other person relate. This is particularly true when you find yourself stuck in an impasse and are unable to complete your communicycles or when you want to prevent an impasse in the future.

The word "meta" means above or about. *Meta Talk is conversation about the process of how you talk, interact, and make decisions with another person.* Meta Talk takes you outside your circle of ongoing interaction to plan, clarify, affirm, reflect on, and restructure, if necessary, what is happening inside the circle of your regular interaction. The purpose of Meta Talk is to create a more mutually satisfying conversation and be more productive.

To Meta Talk, you use all of the speaking and listening concepts and skills introduced previously. However, your exchange jumps out a notch from the issue itself to focus on the process of how you talk about the issue — what is working (getting you what you want) and what is not working. By anticipating and altering actions at this level, you can prevent or repair misunderstandings, as well as enrich and savor the interaction. Meta Talk helps you to be more in charge of your interaction.

When you have a metaconversation with another person about how the two of you relate, interact, work, or communicate together, you are able to:

1. Prepare yourself and the other person for a conversation.

2. Set the ground rules before a conversation or clarify confusion during your interaction.

3. Work out ways to improve how both of you relate by consciously learning from what happens during a particular exchange or meeting.

Meta Talk Skills

Processing how you live or work together can take three forms:

1. Pre-talk about how you *will* interact
2. Now-talk about how you *are* interacting
3. Post-talk about how you *did or have* interacted

Now-Talk

Pre-Talk   Post-Talk

PRE-TALK

Basically, Pre-Talk is a way of anticipating and overviewing a discussion by setting the stage for a constructive conversation. It provides orientation for what is to follow.

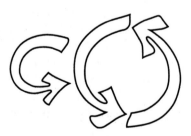

Contracting: Setting Procedures Together

Have you ever launched into a discussion about something of great importance to you, only to find the other person unresponsive? Your first reaction is usually anger as you jump to the conclusion, "My partner's not at all interested in what I am concerned about."

When this happens, people typically either push harder to be heard (despite all the nonverbal signs of unavailability), or they leave the situation upset, believing that the other person will never be interested in the issue.

Rather than assuming a lack of interest or trying to force involvement, there is another alternative — contracting. That means before starting a conversation to get the other person's okay (contract) to proceed immediately or to establish another time and place for the conversation. This is useful whether you are making a brief phone call ("Barb, do you have five minutes to go over our planning agenda for next week?") or setting a time and place to have a more extended conversation about an important matter.

Contracting means informally setting procedures. It demonstrates respect for all parties involved by clarifying several factors which will assure everyone's readiness to focus on an issue. This prevents frustration and the waste of time and energy. Here are the eight factors to consider when you make a "contract":

Issue	1. what
	2. whose
Procedure	3. who
	4. where
	5. when
	6. how
	7. energy
	8. stopping

Figure 11.1 Contracting Considerations

Notice how many procedural possibilities there are to interfere with a good discussion of an issue. Here is what we mean by each of these factors:

1. *What* to talk about

   The "what" is the issue itself. It can have a topical, personal, or relational focus and be the concern of one or both parties.

Identifying the issue and establishing agreement to talk about it is a critical starting point.

2. *Whose* issue it is

Also important is identifying whose issue it is primarily: mine, yours, ours, or someone else's. To answer this, think about who will be affected and what is at stake for whom. It is especially important to do this when the issue is mine and does not involve you, yet I want you to be a consultant to my concern.

3. *Who* is included

Sometimes a conversation should involve only you and one other person, but at other times you will want several people present. To respect relational and organizational boundaries, you will find yourself reserving certain discussions for certain people.

4. *Where* to talk

Place is important. Some places are conducive to focusing on important issues, while others can be distracting.

For example, making critical decisions during a meal may not be the right place; it interferes with savoring your food. Likewise, heavy discussions in bed may be out of bounds; one partner drops off to sleep, while the other cannot get to sleep. Some people save their discussions for an extended walk, and others have a comfortable spot in their house that facilitates productive discussions. The more fast-moving and complex your life is, the more intentional you have to be about contracting. Find a good place that fits for both partners.

5. *When* to talk

Trying to force a discussion at the wrong time or giving an issue inadequate time only generates more tension and dissonance. On the other hand, when both partners are ready and want to deal with something, even in a limited time frame, it is amazing what can be accomplished.

Considering time also gives everyone a chance to prepare adequately for the discussion. Some people prefer, and some situations require, time to reflect on their awareness. For other people, postponing a conversation only creates anxiety about what will be said or what will happen. Think about the other person's needs as well as your own and contract accordingly.

6. *How* to talk

Sometimes it is useful to outline a little plan or strategy for talking together. Previewing (see below) does this. Here you might say,

"Let's start with about five minutes of brainstorming in Search Talk and stay out of Control or Fight Talk. Afterwards we can evaluate and prioritize our ideas and see if any of this stimulates some Straight Talk."

7. *Energy* available for dealing with the issue

   Even with all the other conditions right, sometimes physical or mental fatigue dominates. Often the solution to issues is closely tied to the energy you can put into exploring them. Some issues are best reserved for a time when you both have the energy to handle them. However, chronically low energy may suggest you are avoiding an issue or some dimension of your awareness.

8. *Stopping* the discussion

   Develop a rule or cue for stopping a discussion when one or both of you want to do so. Having an agreed upon way to stop will help you keep issues in perspective with an option to postpone further discussion when you run out of steam.

We are not suggesting that it is necessary to run down this list each time you want to deal with an issue. We do want you to be aware, however, that an informal contract underlies every discussion.

Here are three ways to approach contracting:

1. Check up front to confirm whether this is a good time and place to talk. Be alert to any procedural factor that is not right. It will interfere with a productive exchange.

2. Summarize your understanding of your contract before proceeding to discuss an issue to ensure accuracy and shared meaning around your ground rules.

3. Be alert to nonverbal cues along the way of your conversation that suggest something is amiss. For example, if your partner glances at his or her watch, or starts to wander out of the room as you talk, think contract! Shift to Now-talk (see below) and check the contract. If a conversation is not proceeding well, perhaps you have slipped into a style that is unproductive or your partner is running out of steam.

Giving everyone choice in setting procedures increases involvement. When you and your partner can agree on procedures for discussing issues, often half the job is done. That is because choosing to work together and support each other's concerns is a powerful force in a relationship.

Watch Nonverbals

Whether you are scheduling a time and place to meet or simply asking, "Do you have a minute to talk?" watch for nonverbals. If a person's words say "yes," but his or her head, voice tone, or gesture says "no," you do not have a good contract.

Pick up on the incongruency. "I'm hearing yes, seeing no. What's the no?" This encourages the other person's full input into the contract. If you do not start with a good contract, you will not have a productive conversation, and a subtle part of any dance is the contract. Many people miss cues or do not think to metacommunicate about their underlying contract. Consequently, both parties pay the frustrating price of unproductiveness.

Previewing

Previewing *lets the other person know up front what to expect from you.* It sets the stage before getting into the actual exchange:

"I'd like to start by really listening to your point of view, not interrupting, and then see if I can summarize it accurately. Okay?" (Look and listen for the degree of nonverbal acceptance or rejection.)

"Would you like some positive feedback...."

"I'm going to be tough on you for a few minutes. I'd like you to listen and not react until I've told you what I'm concerned about."

"I think we have some big differences, but first let's see what we've got in common."

"I'd like to discuss how we got into this mess, and have both of us stay out of Fight or Spite Talk."

"Would you be willing to talk about the balance in our checking account for a few minutes?"

Previewing is a form of contracting, but it is generally more directive. While you still look for consent, you mainly tell the other person what is going to happen and how you want them to respond, or you ask them if they would be willing to take a certain approach.

Again, look and listen for small nonverbals that indicate compliance. If you see or hear non-compliance, check it out. Perhaps you need to develop a plan together for how to proceed. By getting the rules straight before proceeding with a discussion, you reduce hidden agenda and surprises, and you set expectations which gain cooperation. Your forthrightness actually builds trust.

Defusing and Disarming Resistance

When you get to know other people's reactions to certain situations quite well and expect that they will resist what you have to say, sometimes you can reduce or possibly eliminate their typical (usually negative) response by anticipating it. You can even give them permission to react as you expect them to. It is important to be aware of your underlying intentions in using this tactic. Recognize if you are trying to control by manipulating or connect by managing.

Here are some examples of preambles that make it harder for the others to respond in their usual manner:

"I'm assuming you won't like this idea for fundraising, but I'd like you to hear me out, okay?" (This prepares the other for what is to follow. The person might think, "I'll listen and see if I like it or not.")

"Can I ask you a question you might find difficult to answer? (Watch nonverbals, perhaps move closer, drop your voice a bit, and continue) I've been wondering what you ...?"

"What I expect you to do from past reactions is..."

"If I push too hard for my point, and you can't handle it, I want you to raise your hand as a signal for me to back off. But see how long you can keep your hand down."

By being careful to speak for yourself and *make statements about the other, not for the other*, you can make strong statements, give suggestions, and even provide directives with minimal resistance. When you "call the shots" first, and are right on target, it is either tough for the person to respond in his or her usual manner, or the usual response has the person going in your direction. Much of the resistance evaporates with your "warning" or request. In a funny sort of way, you involve your partner in getting past the first hurdle.

The fewer the options in another person's typical behavioral repertoire, the better this form of Pre-Talk works. The purpose of this kind of Pre-Talk is to cut through the usual reaction/rejection response so you can get a hearing in order to negotiate a satisfactory outcome.

Instructing/Coaching

Instructing/coaching sets the stage for someone else to participate in a conversation; you do this to help the other person prepare for the eventual exchange.

"Here's what I would like you to tell Beth..."

"Don't let yourself be intimidated by his anger. Hang in there. Use his anger as a cue to uncover his fear. When you think he's getting angry, ask him 'What do you think is the worst thing that can happen in this situation?' "

In summary, all types of Pre-Talk boil down to some form of contracting.

NOW-TALK

Now-Talk focuses on what is happening in the interaction at that moment: what you are immediately sensing, thinking, feeling, wanting, or doing in relation to the dance. Comments can be positive feedback about how the dance is going or requests for change or help.

Observing and Giving Feedback

Think of stopping and stepping outside the circle of your immediate exchange and commenting on the "now" when you are:

Locked into an impasse: "I don't think we're getting anywhere. I'm blaming you and you're nailing me. I'd like to shift into trying to help each other solve this problem. What do you think?"

Pleased with what is happening: "I'm feeling very optimistic about our decision. I really like your ideas, and appreciate how you are taking my concerns seriously."

Experiencing strong negative emotions: "You really sound upset to me. What's going on?" or "I am really frustrated. I don't think you are hearing what I'm trying to say. Am I doing something to interfere with your listening?"

Seeing or hearing incongruencies or mixed messages: "You say you're satisfied with the results, but you don't look satisfied to me. Am I accurate?"

Being interrupted: "I'm having a hard time telling you what happened because you keep interrupting me with questions or comments. Could I just describe the situation first and then answer your questions?"

Stuck: "I don't know what to say next." (Be silent and see what happens.)

On the telephone: "You sound rushed right now. Should I call you later?"

Clarifying

Little questions can serve as check points along the way to clarify the process and keep things running smoothly and efficiently.

"What's going on between us right now that we can't make this decision?"

"Am I being impossible to work with?"

"Are we sticking to the issue?"

"I think my remark about your hair a few moments ago may have offended you. Did it?"

Summarizing

Summarizing is a way of facilitating the interaction by ensuring that the content of the discussion is being accurately understood. You step aside for a moment to be sure you are on track with a shared meaning.

"Let me see if I've got your point." (Then follow with a summary of what the speaker just said to assure accurate understanding.)

Describing

Descriptions are metacomments about the meaning of your actions. They help others understand the meaning of your behavior:

"I'm thinking about what you just said.

"I'm looking over your shoulder to help you catch the math mistake."

Counselors, medical doctors, and process consultants (skill trainers, mediators, facilitators) occasionally tell their clients what it is they are doing as a part of their intervention.

POST-TALK

After you have resolved an issue, finished a task, or ended a meeting, Post-Talk allows you to reflect on the event. You often do this with an eye toward continuing or improving your interchange in the future.

Recounting

(While you are doing the dishes after your dinner guests have gone.) "I really liked the way we planned and served dinner for our guests tonight. It seemed so coordinated. I think our planning the menu together, then having you cook and me clean the house worked well."

"Remember how much fun we used to have when we were all in graduate school, and didn't have any money, and didn't care?"

Analyzing

"I think we could avoid much of the stress we just went through if we would regularly sit down together and go over our calenders for the next few weeks."

"Jack, when you and Harold get into one of your disagreements, everyone else in the group seems to mentally check out. I think we end up wasting a lot of time. Is there something we could all do to avoid this at future meetings?"

Clearing The Air: By Acknowledging, Apologizing, Or Asking For Forgiveness

Occasionally you have a misunderstanding, embarrassing moment, disagreement, or argument, or you do something which disrupts or even damages your relationship with another person. You are at an impasse or have left a communicycle dangling.

The hiatus can last a few minutes, hours, days, or months. Occasionally events go back years and become grossly distorted over time in each player's mind.

In order to get back on the track again together, you or the other person must take the initiative to acknowledge the disruption (close the communicycle) and make amends. If you do not do so, future exchanges will be conditioned by the unfinished business. Your conversation about the past event is a form of Post-Talk:

> "Jane, I want you to know that I am aware of my not calling you as I promised. I imagine you have been wondering what ever happened to me. Here's what's been going on with me..."

> "Pete, I want to apologize to you for not involving you in the planning. It didn't occur to me that your department would be affected by the new policy."

> "Bob, I think I really offended you in front of our friends when I made the offhand comment about your knack for poor investments. Would you forgive me for what I said? I won't do something like that again."

STORIES

Story telling is a very powerful form of metacommunication: it is talk about life. A good story will transport you to funny times, hard times, good times — life times.

Most people think that stories exist outside themselves in the form of jokes or fables. They overlook their own wealth of experience as a source for stories. To learn how to tell an engaging story, listen to some good story telling. Notice that many of the communication concepts and skills presented in CONNECTING are used.

First of all, think of yourself as a story teller. Your stories can take any *focus* — topical, personal, or relational — and use any or all of the communication *styles*. Good stories include vivid descriptions of *sensory data,* capture people's *thinking,* and in the process stimulate your *emotions* as they reconstruct circumstances and events.

Tell stories about people who influenced your life and what you learned from them. Recall important, funny, and moving moments with them. Tell stories about embarrassing situations, funny events, and spiritual experiences.

As you tell a story watch other people's nonverbal response to the way you tell your story. Modulate your energy, space, and timing. Notice what is effective, and what you do that loses your listener.

Stories are metaphors about implicit realities. Their force carries over and applies to other areas of life beside the immediate sights, sounds, thoughts and feelings you are describing.

The stories you choose to tell reveal a lot about who you are, who you are not, and who you wish to be. Stories open the door to deeper communication and connection as you stimulate other people's associations with your tale. A good story encourages other people to tell their stories. Do not tell all the stories yourself. Learn from others' stories as well.

Tips

1. Schedule and prepare for a relationship talk. If you are having a difficult time relating to a friend, sibling, teacher, boss, or colleague, establish a contract to talk about your relationship. Schedule a time and place for a lunch, coffee, or a time away from your daily routine. Before meeting, use your Awareness Wheel to map the difficulty you are having.

2. Consider the risk. It can be hard to Meta Talk with someone who has real or potential power over you. The more dependent you are on the relationship, the tougher it is to change things because there is a risk that bringing a concern into the open may damage or destroy your relationship.

3. Reflect on the potential outcome. To improve a relationship, sometimes you must be willing to lose the relationship (or job). You have to decide if you want to live with things the way they are or try to improve them. With wisdom, tact, and communication skill, you may be surprised at how effective you can be and how responsive the other person will be to your concerns.

RELATIONSHIP MAPS

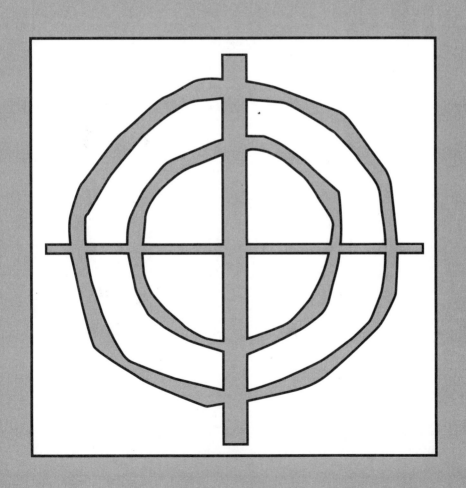

12

RELATIONSHIPS AS SYSTEMS

Every relationship has a life and a set of characteristics all its own; relationships are like organisms in the process of growing or dying. A framework which helps us understand relationships has emerged over the past twenty years. Called systems theory, the paradigm characterizes different kinds of relationships in terms of their dynamic interaction.

Think for a moment of all the different people you interface on a day-to-day basis — from two-person interactions to the small groups to which you belong and the larger organizations you enter or encounter. These are all systems, or subsystems within systems, which are influencing you and being influenced by you.

In this chapter we present some properties which characterize human systems and a major map for helping you better clarify the dynamics operating within your own relationships. This map can be used to help you understand your family and marriage, as well as your friendships, school, work, professional, and other relationships.

Properties of Human Systems

Systems theorists speak of pairs, groups, and larger organizations as being "open and complex" human systems. These terms are used to distinguish human systems from "closed and simple" entities such as many mechanical systems which are less influenced by their internal or external environments.

All open and complex systems have several characteristics in common. Think of human systems as being:

1. *Purposeful.* Although its mission and goals may be rather unclear or confused at times, every system has some reason for being. Much of its activity revolves directly and indirectly around strategies for achieving its ends.

2. *Interconnected.* Whatever affects one member influences all other members in the system, at least to a minimal extent.

3. *Bounded.* Human systems have semi-permeable boundaries which help the system maintain its identity and survival while continuously exchanging energy within and between the system's inner and outer environments. These boundaries are composed of formal and informal rules and expectations which regulate day-to-day activities.

4. *Self-monitoring.* Human systems have the potential for *maintaining, repairing, and directing themselves.* These processes are enhanced when system members have the capacity (motivation and skills) to communicate and metacommunicate effectively about their dance together, and when system rules support this communication.

5. *Information-processing.* Human systems generate, amplify, govern, distort, and transmit information. Most of this activity is conducted through processes of internal and external feedback loops or communicycles.

6. *Greater than the sum of its parts.* At any point in time, the potential presence or influence of a system adds up to something greater than the sum of its individual members' activities. The interaction among members creates something more. This is part of the reason why teams, families, and other systems are viewed as being entities and have reputations. A system's collective force can have positive and negative impact both on individual members and on the output of the group.

These six characteristics, common to all systems, are played out in an infinite variety of ways.

Pick two important groups or relationships in which you are a member at the present time and spend a few minutes comparing them in terms of these six properties.

The reason we outlined these six characteristics is to help you get a handle on what it is we mean when we talk about relationships as systems. Now, we want to introduce you to a more elaborate map which will help you understand the dynamics operating in your unique relationship systems.

THE CIRCUMPLEX MODEL OF HUMAN SYSTEMS

In recent years, Dr. David Olson and his colleagues in the Family Social Science Department at the University of Minnesota have developed a model for studying and understanding relationship dynamics as systems. In the process, they reviewed hundreds of books, research articles, and dozens of models. Their search revealed that, although different analysts used many different terms, their concepts could collectively be boiled down to three dimensions or variables: adaptability, cohesion, and communication.

This synthesis is the basis for the Circumplex Model of Marriage and Family Systems,* or "The Systems Map." (This map has been used in over 700 marriage and family research studies around the world and is equally applicable to other non-family relationships and organizations.) The Systems Map focuses primarily on the first two dimensions: *adaptability* and *cohesion.* CONNECTING treats the theoretical and practical aspects of the third dimension, *communication,* along a scale from negative (destructive) to positive (constructive) communication. Within relationships communication either facilitates or inhibits appropriate system movement on the two other dimensions.

Balancing Adaptability and Cohesion

To thrive in the uncertain and complex world in which we live, *systems must constantly balance change with stability and separateness with togetherness.* The Systems Map charts this balancing act. As you read through this chapter, pick a system with which you are familiar. You might focus on (1) the family you grew up in, (2) your current work group, (3) your most significant relationship, or (4) a committee or board at church. Consider how it *deals with change* and *stability* and manages *closeness and distance.*

---

*See the Appendix for more information on research instruments and the practical relationship feedback tools PREPARE (for engaged couples) and ENRICH (for married couples) which are based on the Circumplex Model of Marriage and Family Systems.

SYSTEM ADAPTABILITY

Adaptabililty represents the extent to which your relationships and systems are *flexible and able to change their dance* to meet different circumstances. The four levels of adaptability range from *rigid* (very low) to *structured* (low to moderate) to *flexible* (moderate to high) to *chaotic* (very high).

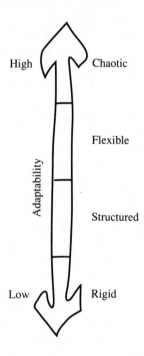

Research and clinical experience demonstrate that the middle levels of adaptability (structured and flexible) are more conducive to viable system functioning. The extremes (rigid and chaotic) are more problematic for relationships as they move through their life cycle.

You can locate your marriage, friendships, family, or work group at some level along the adaptability continuum by rating how your system deals with the following five characteristics of adaptability:

- leadership
- rules/roles
- negotiation
- organization
- values

To define and illustrate each of these characteristics, we will first compare and contrast the two middle levels (structured and flexible). Later we will describe the two extremes (rigid and chaotic) in terms of the five characteristics.

Leadership — Who is in charge?

Leadership or power is reflected in the way that goals and directions are determined. In more *structured* systems, leadership is rather authoritarian and quite stable with the same people making most of the important decisions. A high degree of planning and predictability characterizes structured relationships. Consequently, few options for spontaneity exist; change occurs when it is demanded. Large departments in organizations and the parent-child subsystem of families with small children often operate in this category.

Democratic norms are likely to exist in more *flexible* relationships. Everyone has input, and the responsibility for coordination and decision-making is likely to be shared or rotated. Flexible systems do plan, but plans are readily changed and people are more spontaneous; change happens when necessary. Many American marriages involve flexible relationships. Also as children become older, the parent-child subsystem within the American family typically becomes more flexible in order to accommodate the more independent activities of the children.

Rules/Roles — Who can do what?

System members set boundaries to exercise control over one another in the form of formal and informal rules and roles. The rules and roles let members know *who can do what, where, when, and how.*

Structured relationships are consistent and often quite explicit in the rules and roles which they establish to cover most situations. Rules are slow to change and are consistently enforced. A person who moves from being single, with few informal rules and expectations placed on him or her, into a more structured relationship in a marriage role may balk at the new set of rules which he or she finds constraining (less time with old friends, regular visits to in-laws, careful spending, more regular meals, etc.).

Control is less stable in more *flexible* systems. Rules and roles are adapted to the situation, based on general principles which are used as guidelines. Changing rules and sharing or modifying roles is commonplace and rules are also flexibly enforced. For example, a work group may develop its own system of flex-time, allowing individuals to back each other up and come and go as they wish, as long as the arrangement does not interfere with their performance or the productivity of the group.

Negotiation — How are decisions made?

Negotiations are necessary in relationships to plan and to solve problems. In *structured* relationships, negotiations are more limited in terms of who is involved, what specifically is considered, and how the actual decision-making process is carried out. Typically, responsibilities and commitments are established with minimal discussion. Consequently, problem-solving is efficient and minimizes emotional considerations. Reliability and dependability are important features of structured systems.

Flexible relationships usually involve considerable bargaining, trading, and exchanging. More members are actively engaged in decisions; this often results in new options surfacing during discussions. Open and sometimes extended negotiations also characterize more flexible systems, and arrangements can be restructured easily to accommodate change. These open negotiations require that members trust each other to carry out agreements.

Organization — How orderly are things?

Organization refers to the degree of orderliness and coherence in the system around its basic goals or objectives. Over time, systems work out procedures for carrying on those everyday activities; these procedures contribute substantially to the system's stability over time. Different systems contain varying degrees of organization and hence stability.

Structured relationships emphasize stability and purpose. They work out procedures for handling daily routines and attempt to prevent problems from arising. For example, a structured couple is most comfortable with using a budget to guide their spending and having money in savings. When crises develop, structured systems can weather the crisis well, but it usually requires some time to make necessary adjustments.

Flexible relationships are less orderly and place less emphasis on purpose. They have fewer routine procedures and handle problematic matters as they arise. For example, while a flexible system may review its finances periodically, it tends to play spending "by ear." When crises develop, these families or organizations rally their resources to resolve matters rapidly and recover quickly from the crisis. Because of their confidence in meeting difficulties, a crisis seldom challenges the adequacy of the system's organizational structure.

Values — What is important?

Just as a person's values are central to his or her personality, a system's sense of identity — who we are — is based on a common set of values. *Structured* families preserve their stability by strictly adhering to their traditional beliefs. They establish rituals and resist changing them. This may range from religious practice and holiday rituals to ways of going about cleaning the house.

More *flexible* groups try to preserve what they value too, but they are more interested in understanding new possibilities and, perhaps, incorporating them into their on-going belief system. For example, flexible project teams are more likely to consider unconventional ideas or pursuits, believing that this may produce a new discovery and therefore increase productivity or profitability.

TOO STRUCTURED OR TOO FLEXIBLE: SYSTEMS AT THE EXTREMES OF ADAPTABILITY

Up to this point, we have been talking about the two middle levels of adaptability. Most couples, families, professional staffs, and other work groups operate within this range of the continuum. Sometimes, however, systems operate primarily at one of the two extremes on this dimension. Occasionally this occurs when a system is thrown into crisis or is moving through a transition. If the system continues to operate at the extreme, it usually portends severe difficulties.

Rigid (Very Low Adaptability)

When a relationship becomes extremely structured, it can become rigid. For example, *rigid* families are characterized by authoritarian leadership and highly controlling parents who set tight rules and impose decisions with no input from or negotiation with children. Roles, which generally run along traditional male-female lines, are strictly defined. Rules are unchanging. Furthermore, rules are carefully enforced and carry severe consequences if they are violated. Parental values are so highly cherished that others who have differing values are usually distrusted. When children or adolescents bring new information or values back to the family, it often creates a family crisis leading to even higher levels of rigidity. In summary, very rigid systems are too tightly organized and too closed to change.

A central conviction of those who establish rigid patterns is that people will not act responsibly without a high degree of control. Because of the underlying distrust of others, elaborate efforts are made to guarantee that others will behave properly. For example, in rigid schools, standards are inflexible and rules are enforced to the letter in order to build character and responsibility in students.

Chaotic (Very High Adaptability)

At the opposite extreme of the adaptability continuum is chaos. Leadership in a *chaotic* system is erratic or nonexistent. Members relinquish responsibility for control, and instead, often rely on external constraints established by other systems to govern their behavior. These external sources include other departments in companies, schools, churches, and police. Decisions are made impulsively, in a context of endless negotiation, without the benefit of any consistent values, principles, or perspectives. Roles within the group lack clarity and are frequently reversed. Rules are unclear, inconsistently applied, and constantly change. In addition, different rules can be called into play at any point. As a result, discipline and the consequences for breaking rules are quite erratic. In short, chaotic systems are too loosely organized and too open to change.

Unlike the rigid system in which distrust of others is pervasive, a basic distrust of self haunts those in chaotic relationships. A continuing pattern of failure in setting goals, creating plans, accepting responsibilities, and fulfilling commitments creates a pervasive sense of despair. Repeated disappointments at their own inability to order their lives undermines self-confidence, resulting in a loss of self-respect.

An example of a small business with an underlying chaotic system came to our attention when we moved our publishing company and needed some quick printing. The seemingly competent owner of the printing company promised the work by a certain date, but the deadline was missed. Phone calls to inquire were not returned, and when we finally got through, one person told us one thing, someone else another. Another deadline was missed. The printer complained of turnover in personnel or made other excuses about his suppliers. Two weeks later the work still was not complete. When we decided to give up on the printer, pick up the artwork and go elsewhere, the artwork could not be found. One person blamed the other and spoke of how bad the printing business was becoming. Someone else mumbled that they should not have taken the job in the first place.

SYSTEM COHESION

Cohesion refers to the *amount of togetherness* operating in your relationships and how your systems *balance autonomy (separateness) with mutuality (togetherness)*. Cohesion deals with the issue of how "I" versus "we" is worked out in your relationships. The four levels of cohesion range from *disengaged* (very low) to *dispersed* (low to moderate) to *connected* (moderate to high) to *enmeshed* (very high).

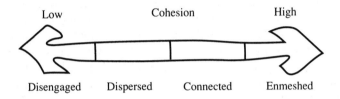

Again, research and clinical experience demonstrate that the central levels of cohesion (dispersed and connected) are more conducive to viable system functioning than the extremes (disengaged and enmeshed). These two extremes are problematic for relationships as they move through their life cycle.

You can locate your marriage, friendships, family or work group at some level along the cohesion continuum by rating how your system deals with the following five characteristics of cohesion:

- closeness
- support
- decision-making
- commonality
- unity

To define and illustrate each of these five characteristics, we will first compare and contrast the two middle zones (dispersed and connected) and then describe the two extremes (disengaged and enmeshed).

Closeness — How much involvement is there?

Closeness is the feeling of warmth, affection, and concern between members of a group. This descriptor also includes intimacy but members can be close without necessarily being intimate.

In *dispersed* systems, positive emotional bonds exist among system members, demonstrating a clear sense of concern for one another. But often the strongest emotional ties exist with people outside the unit. Within the system, interpersonal involvement favors privacy, separateness, and emotional distance over closeness.

More *connected* systems have a stronger bonding among members. More emotional energy is focused on members inside the system than on relationships outside the group. Here interpersonal involvement favors togetherness and emotional closeness over distance.

As an example, people who work in a department or on a staff together vary considerably in the degree to which they are involved with each other. In some units that are more dispersed in nature, people are pleasant with each other as they exchange work-related information, but they know very little about what makes each other tick away from the job. Their interaction is typically more Shop Talk than Small Talk. At noon, they usually join someone from another department for lunch or to play cards. Other more connected work units, however, can extend their conversations and get-to-gethers far beyond the job. They share day-to-day information about their personal lives, often get together informally off the job, and usually eat lunch with someone from their department.

Support — How much backup is there ?

When system members support each other, they affirm, encourage, and back each other up. This is particularly critical when a person is dependent or feels vulnerable. Support is also important as encouragement for new ideas, ventures, and experiences which can enrich individual members and the system as a whole. The way support is given to or drawn from members distinguishes dispersed from connected relationships. Sometimes it is expressed in formal or informal rewards.

In *dispersed* systems, support is rather formalized and ritualized within the system. It tends to be available in ways specified by rules. Backup is often drawn from people and groups outside the system, not just from members within the group.

In closely *connected* systems, encouragement and affirmations are spontaneously and freely given, often in an informal way when they are needed by members of the group. Members are more ready to reach out and back each other up with their time, goods and emotional support.

Decision-making — Who benefits?

In terms of cohesion, decision-making varies according to whether a decision is an individual or group matter. It also changes depending upon who is the primary beneficiary of a decision — the individual or the group.

Individual decisions are typically made without consultation in *dispersed* systems, and the decisions often benefit individual members as they engage in separate activities. When decisions involve the entire system however, joint decision-making occurs.

In *connected* relationships, more decisions are made by the group, and the benefit to the group often outweighs individual benefits. In addition, many individual choices grow out of consultation with other members of the system.

For example, when a person is considering marriage or re-marriage, there will be more involvement and more opinions voiced within a connected family system than is true of a dispersed system.

Commonality — What is shared?

Time, space, interests, activities, and friends are among the chief things members of a system can share in common or have separately.

Members of *dispersed* systems share less in common. Typically individual members each have a number of separate activities, interests, and outside relationships. Nevertheless, although each person spends considerable time away from the group in individual pursuits, most dispersed groups value and seek some "group" time together.

In more *connected* systems, many experiences are shared by some of the members as a subgroup or with the group as a whole.

For example, a couple with a dispersed system may be very active in a sports and health club but seldom go to the club together to exercise or play tennis. Their schedules make it difficult for them to visit the club together, and each really prefers different types of exercise and sports. On the other hand, another couple from a connected system stays in shape by exercising regularly together. They may also use their membership as a way to socialize with other couples at club functions.

Unity — How is morale?

System unity grows out of pride in membership, esprit de corps among members, and commitment to the group.

Dispersed systems have a moderate sense of unity. Although members may attach considerable importance to being part of the group, little effort is made to build or preserve system customs and rituals. In work situations, for example, members' commitment to their own careers is greater than their concern for the work group itself. If a better offer comes along, individuals readily leave the department for another opportunity.

In addition, group members may have little knowledge about the department's history: how it got started and how it has evolved. This information is scattered among a few system members, but they seldom say much about the past. Furthermore, little direct attention is given to maintaining or enhancing the group's reputation.

The meaning of membership is more significant in *connected* systems, and the unit's name evokes considerable pride. Commitment to the group is taken seriously, and group loyalty is expected. The group's history is known and significant historical events are recounted on appropriate occasions. In addition, the unit's reputation is important, and attention is given to maintaining and enhancing a positive reputation. In short, members are proud to be associated with the group.

TOO DISPERSED OR TOO CONNECTED: SYSTEMS AT THE EXTREMES OF COHESION

Dispersed and connected systems operate in the *mid-range* of the cohesion dimension. Most healthy couples, families, professional staffs, other work groups, and organizations function within this range. Occasionally systems operate primarily at one of the two extremes on this dimension. Relationships become *disengaged* on the one hand or *enmeshed* on the other. Being at either extreme may signal movement through a transition or, if the system remains at the extreme, severe difficulties probably will arise.

Disengaged (Very Low Cohesion)

Members of *disengaged* systems live separate and isolated lives with different interests, activities, and friends. System members proceed like "ships passing in the night." With little in common and a lack of emotional bonds between them, members of disengaged systems do not energize or nurture each other. Their sense of belonging and commitment to the group is almost non-existent.

Disengaged members prefer to make decisions alone without regard for others in the unit. They seek minimal interpersonal involvement and lack any loyalty to the group. The predominant feeling within this system is indifference. The system operates as though a centrifugal force pushes people away from each other.

For example, the student body of a large urban commuter campus is generally disengaged (especially compared to that of a small residential college). Unless individual students seek out special situations or make a particular effort to interact, they will probably not experience meaningful personal connections there.

Groups sometimes become disengaged over time and disintegrate through their inability to set goals, establish appropriate and productive procedures, or manage conflict. For example, this could happen in a volunteer service organization.

Enmeshed (Very High Cohesion)

Enmeshed systems are at the opposite end of the cohesion continuum. Members of enmeshed relationships are overly involved with one another and often become extremely dependent upon one another. Individual boundaries blur and people think and feel for each other, frequently over-reacting emotionally to each other. There is no respect for privacy. Everyone knows everybody else's business. Anxiety creeps in when one member begins to think for himself, spends time away from the group, or develops separate interests.

Decisions are subject to the wishes of the whole group, and individuality is denied. This heightened sense of unity is suffocating. Partners "own" each other. This results in a sense that each person is an immediate extension of everyone else. Energy is mainly focused inside the group and outside contacts are discouraged. Loyalty to the system is demanded and group pride is so great that a black eye for one member becomes a black eye for the entire unit. The system operates as though a centripetal force pulls members into its middle binding them together.

For example, a minister's family who fit the enmeshed description went for counseling because a teenage son had been caught smoking marijuana with some school friends at a party. The minister thought his ministry would be ruined by the son's behavior. The mother was embarrassed by the poor example to other kids in the youth group and was in tears over what their parents would think of her and her husband. The son had always been very involved with the family and church program and had few outside activities or friends, yet he wanted to see what some other teenagers found to be fun. The party provided the opportunity. The incident threw the entire family into a state of crisis.

THE SYSTEMS MAP

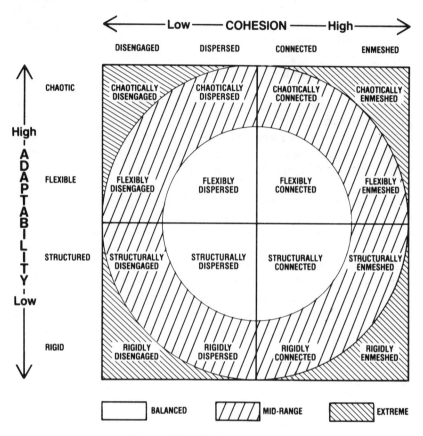

Figure 12.1 The Systems Map

As you can see in figure 12.1, The Systems Map combines the dimensions of adaptability and cohesion into sixteen distinct types of relationship systems. A key feature of the model is the designation of four *balanced,* eight *mid-range,* and four *extreme* types of systems. These three system designations refine and parallel the three types of relationships — *viable, limited, and troubled* — discussed in Chapter 1, "The Interpersonal Dance."

Here is a way of further integrating The Systems Map with The Interpersonal Dance Framework discussed in Chapter 1. Think of all the steps in Figure 1:1 from Separateness to Togetherness as the *cohesion* continuum. Further, the different steps in a partnership's repertoire within a situation correspond to the *adaptability* continuum. Hence the more steps partners use in their relationship as they dance, the more balanced and viable the system.

System Types Illustrated By Movies and TV

Movies and television programs often provide excellent examples of extreme types of couple and family relationships because these are often more dramatically interesting than the balanced types. Here is a list of movies that illustrate the four extreme types:

Rigidly Enmeshed	*Great Santini*
Rigidly Disengaged	*Ordinary People*
Chaotically Disengaged	*Shoot the Moon*
Chaotically Enmeshed	*Who's Afraid of Virginia Wolff?*

The following TV show illustrates how a balanced family operates:

Balanced Type	*The Cosby Show*

Consequences of System Types

A central hypothesis of The Systems Map is that pairs, groups, and organizations with balanced (middle positions) cohesion and adaptability will function more adequately and productively over time than those systems at the extremes on both dimensions. The notion of "balance" does not mean that a group *always* operates in the middle position on both dimensions. Rather, it means these relationships can function at the extremes on one or both dimensions when it is appropriate, but they do *not* typically function at these extremes for extended periods of time.

Extreme systems, however, function at the ends of both dimensions for long periods of time. Their basic pattern of operating involves either rigidity or chaos on the adaptability dimension and either enmeshment or disengagement on the cohesion dimension.

Olson and others have conducted a number of studies to test the general hypothesis that balanced family types will function more adequately than extreme types (Clark, 1984; Bonk, 1984; Garbarino, Sebes, and Schellenbach, 1985; Carnes, 1987). Most of the research has compared non-problem families with families in which at least one member exhibits some sort of problem with mental illness, chemical dependency, or criminal behavior. The results across all the problem categories strongly support the hypothesis.

USES OF THE SYSTEMS MAP

The Systems Map has many practical uses besides its utility as a theoretical and research model.

Increasing Awareness and Understanding

We live out our lives in systems. Often we have very little conscious awareness of how our most significant human groups have influenced us until we leave a group or join another. Then we encounter dynamics different from the ones to which we have grown accustomed. When we meet differences, we begin to realize the advantages and disadvantages and the strengths and weaknesses of all the systems in our life. The Map is good for reminiscing about fun times, getting a handle on painful moments, and visualizing or planning for different arrangements in the future.

Here are some systems that influence your everyday life which The Systems Map can help you better understand:

1. Your own (and your partner's) *family of origin.*

2. *Current significant relationship(s).*

3. *Former relationships* that have ended or gone sour.

4. *Movements between systems* — family, school, friendship groups, work — and their different cultures.

5. *Experiences with different subsystems* within a larger system — different types of groups or departments above, below, and next to your unit at work.

6. *Encounters with coalitions* within various systems.

The following notions may further stimulate your awareness and understanding as you think about where each system or subsystem operates on The Systems Map.

Understanding Systemic Comfort Zones

Rarely does a system operate purely as one of the sixteen types on the Map over long periods of time. Usually, different members within a relationship or group have different perspectives, preferences, and expectations about how the system does or should operate. Some members are typically at least one system type away from the majority because of different family backgrounds, educational and work experiences, and psychological types. In effect, individual members have different "comfort zones" on the Map.

For example, some members may prefer flexibility while others wish for more structure. Some members thrive on separateness while others long for more togetherness. The aggregate cluster of these cells, from which all members operate with reasonable comfort, represents a particular system's comfort zone on the Map.

Unless all members have considerable understanding and acceptance of each other's ways, they will negotiate with each other periodically — perhaps even constantly — to change the way the group operates as it confronts new issues. Some groups typically develop a certain type of system based on their goals and function in the organization. For example, the hospital staff in an emergency receiving unit may be characterized as *flexibly connected,* while nurses and doctors in an intensive care unit may be more *structurally connected.*

Attending to Change

Change originates from both *outside* and *inside* the system. Every system operates within a larger social, economic, political, and religious network. The more complex, uncertain, and active this environment is, the more a system has to simultaneously *adapt* and *maintain* itself to function effectively.

Change from the inside has many sources. Members may be added or subtracted and they mature and develop new interests and competencies. The group handles crises, meets opportunities, and arranges work or study schedules. Throughout the group's history, members play out their various personality types involving changes in thoughts, feelings, wants, and actions. When one member desires change, other members must somehow deal with that request.

One of the biggest challenges facing any system — couple, roommate, family, work group, or larger organization — is the blending or merging of two systems. Every time a new system is established, through *voluntary* association as in marriage, or through more or less *involuntary* restructuring as often happens with departmental reorganizations or the children of second marriages, there is a reshuffling of system dynamics.

Mergers can be traumatic for members. Former expectations, routines, positions, and rituals are lost, modified, or challenged. How members attend to, nurture, and communicate with each other as they handle their issues during this transition time will have great impact on the success of the new system in the future. (See Chapter 13, "Relationship Phases," for more information on the process of system formation.)

Likewise, the division of a system or loss of members within systems (congregational splits, company layoffs, divorce, and death, for example) often has enormous repercussions for the system. Members are forced into dealing simultaneously with the loss or alteration of an old system and the formation of a new system. Careful attention must be given to individual *and* system needs as members work out new arrangements, roles, and rules.

Spotting Systemic Stress

The wider the spread between members' preferences around the dimensions of adaptability and cohesion, the greater the potential for conflict and strife. Constant and unresolved jockeying for more or less structure or for greater or lesser togetherness is fatiguing to all members and drains their productivity.

As members of the group change and as the environment changes, systems must be flexible to change their orientation. During stress or crisis members may polarize, constrict their comfort zones, and form coalitions in an attempt to right the system. Prolonged or intense systemic stress is an organization's way of calling for help.

It is particularly important during times of stress for a system to exercise its capacity to self-monitor and metacommunicate in order to remain viable. Sometimes groups are unable to self-correct and must seek the help of an external counselor or consultant to help regain balance. The Systems Map can be useful in spotting stressful differences and heading off potential conflict by helping members identify how they would like their system to be functioning.

As you can see, system membership has its tradeoffs. Systems provide solace for members but also can cause great stress. The ability of members to communicate together and process and accommodate competing forces determines to a large extent how well the system will serve its members.

Recognizing Choices

Some systems work better than others and are more satisfying to its members. If you like what you have found in most of your relationship-systems, congratulations! What you have gained from applying The Systems Map is new insight into what makes your human systems work so well. Be sure to tell your spouse, parents, kids, friends, boss, and employees what you like about the system you share with them.

On the other hand, if you have gained new insight into why one or more of your relationship-systems is not working well, you have some choices:

1. You can say to yourself, "This is the way it is. I don't have the energy, influence, or inclination to try to change things, so I'll

accept things as they are and *appreciate* the benefits that do exist."

This choice requires letting go of any Spite Talk which only spreads destructive negative energy. It also means that you will be only a limited but positive force in the system. Recognize also that dissatisfactions sometimes stem from legitimate individual differences. Do not overlook this. Try to take a wholistic view and see what everybody brings that is useful to the system.

2. You can take some concrete steps to *plan, anticipate crises,* and *initiate* change. Perhaps you have discovered that your family really operates too loosely and does not give your children the structure you would like to provide for launching them successfully in the world. Or you may find your work group is too dispersed to generate creative ideas and keep information flowing productively. Or your staff would benefit from hiring a person with a certain personality type who would balance your group better. Planned change requires wisdom, good will, and communication skills. Much of the material throughout CONNECTING is written to help you with this process.

3. You can realize that not every system works. Some systems never blend. In other situations, relationships and groups run their course meeting goals and benefiting members, but eventually lose their purpose. Recognizing this and ending a relationship, even though it may be very difficult, can be the best step. Be careful, however: *many relationships end just when they are really ready to begin.* (See the next chapter on "Relationship Phases.")

13

RELATIONSHIP PHASES

Over time the important relationships we have in life go through transitions. If you think about someone you have been involved with for a length of time — several years perhaps — you recognize the reality of change. Seldom does a relationship ever stay the same; because life changes, we modify the ways we connect, too.

We can experience four distinctly different phases during the course of a relationship. Each phase increases or diminishes our satisfaction with the other person. We may spend a long time in a particular phase, experiencing contentment and even finding joy there. Or we could have periods in which we move back and forth between a couple of the phases. We may get stuck in a phase and without moving to the next phase, we end the relationship. For the most part, however, the movement from one phase to the next occurs in the general progression we will discuss here.

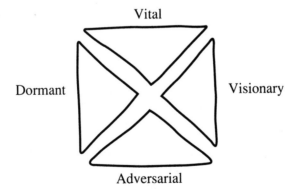

Figure 13.1 Phases of a Relationship

This chapter presents a map of phases of a relationship occurring over time. These phases are typical of close relationships, whether personal or career-connected. You will probably recognize their features when you think about a partner, perhaps your spouse, or a good friend on your work team.

Once you understand the phases, you can be aware of both the positives and negatives each phase involves. Then by using communication skills, you can make the most of the positives and reduce the negatives. Also through awareness and by using skills, you can even move out of a particular phase into a more satisfying one.

VISIONARY PHASE

Close relationships often begin with a visionary phase. As the word "visionary" suggests, we have an imagined view — fantasies — of how the relationship will be. We picture a satisfying future together. We emphasize the value of our similarities and enjoy the way they bond us together. We find our differences stimulating and energy-producing.

We see what we want to see in one another. We also see what we think the other person visualizes in our relationship, and we are attracted to what we see. For example: "We both have good career offers. With this assured income, we can build a dream house."

Or, "You'll make a great marketing addition to our consulting team. With your ideas, new customers will discover our services, and with our high-quality planning, we will deliver them. Together we will find more success than we could separately."

During this visionary phase, we experience a high level of excitement. Our feelings are light-hearted, sometimes even to the point of being euphoric. There is playfulness, and it feels good. We delight in the fact that we make a difference to someone, that we have a common purpose, and that we are sharing something special. Our expectations are high. Small Talk and Search Talk often characterize our conversations.

The Focus

In the visionary phase the focus is on *us and our immediate future.* We look at what we will do — and at what we will be together. We pay attention to the good features of our relationship, even if that involves ignoring other parts of reality.

Positives and Negatives

The visionary phase definitely provides a positive impact on a relationship. It gets us off to a good start. In this phase we set a direction and often make or clarify our goals. We find motivation to make changes, and we experience optimism about life. In this phase we sense our possibilities. We create a shared vision.

Yet while we have heightened vision, we may also have "blurred" vision. When we see what we want to see, we may miss other parts of what is there, especially anything negative.

Often we believe that we have found *the one — the answer* to life. This answer revolves around the other person and lies outside of ourselves. We do what we can to please the other person — to keep that person happy, even if it does not take our own longer-term contentment into account.

During this phase, we often deny aspects of our relationship that do not fit right. We discount or ignore parts of ourself or of our partner that interfere with the vision coming to pass. To protect the vision, we may unintentionally live with a measure of personal dishonesty. If we do find something negative, we deny its importance or say to ourself, "That will change later."

For instance, "Your marketing ideas for our consulting business require more cash flow than anticipated. That makes me nervous, but I don't want to discourage your enthusiasm so I laugh off the fear."

Furthermore, in this phase a pressure can begin to build to live up to the expectation that my partner holds for me or that I hold for myself. For example, "My good job requires extra long hours. Making decisions involved in building our house becomes a demanding chore rather than a step on the way to our dream, and as a result, I procrastinate on activities involved with the house. However I won't admit that this is so for fear of ruining our dream — and perhaps our relationship."

Even with the negative aspects, the visionary phase can be a heady, wonderful phase in the course of a relationship. The relationship holds high priority for us. We hope; we dream. We can overcome any obstacles.

The visionary phase can also occur at times other than the beginning of the relationship. It may occur at important turning points, for example, such as when the last child leaves home or when we anticipate a major move.

Your Visionary Phase

Think back to the beginning of an important relationship in your life. Reflect on the visions you shared with the other person. What did you think you would be like together? What did you anticipate accomplishing? How did you see one another?

ADVERSARIAL PHASE

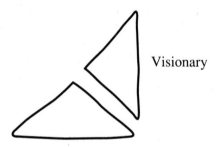

Visionary

After awhile we find out that maintaining the vision is not so easy. Things are not quite the way we thought they would be. Reality sets in. The issues of life give rise to struggles about how to handle those issues.

The adversarial phase is triggered by frustration, disappointment, or disillusionment that life is not what we expected it to be. Often we have negative thoughts about our partner: "You don't put me and my wishes at the center of your world anymore." Or, "you don't appreciate me for who I am."

Now, instead of denying the incongruent parts of our relationship or about other realities, as we did in the visionary phase, we see them clearly. Perhaps, we even see the incongruencies as larger than life. Our differences come to the foreground while our many similarities recede into the background.

In this phase our differences clash, and we really feel their impact. Instead of intriguing us, differences annoy. Our similarities do not provide enough new energy. Someone must be at fault. We find it easy to blame one another for not living up to the fantasy.

For instance, "Although I am working hard and want to relax during my free time, you still want me to do projects on our new house. To me it is no longer a dream but a burden. You should be more accepting of my wish for fun. I think you're too rigid about completion anyway."

Now we try to change each other to be the way we expected or to treat us the way we anticipated. Perhaps we simply spar with one another about issues. Maybe we become meaner and use manipulation and threats — or we may even "punish" one another. We might attack each other's vulnerabilities — whatever it takes to make one another be the way we want.

For instance, "If you go ahead with costly marketing ideas without enough research on their results, I'll make sure that you're on a tight budget so you will have to make tough choices."

The Focus

In the adversarial phase the focus is on *you and your impact on me.* *You* should change. You should *let me be* as I am.

While issues of life arise during any phase, the tone in this phase is adversarial: to win and to have things my way.

Positives and Negatives

On the positive side, each of us finds the means to show who we really are. At the same time, like it or not, we are forced to recognize our partner's separate wants, intentions, and modes of operating. These may not be as we envisioned previously.

But if we apply communication skills for gaining awareness and for negotiating about issues, we can come to know and appreciate one another better. Energy and even a deeper understanding of each other can emerge out of the conflict.

But without those communication skills our relationship can reach an impasse. A negative spirit may accompany the adversarial phase. When that happens we may start talking as though we believe in the win/lose idea, in the good/bad person notion, and in the right/wrong behavior. We may begin believing that we really do not need to respect the other person's differences, and in so doing, we communicate the sense that our partner is a loser, bad, or wrong.

Another negative part of this phase grows out of the tendency to start thinking that we can *make* someone be what he or she is not. "You could become general manager if you just put more into your work, if you showed more drive! You've got to sell yourself!"

Without awareness and skill, we may turn the negative spirit inward and believe those ideas about ourselves too. Instead of using Style II words in outward Fight Talk, we may turn them inward in Spite Talk.

For example, "Since nobody around here appreciates my marketing ideas, I'm not going to waste more of my creative energies with this company. I'll just put in my time."

Finally the negative energy extends beyond our own relationship to others around us — to our family or throughout the work team. Like a pollutant, it spreads.

Unless we find realistic solutions during this phase, each of us is vulnerable to becoming attracted to an outside alternative, partly to spite the other person. It is tempting to turn to an affair or to an offer to moonlight on other jobs to escape the unsatisfying situation. Frequently the alternative is no better or worse, only different.

The romance and excitement of reentering the visionary phase with a new partner usually overshadows the fact that we will have to recycle the relationship phases — including the adversarial phase — with this new person or job. Never really understanding this, some people run from situation to situation unable to make a commitment to work through differences effectively.

Many relationships end with the adversarial phase. Others remain in this phase for long periods, bringing bitterness and underlying pain. The relationship continues in this unsatisfactory condition, often maintained by circumstance or other values, such as religious convictions, social expectations, children, or fulfilling economic commitments. Still other partners learn from the phase, and then move on to a new phase in their relationship.

Your Adversarial Phase

In looking at an important relationship of your own, consider the ways you each have attempted to change the other. When issues would arise, how have you tried to win? How has your partner?

DORMANT PHASE

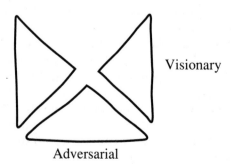

Visionary

Adversarial

Once we have survived some of the struggles characteristic of the adversarial phase, we begin to develop more acceptance of life — and more acceptance of ourselves as we are. I accept myself for who I am. I also know that my partner will not always live up to my expectations, and yet I still recognize and value my partner for who he or she is.

We enter a phase in which we have more perspective about various events connected to our relationship. Any single event, which in the past might have been potentially damaging, now probably does not threaten the relationship. We are less apt to feel hurt, anger, or discouragement by one situation. Rather, we view situations in terms of a larger whole. Surprises are few, and we know that life will go on.

We live and work more peacefully with one another, even if the peacefulness sometimes covers an inner discontent. We are aware of our patterns of behaving, and during this dormant phase, we quit pressuring one another to change. We are more congenial with each other and do not rock the boat. For example, "I don't say anything about your choosing wallpaper that I really don't like for the hallway because with my busy schedule I wouldn't take time to help select it."

Or, "You spent considerable energy chasing a foreign project that had little payoff for the business except for some travel. Since that is rewarding for you, I won't bother about discussing the lack of analysis of financial return, even though that was our agreement on accepting projects."

We maintain an obvious structural commitment to our relationship. Others take for granted our relationship to one another. We are known as a pair or part of a work team. But often our time together is "duty" time: if in the work world, being together at business meetings or social functions; if personal, coming to family get-togethers.

However, we may not spend very much time together alone. Our activities and interests are more separate now. We each go our own way — in career interests, in community affairs, in being involved with children's activities, and so on. Any of these other parts of life can draw our energies in directions away from each other.

We probably share less of the intrinsic aspects of work or of whatever it is that helps make life worth living for each of us. Consequently, our relationship together receives little nourishment. While other parts of life may be full and vital, during this phase the relationship stays relatively inactive and lifeless. If our relationship is a basically viable one, we are likely to feel peaceful and serene during this phase. Otherwise, we may feel empty and void about the relationship.

The Focus

The focus during this phase tends to be upon *me* — upon developing the interests I find important. These interests may even come under the guise of other demands (financial, children, community needs). I go my way, and I permit the freedom for you to go yours. We do not bother each other.

Positives and Negatives

Similar to the other phases, this dormant phase offers some positive aspects. During this time each of us can develop real individuality as an adult. We can discover strengths and explore interests, and generally do so with the security of having relationship and emotional needs already met. The phase provides a context to find out "who I am," or what my individual style really is. That allows me to be appreciated for who I am now — not for who you thought I was or who I should be.

The dormant phase also provides more economy for the relationship system, especially when others are involved. Only so much energy exists in any one pair, and in busy periods many things draw on that energy. It simply makes good sense to have separate areas of concentrated attention by each partner.

Also on the positive side of this phase, we each learn to take more self-responsibility for contentment in life. Our individual personality type can get full play, and we must account for it. As this occurs, we start to realize that some of our own responses to the world shape our satisfaction, and we lessen our tendency to point a finger of responsibility at our partner when something goes wrong. We accept our own strengths and limitations: we recognize where we flourish or have difficulty in meeting issues and challenges of life.

However, a negative dimension comes into the dormant phase too. Sometimes each of us takes on so much self-responsibility for making life be the way "I want" that we shut out our partner. Since neither of us wants to make waves, we may both avoid dealing with real issues. Issues resolve themselves by default, or the one for whom the issue is most pressing at a particular time handles it in the most expedient way for the moment, regardless of whether it is best in the long run for our relationship.

For example, "I believe our company should have more visibility in the marketplace and think we should send representatives to a major trade exposition. While you don't object, you think other kinds of promotional approaches bring more immediate return. Even though marketing is your responsibility, you don't take time to plan for the promotion. The exposition comes and goes, and we're not part of it. Although I think you made a mistake, I let it pass."

Another negative aspect of this phase occurs when personal distance from each other becomes a habit. Once our patterns of separate behavior become well established, this habit may prevent real intimacy from occurring during the dormant phase when it might otherwise be possible. In terms of The Systems Map (see Chapter 12), we are in a *dispersed — perhaps even disengaged —* cohesion mode.

Until something brings it to life again — or until through atrophy it withers and dies — our relationship stays in the sleeplike state of dormancy. This phase can extend for years, and people live out their lives with mild but relatively lifeless connecting. On the other hand, the dormant phase can be a brief season between other phases, a necessary preparation for renewed energy and growth together.

Your Dormant Phase

Think about an important relationship to you. Where did you and your partner each put separate energies during a dormant phase between you? Also think about what you each have done to promote or maintain that dormant period.

VITAL PHASE

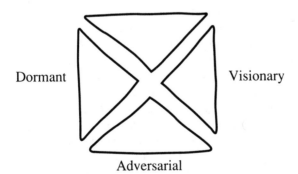

Dormant   Visionary

Adversarial

The vital phase usually grows out of some form of challenge to the relationship as it has been. We are faced with a question about its personal value to us. Something forces us to test its resilience. No longer can it stay quietly asleep.

A relationship may enter into the vital phase at a time of high stress. For instance, it may occur when one person loses a job or a major contract, when an accident or serious illness arises and forces priority-shifting, or when an opportunity comes which benefits only one of the partners but affects the other as well. Other challenges include the birth of a child, discovery of an affair, financial reversals, spiritual conversion, confrontation about chemical dependency, and retirement.

For example, "You get a job opportunity that requires you to move to another city. My best career opportunities are to stay here, and neither of us wants a long distance relationship. A choice has to be made."

We come to a point of active choice, and, recognizing that we do have options, we make a conscious decision to commit our energies to the relationship. With eyes wide open, both of us take responsibility to make it work.

Now we place a higher value on blending as a pair and on balancing our individual similarities and differences to be mutually supportive. We recognize the complementarity of our differences and understand how both of us contribute to the vitality of our relationship.

For instance, "As business partners we sit together to plan a marketing promotion in terms of time, budget, personal rewards, and the company's needs. We come to a realistic plan that maximizes your creative abilities and builds my confidence in its potential effectiveness. In planning, we listen to each other's ideas as well as bring up our concerns in a straightforward way. We really get behind one another's efforts to make the project a success."

In the vital phase, we put effort into discovering who our partner is *now,* and into how we are together. We see ways that our relationship system works well for us, and we take satisfaction in the life we live together.

Our commitment to our relationship is founded on knowing ourself and our partner in realistic terms. With this awareness we truly have self-respect and respect for each other. We realize that we can be mutually honest about our own deepest truths and still appreciate one another. We acknowledge our interdependence and thrive together, realizing that together we are better than each of us is alone. In this phase, we experience a paradox of freedom: our committed togetherness supports and nourishes each of our separate identities.

During the vital phase our interaction with each other increases — we pay attention and bring energy to our conversations. If we feel angry or upset, it typically signals an issue to resolve and poses little danger to the relationship.

And interestingly, during the vital phase we can experience times of intensive conflict. Conflict is greater now than during the quiet dormant phase when we kept more personal distance. But compared to the conflict of the adversarial phase, the disagreements now revolve around more important issues. Usually we can settle them quickly by using Straight Talk. To make life better for both partners, we collaborate more.

The Focus

In the vital phase the focus is on *who we are — what we are about in the present*. We place priority on what our relationship requires now.

Positives and Negatives

Positive outcomes of this phase include a sense of robustness and contentment in being together. We experience more wholeness from the blending of our differences and similarities and we project less compartmentalization to others. Our vitality radiates outward to others.

As a pair we stand together to face the pressures from the rest of the world. We can turn our combined force to make better, more satisfying decisions, whether as a couple or a work team. Some pairs even intentionally extend their vitality into service for others.

While the positive aspects of the vital phase dominate, some negatives may occur. Perhaps a kind of negative aspect might be experienced by those outside the pair who may be envious or want some of the vitality directed toward them. The pair maintains a kind of selfishness (for the sake of the relationship) about time, energy, productivity, wisdom, and joy — and others may want to tap it more than it is available. The pair may believe they exist as separate from the rest of the world.

Your Vital Phase

Consider how you place your relationship in priority to other parts of your life. What implications does giving it high priority suggest for other areas of your life? What kinds of arrangements have you made which take the needs of both people in the relationship fully into account? When, for the sake of your relationship, have you said no to outside pressures?

Concluding Tips

Understanding and identifying the phases of a relationship can be useful for several reasons. You gain perspective on your own relationship(s); you realize that your situation is not really so unique and you develop insight into the patterns you now find occurring. Knowing that as a pair you are not alone can give you confidence about your relationship.

Once you understand the phases, you can do the following:

1. Take a few moments to identify what phase you are mainly in now in your relationship. How long have you been there? Where do you think you are headed next? Where would you like to be? What specifically could you do to move to the desired phase? Sit with your partner and reflect together on these questions.

2. Highlight what you like. Once you identify the phase you are in, you can take steps to emphasize the positive elements of the phase. Use your speaking and listening skills with your partner to round out your understanding of your relationship.

3. Decide what you want and take action. Your awareness gives you increased options. Instead of being stuck in one phase when you wish you were in another, make a personal change which can begin to alter the situation or your view of it. Realize that if you took on a new partner, you must recycle the phases with that new person too.

RELATIONSHIP PROCESSES

14

COMMUNICATING UNDER PRESSURE:
Reducing Interpersonal Stress

Communicating in pressure situations is the real test of your interpersonal competence. The more you learn about how to relate to others effectively when the pressure is on, the more you will enrich your own and others' lives, as well as enhance your professional value.

WHAT CAUSES PRESSURE?

Pressure increases as demands — real or imagined — exceed our available resources to handle situations.

Demands include anything out of the ordinary — change, novelty, or conflict — or the accumulation of events which require our attention. They are commonly called "stressors." In former times stressors were primarily physical — assuring food, clothing, shelter and protection from identifiable dangers. While these basics still preoccupy some individuals, technology has buffered many of these so that today most of our stressors are interpersonal — social and psychological in nature.

Available resources include our life's learnings (jobs, education, training, crises), intellectual ability, emotional resilience, physical health, spiritual attunement, and support from other people. Time, money, space, technological information, and equipment are other important resources. People skills are significant too.

Managing stress is an individual matter because all of us have different and varying degrees of resources — strengths — for meeting demands. An issue that strains one person may barely stretch someone else.

Hans Selye, the father of stress research, identified two general types of stress, "delightful eustress" and "painful distress." Surprisingly, happy events initially create the same physiological reactions as sad ones. However, since happiness is more acceptable and easier to express, more devastating physiological effects stem from prolonged unexpressed distress. The most lethal stressors include feelings of extended humiliation and frustration, unresolved fear and anger, or a relentless sense of failure.

Three Stages of Stress

Selye identified three stages which the body goes through as it tries to adapt to stress.

First is an *alarm reaction* — a mixture of alertness, anticipation, curiosity, and fear. Blood pressure and blood sugar rise, muscles tense, pulse quickens, breathing accelerates, adrenaline is released, and the senses become more acute as you get ready to do something about the stressor. This response can save your life in a true crisis or improve immediate performance. The action you take to deal with the challenge depends both on how you size up the situation and on what personal resources you bring to bear.

The second stage is called *resistance*. As your body enters this next stage, it begins *to adjust to and resist* the pressure. At this point, the body attempts to return to equilibrium. If your action is effective, your body returns to normal function (the communicycle is completed); it rests and restores itself before the next challenge or threat occurs.

However, if your action is not effective, and the stressor and your negative feelings about it continue, your body soon returns to stage one: the alert, ready state. You use additional energy to maintain this state, and as you expend energy, your body strains its ability to cope and adapt. Eventually you pass the physical threshold of adjustment and your body is unable to rebalance itself. You then enter the third stage, *exhaustion*, in which continued stress can have a deleterious effect on the immune system, causing illness and sometimes even death.

Predictability and Control Reduce Pressure

While some surprise and uncertainty is stimulating and exciting, most of the time we order our lives and relationships to be as predictable as possible. *Control is a very important element in managing pressure.* When you have some confidence that you are able to influence situations, you are better able to withstand stress and respond effectively to pressure. If you are interpersonally aware and have skills to connect with others, you have more options for participating in and influencing decisions. Whether you actually exercise some control does not matter as much as knowing you can if you choose to do so.

Stress is created when your plans fail, when you are bombarded with unpredictable events, overloaded with decisions, or trapped in an unsatisfactory situation. If the actions you take do not resolve the issues or solve the problems, pressure grows. Being out of control — plagued by continual uncertainty — is a very frightening, unnerving, and wearing experience; living in a state of heightened vulnerability is extremely stressful.

Pressure Is Communicated

We first signal distress nonverbally, then verbally. In prehistoric times physical danger aroused an appropriate but limited "fight or flight" response. For many people, this is still their primary response even to social and psychological threats. They use Style I to flee from the danger or Style II to fight.

As you can see from the Communication Styles Map, however, increased interpersonal awareness and communication skills give you more options for responding to today's pressures. You can float with the pressure in Style III or focus directly on it in Style IV.

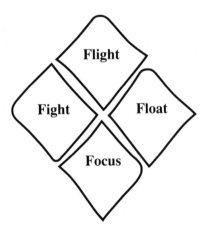

Here are some typical ways people respond to pressure when they use different communication styles.

Small Talk: see the humor and let the tension go; joke or change the subject to avoid conflict; deny or run from tension.

Shop Talk: get busy discussing routines and details; lose the big picture.

Control Talk: attempt to take charge by giving directions, instructions, advice; push for their own point of view.

Fight Talk: attack, blame, demand, threaten, force, abuse.

Spite Talk: angrily withdraw; drag feet, snipe, or sulk; gossip or complain; become cynical, sarcastic or defiant; retaliate or placate.

Search Talk: try to gain an overview; consider options; suggest possible solutions.

Straight Talk: candidly share their own experience; encourage others to express thoughts, feelings, wants; commit to what they can do to improve the situation.

What is your typical pattern for dealing with uncertainty and conflict? Notice how the communication styles you use to meet pressure and resolve conflict either increase or reduce stress — for yourself and others.

Response Is More Important Than Cause

Whether stress is created by an angry outburst directed at you, a complicated issue, or the accumulation of many demands, when you feel stretched and question your ability to cope, pressure rises.

The way you respond to and deal with pressure is much more important to your well being than any particular source of the stress itself. The skills and concepts discussed here will equip you to respond more flexibly and effectively *on the spot* to reduce interpersonal stress and create more mutually satisfying outcomes for yourself and others.

HANDLING PRESSURE AND RESISTANCE: YOUR OWN AND OTHERS'

Selye's three stages of body-stress response also give us a framework for understanding and monitoring stress in interpersonal exchanges. We can monitor our stress in part because interactions with others register and are reflected in our bodies.

FOUR STEPS TO MANAGING YOUR OWN PRESSURE

Step 1. Recognize Pressure Cues

The first step in dealing effectively with interpersonal stress is to attend to what you see and hear from others as *external stress cues* and to use *internal reaction cues* inside your own body as early warning signs to the first stage — the alarm reaction.

Typical *external stress cues* include:

- anxious body movements
- forceful or despondent gestures
- tense facial expressions
- higher-pitched voice tone
- markedly faster or slower rate of speech
- irregular breathing
- changes in skin coloring
- physical crowding or distancing
- tense or angry words and phrases

Typical *internal reaction cues* include:

- muscle tension (even slight pain) in your upper body — stomach, chest, shoulders, neck, or face
- faster and more shallow breathing
- a sense of being stuck or blocked
- doubts about your self-worth or competence
- feelings of anger, impatience, fear, frustration
- intentions to attack or defend
- ineffective listening or speaking behaviors

The earlier you spot your own and others' stress cues, the quicker you can act to reduce distress in yourself and others.

Think for a moment about the main spot in your body where you usually accumulate tension and strain. For most people this is somewhere in their upper body — around their eyes or temple, in their neck or the upper part of their shoulders, or in their chest or stomach. These spots become tender and painful from the accumulation of repeated stress responses.

Step 2. Go To Center.

Instead of accumulating blocked energy in your upper body and broadcasting your distress to others, at the first sign of pressure, learn to *go to center.* Your physical center of gravity generally is located about one inch below your navel, and one-third of the way back toward your tailbone. From this centering point you can literally attain optimal performance with minimal effort. Being centered means that you are *relaxation in motion,* balanced and strong without trying to be powerful.

To go to center, actually shift your attention to your physical center of gravity and bring your locus of energy there. This takes some practice, but it usually means letting go of the tension you are maintaining at some point in your upper body, and allowing it to drop vertically, to the point of equilibrium at the physical center of your body. As this happens you will experience your energy expand as you operate from this more effective point.

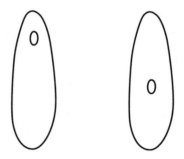

Going to center counteracts your body's tendency to become unbalanced in stressful situations. In the alert stage, your energy naturally shoots into your upper body as you become ready to protect and defend yourself which throws your body off balance. However, if you immediately rebalance yourself by consciously relaxing your upper body and allowing your energy to return to your physical center of gravity, you will bring strength rather than stress to difficult situations.

Straight Talk flows from the center or heart of your being, while the locus of Fight, Spite, and Control Talk tends to be higher in your body. Depending on your communication style, your body will register calm or tension in the respective areas.

Any real or imagined issue can knock you off balance. When you feel your stress response shoot upward into your chest, shoulders, neck, or face, take a breath and go to center. When you find yourself in Fight Talk, center and take a breath. The secret of keeping your balance is consciously going to center.

Step 3. Breathe Fully

When you are feeling stressed, your breathing becomes more rapid, shallow (from the upper chest), tentative, and stifled. When you are centered and balanced, your breathing is fuller and deeper (from your diaphragm). Like muscle tension or pain, your breathing can also tell you when you are out of center and off balance. Breathing can also bring you back to center and balance.

Place one of your hands just below the middle of your abdomen, and the other, at the same level, on your side. As you breathe in, let your diaphragm and lungs act as a bellows. Expand your diaphragm down and your stomach out, drawing in a large amount of air. Feel yourself being energized as you inhale. Then relax as you exhale. Be careful not to breathe from your upper chest by raising and lowering you shoulders. As your breath flows in and out, let the incoming oxygen nourish any strained muscles throughout your body as tension evaporates.

Going to center and then continuing to breathe fully take conscious attention and practice before you can readily alter your typical stress response. However, when you learn to do them, you can be more in charge of yourself during difficult interpersonal exchanges.

Going to center and breathing fully have several advantages:

1. You can center yourself anywhere during any activity. Professional athletes in many different sports use centering and deep breathing to attain peak performance. All you have to do is recognize tension, then consciously go to center and alter your breathing. They can be done in a split second with practice.

2. When you breathe fully, more oxygen goes to your brain to support clearer and more creative thinking. (Your brain weighs about two percent of your body weight and consumes about twenty-five percent of the oxygen you inhale.)

3. As your pressure subsides, you stop broadcasting your anxiety to others as well.

4. When you and another person are in an anxious state together, if you shift to a more relaxed state by centering and breathing fully, the other person will often unconsciously match your breathing and become more relaxed too. Centering and breathing fully are unobtrusive ways to manage a situation.

In summary, centering and breathing transform an "alarm reaction"and the urge to fight or fly into a less stressful and more manageable form of energy. You become reintegrated and balanced for productive action.

Step 4. Expand and Act On Your Awareness

When you are centered, you are relaxed yet alert; in this state, you are better able to expand and use self and other information. Since the Awareness Wheel is a tool to help collect and organize information, it also helps you to center. Ask yourself, "What is happening right now?" Use your Awareness Wheel to fill in the blanks. Also ask yourself, "Where is my resistance?" Identify blind spots, incongruencies, and blockages. (For more discussion about blind spots, incongruencies, and blockages, see Chapter 7, "Partial Awareness.")

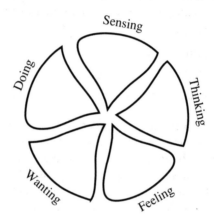

```
UNDERSTANDING YOURSELF
TAKES PRESSURE OFF OTHERS
```

When you are off balance, you may impulsively *act out* negative emotions with unproductive and often regrettable consequences. Operating from center and *acting on* your awareness will help you to be less defensive and to use your energy to take positive action. It will also help you integrate and naturally use all of the skills and principles you have been learning in CONNECTING.

The main point of what we have been saying about dealing with your own pressure is this: *manage yourself to bring about the kind of behavior you want in others.* Although it is hard to force others to change, you can often stimulate change in them. The key is to start with yourself; changing one part of the system — yourself — changes other parts as well. Remember that it only takes one person to alter a relationship. The big question is: who will change first?

DEALING WITH RESISTANCE

Recall that Selye labels the second stage in the body's stress response, resistance. *Wherever you find pressure — inside yourself or emanating from others — you will find resistance!* Recognizing and knowing how to put your own and others' resistance to work for you can transform stress into a resource and impasses into communicycles.

Change Creates Resistance

As we have seen in previous chapters, members of pairs, groups, and larger systems frequently *act, react, and interact* to alter:

- closeness and distance
- sameness and difference
- stability and change
- resources and demands

Unless people are immediately persuaded by overwhelming evidence of the benefit in a change, there is almost always some resistance to proposed or actual change. *Resistance serves to protect and preserve personal and relational equilibrium.* Change challenges the status quo. It often stimulates uncertainty and creates fears that stir up such questions as: "What will I lose?"; "What will I gain?"; and "How will I fit in?"

Much of our communication with others is aimed at gaining agreement and initiating change, both of which run the risk of generating resistance. (See the section on Transition States in Chapter 1, "The Interpersonal Dance.")

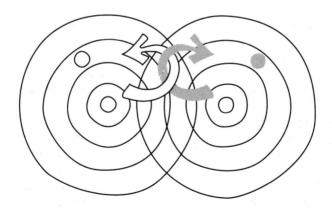

Disagreement and noncompliance — hesitation, objection, opposition, indifference, or rejection — are all forms of resistance which create some degree of distress. Not every hesitation or objection is a major threat or challenge, of course. Nevertheless it is amazing how quickly and naturally disagreement and noncompliance stimulate counter resistance.

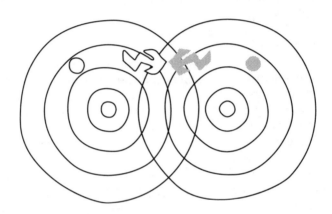

Change Threatens Individual and System Comfort Zones

People are slow to accept what they question, do not value, or do not trust. Comfort zones are the physical, emotional, intellectual, and spiritual "space" (beliefs and behaviors) which we *value* and *trust* the most. They are grounded in our psychological type, shaped by our family of origin, and reinforced and enriched by life's experiences — perceptions, thoughts, feelings, wants, and actions. (See Chapters 6 and 12, "Individual Similarities and Differences: Conflict or Collaboration" and "Relationships As Systems.")

While the breadth and flexibility of your beliefs and actions may vary somewhat from situation to situation, *your comfort zones always have boundaries.* You can encourage or tolerate only a certain range of ideas and behaviors. Too much is too much, and too little is too little. If someone goes too far with an idea or behavior, he or she bumps into your boundary, either on the near side or the far side. This explains why we often like and trust those people who share our basic beliefs, values, and experience (our comfort zones) more than people whose views do not coincide with our orientation. The more alike we are, the more we affirm rather than jostle others' boundaries, and the less distressful the relationships are for us.

Comfort zones are very individual and subjective. Nonverbal messages are the best indicators that you are approaching, encroaching on, within, or leaving another person's boundaries.

Comfort Zones Constrict Under Pressure

All of us regress under pressure and stress; our comfort zones constrict and become more rigid to protect us and preserve our equilibrium. Under pressure, we typically resist any message or demand that discounts, threatens, or stretches our boundaries. In short *resistance serves as protection from actions and ideas that we fear might hurt us or destroy a relationship.*

Resistance Is Your Friend

Resistance serves a very important function — it tells us where we are with another person at any moment. It slows things down until we understand what is going on, what the change will mean for us, and how we will fit in. When we feel uncertain, afraid, or loss of control, we resist. This is true for us when others ask us to change, and it is true for them when we ask them to change, so expect a short-term negative reaction — in yourself or in others. Remember, change requires adjustment and adjustment takes time. Often when understanding of what a change would mean is achieved, comfort returns and resistance evaporates.

Once you begin to recognize and understand the function of resistance, the resistance becomes your friend. If you will let it work for you, it will direct you to the critical information — inside yourself or in others — which is central to working through issues and impasses. *Resistance tells you where and when to focus to find the key(s) to unlock an impasse.*

Most people react to resistance with fight or flight. It is seen as an enemy rather than as an ally and guide to the next interactional step. They do not realize that when they encounter resistance they are on the trail of vital information.

No is the Connecting Point

In interpersonal and intergroup conflict, resistance actually represents potential exchange points. When someone says or suggests nonverbally that the answer will be *no* to a proposed change, the objection tells you where you must connect if you are going to negotiate the change successfully — make a decision, mediate a dispute, or close a sale. *No* surrounds the critical information that must be recognized, accepted, and resolved. Use the Awareness Wheel to identify if the other person's resistance is stuck around data, beliefs, interpretations, expectations, feelings, or wants.

For example, when we as consultants are asked to make a sales presentation to a company about our WORKING TOGETHER: PRODUCTIVE COMMUNICATION ON THE JOB program, near the end of the presentation we usually ask the client what his or her objections or hesitations about the program are. We often just simply ask, "Now that you have had a chance to see the program, what are the 'No's'?" If there is any misfit between client and program, this question draws the difficulty out into the open so that it can be addressed.

In short, the content of resistance is often the basis of effective negotiation and collaboration. The sooner you understand and deal with *no*, the quicker you can get to *yes*. If resistance is not reframed into a resource, power plays usually occur, generating anger, resentment, and possible retaliation.

Leading Rather Than Following — Control Is Often the Problem

As the two preceding graphics suggest, both people are trying to exert control. As we noted earlier, being in charge or having a sense of control mitigates stress. However, when each person:

- shoots for agreement rather than understanding
- attempts to lead rather than follow

their mutual resistance escalates their distress by setting off stronger alarm reactions in each other.

IF YOU WISH TO BE AN EFFECTIVE LEADER
YOU MUST BECOME AN EFFECTIVE FOLLOWER

Allow The Other Person To Lead You

There may be a number of reasons why you hesitate to let the other person "take the lead and tell his or her story":

- perceived shortness of time
- fear that your issue will be overlooked by focusing on the other's issue
- concern that your willingness to listen and understand what the other is saying might be mistaken for agreement with what he or she is saying
- fear of "what is" — that some information will be "discovered" that you will not know how to handle

- recognition that you might have to change your ways
- apprehension that if you really listen to what the other person is saying, you will reduce your control over the other person or the situation

If giving up control is a problem for you, you can still be in control *while* the other person leads you. Play a mind game with yourself: *be in charge by allowing the other person to lead you.*

The more you shoot directly for control and agreement, the less you actually achieve it. Paradoxically, real power and mutually agreeable outcomes result quickest by your releasing control and focusing on understanding the other person accurately.

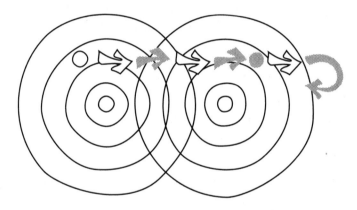

The diagram above illustrates an effective approach to handling resistance, although most of us find such an approach to be somewhat unnatural. When you feel resistance:

1. Shift (stop doing what is not working), go to center, and breathe fully.
2. Invite, match, and keep inviting. (See Chapter 10, "Listening Skills.")

Let the other person lead you temporarily out of your comfort zone into his or hers. As you follow, keep inviting the other person to speak — telling you what he or she wants you to know about the concern(s).

If you feel anxious about what the other person is saying, manage yourself — go to center and breathe fully. *Resist* your urge to defend yourself or correct the other person by saying something like, "Let me tell you why I did that," or "That's not right," or "You can't possibly feel that way." These comments will not relieve the other person; instead, they will immediately place you back into a pulling/dragging or pushing/blocking dance and move you away from useful information.

When you think you are at the heart of the other person's concern, summarize what you have heard (as a check for accurate understanding). Then either sit silently and wait to hear what else might be said, or invite the person to tell you anything else he or she wants you to know about the issue. Here is where you will find the gold — the information you would never have heard if you would not have been willing to follow rather than lead.

To be sure you have all the important information, invite again. When you reach the point where you begin to exceed the real concern, the person will say so and begin pulling you back into bounds. You are starting to exceed his or her comfort zone.

The key to gaining vital information is to invite and follow. Inviting encourages free association and communicates a readiness to listen. People have their reasons for doing what they do and for resisting what they resist. Inviting and following the other person's lead will get you to this crucial information the fastest way.

Advantages of Following

Allowing the other person to lead has several specific advantages:

1. You begin dealing with the real issue faster.
2. You do not have to be thinking about what you are going to say. Instead you just listen. Then, what you eventually say can relate better to the other person's legitimate concerns.
3. You earn the right to be heard after you have listened to the speaker tell his or her full story.
4. The other person ends up feeling good, or at least better, about you, and you have strengthened the relationship.

Agreement Versus Understanding — Your Resistance Versus My Resistance

When we shoot for agreement, we usually pay little attention to understanding the other's comfort zone. We treat understanding as if it takes too much time but then we waste considerably more time and energy trying to pull others in our direction or push them into new space. We fail to recognize that the harder we pull or push, the more others resist in order to maintain their balance. And the more they counter our actions, the more we resist them. Meanwhile neither is getting to the core of what is going on within and between us. We are all pressing for agreement without really understanding what it is that others are protecting or preserving.

Understanding Precedes Agreement and Action

Understanding becomes the first step and foundation for developing collaborative and mutually satisfying solutions to problems. After you have connected by demonstrating that you accurately understand (even though you may not fully agree with) the other person's concerns, it is time to share your concerns.

Recall the Mapping-An-Issue process discussed in Chapter 8. It is very important that you explore and accurately understand any resistance you can identify in Step 3, "Understanding the Issue." In our experience, we have found that you cannot freely proceed to Step 4, "Identifying Wants," if unidentified or misunderstood beliefs and feelings are festering.

Finally, as you proceed in any process of negotiation, decision-making, consulting, or selling, be alert and ready to deal with resistance whenever it appears. (This includes later steps in the Mapping-An-Issue process as well.) Repeated failure to deal effectively with resistance and to resolve issues leads to Selye's Stage three — exhaustion.

Stop for a moment and recall your most recent argument or difficult exchange with another person. Focus on your own behavior and answer these questions:

1. *Were you primarily trying to control or connect?*

2. *Was your energy high in your body or at center?*

3. *Were you shooting for agreement before understanding?*

4. *How much were you leading? How much were you following?*

5. *What styles of communication did you use? Were there any mixed messages, mixing Style II with Style I, III, or IV, for example?*

6. *If you could repeat the exchange, what would you do differently?*

Tips

1. Listen for objections and acknowledge obstacles. Ask for others' solutions and explore them as well.

2. Anticipate and look for resistance when you seek or plan change. Build "handling resistance" into your planning, negotiating, and selling strategies.

3. Determine the percentages. During an exchange, when you think someone is partially agreeing with you, put a percentage on it. For example, 60 percent *yes* and 40 percent *no*, or 80 percent *yes* and 20 percent *no*. Ask the other person if the percentage is accurate. Then invite him or her to tell you what the *no* is about. In many instances, a certain percentage of *no* is realistic, and it will not interfere if you understand what the *no* means and can live with it.

4. Face the *no*. A *no* as really *no* may be very disappointing. But the earlier you can discover this the sooner you can take it into account to plan, adjust, or move on to another point, job, customer, friendship, and so on.

5. Involve others and give choices. In addition to gaining accurate understanding, *involvement and choice* are two big antidotes to resistance. Involving others in planning activities and solving problems gains their input and commitment. Giving them real choices lessens trapped responses because people like to have as much control over their lives as possible.

6. Identify additional resistance. As a way of identifying further points of resistance in a situation, ask the person with whom you are negotiating, "If the present concern (whatever it is) would be taken care of, would you agree with (comply or buy into) what I am proposing?"

7. Respond positively and unexpectedly in pressure situations. Do the opposite of what is typically anticipated — a negative reaction on your part.

8. Watch for and act on nonverbal "turning points" which signal increased or decreased resistance during an exchange.

9. Let resistance be a cue. Continued resistance is useful feedback to you. It may indicate you are pressing too hard. It may tell you that you are not addressing the other person's concerns. Resistance may be more of a statement about your inflexibility than about the other's inflexibility. Use resistance as a cue to stop doing what is not working.

RESPONDING TO FIGHT TALK:
DIRECT PRESSURE FROM OTHERS

Our research indicates that people find Fight Talk to be the most difficult communication style to handle. They fear two things: (1) not being able to control the situation; (2) being hurt verbally or physically. The secret of dealing effectively with other people's pressure is to relate to them in a way that takes their concerns into account and, in the process, makes them your ally rather than your adversary.

> UNDERSTANDING OTHERS
> TAKES PRESSURE OFF YOU

Most approaches to self-defense of martial arts (karate, kung fu, and judo) involve direct linear attacks on others and may be used to inflict injury or death upon the attacker. Aikido, however, a relatively new Japanese art of self-defense, is more circular. When practiced in its most masterful form, it is used to merely neutralize and harmlessly redirect the aggression of the attacker.

The aikidoist does not perceive a challenge as a competitive attack but rather as an opportunity both to learn and to teach. Spinning and rotating, the aikidoist maintains control of the interaction with the challenger, however, often it is not clear who is the attacker and who is attacked. "The quick blending of forces makes indistinguishable the cause-effect relationships and makes apparent only the circularity of forces blended together for mutual problem-solving — neutralization of aggression and redirection of energies" (Saposnek, *Family Process*, Vol. 19, September 1980, page 229).

ACCEPTING, BLENDING, AND REDIRECTING

An aikidoist does not block or clash with the aggressor. Rather, the aikidoist accepts, joins, and then directs the challenger's energy flow.

By blending, resistance evaporates because the aikidoist returns nothing for the antagonist to resist. It is like letting air out of a balloon. No additional force is added; only the challenger's energy is used. As a result, potential resistance is converted into free energy which can be guided into more productive directions.

The principles of aikido can be useful in a situation of communicating under pressure. With these in mind, if you are verbally challenged or attacked, go to center, breathe fully, and then do the following:

Step 1. Accept (listen non-defensively) by:

Displaying calm nonverbals: open posture, gentle eye contact, relaxed facial expression

Acknowledging feelings: "Yeah John, I can see you're really upset."

Assuring: "I'm sure we can figure something out to take care of the difficulty."

Inviting: "Tell me more about the problem."

Now Talking: "This is hard for me to listen to but keep talking."

Encouraging: "Tell me everything you think I need to know."

Step 2. Blend (see the world from the other person's point of view) by:

Paraphrasing: "You're angry because you don't think you've gotten a fair deal." (Use this only to check the accuracy of your understanding; otherwise it will escalate the other person's anger.)

Agreeing: "You're absolutely right. Things shouldn't be that way."

Admitting: "Yes, I made that decision."

Extending: "I'm surprised that you are not more upset and hadn't come to me sooner."

Crediting: "You've done me a favor by bringing this to my attention. Thank you."

Summarizing: "I understand that you're concerned about three things. The first is ..."

Sharing: "I've been unhappy about this situation too."

Step 3. Redirect (ask and act toward a joint solution) by:

Offering choice: "Do you think you and I can handle this, or should we turn it over to someone else?"

Involving: "How can we solve this?"

Specifying: "Exactly what would the change you want look like."

Asking for help: "I'd like your cooperation to change the situation."

Putting others to work for you: "I'd like you to keep an eye out to prevent this from happening again in the future."

Taking action: "I'll talk to Pat and get it done."

Accept, Don't Reject; Blend, Don't Defend; Re-direct, Don't Attack

For most people, welcoming an attack does not make any sense. Logically it encourages things to get out of hand, wastes time, and does not get them what they want. But doing what seems to be illogical — inviting, accepting, blending with an attack — is actually the quickest way to get the information needed to work together most productively.

A non-challenging response to an attack is surprising. Usually an attacker expects to be met with a challenge or counter resistance. When the attack is *not* met in kind, this is confusing and disarming.

Operating from your center and sincerely "welcoming" the attack as an opportunity to learn — about the situation, yourself, and the challenger — is unexpected. You do not let the other person's pressure knock you off balance. Rather, you place yourself, as the pivot point. Accepting the attack as a gift of energy transforms negative energy into positive energy, and reframes threat into possibility.

RESPONDING TO SPITE TALK: INDIRECT PRESSURE FROM OTHERS

When people are in Fight Talk, they are actively and directly attacking or challenging you. Your job is to connect with and redirect their energy productively.

When people are in SpiteTalk, they are passively and indirectly thwarting you. Your job is to gather and transform their diffused angry energy into more productive use.

People act with spite when they feel powerless and believe resentful resistance is their only alternative. Spite Talk is their indirect way of saying they want something but are not getting it and they feel resentful and powerless to act directly on their own behalf. Footdragging, complaining, slowing things down, and being negative are the only kinds of power they believe they have. As a result, they get stuck in a state where unproductive thoughts, feelings, and actions breed on themselves and infect others.

Chronic Spite Talk typically reflects one of two things:

1. An individual has negative, low self-esteem and a passive orientation to life.

2. The person is in a situation in which he or she is repeatedly undervalued and discounted.

To deal with Spite Talk, you have four major options:

Option 1. Describe What You See and Hear and Ask What Is Wrong

Spite Talk is often a way of getting your attention by indirectly signaling that things are not right. Do not react or run. Pick up on it directly. Describe what you see and hear and invite the person to say more. Often a simple direct acknowledgement is enough to open a discussion of the "sore" spot and clear the air.

"Mary, the tone of your voice sounds to me like you're really unhappy about something. What's up?"

Despite your invitation, the other person will often deny that there is anything wrong. Instead their denial is an additional spiteful act which tells you something about the degree of resentment. When a straightforward request to talk about what is bothering the other person does not work, the overriding question is what to do next.

Option 2. Realize that Straight Talk Begets Straight Talk

Before you encourage the others to talk — which they will not do until they trust you — be straight with them about yourself. Share your Awareness Wheel. Tell them what has really been going on with you. Acknowledge your own contribution and response to the situation. Ask them if you have done something which offended them. If you are really sincere (no hidden agenda or unstated strings attached), you will build trust and they will usually be straight with you.

"Mary, I think I've been putting down your ideas at our department meetings recently. I'm so intent on making sure that my own ideas are heard that I discount yours. I'm going to work at making sure I hear out your suggestions."

On the other hand, if you are pretending to be straight just to get them to talk or change, it will not work.

Option 3. Break State, Speak About Other, Be Silent

Breaking State

Spite Talk's most aggressive action is no action — saying nothing and doing nothing while looking and feeling hurt. When you ask, "What's wrong?" the response is, "nothing." The silence could kill.

When someone is in a physically and emotionally "stuck state" like this, no amount of talking will get through to the person. You need to get him or her up, moving, breathing, and often into a different context to make connection. There are many ways to do this:

Change posture: if the person is sitting, do something to get him or her to stand.

Get the person to do something: tell the person to hold a tool, look up some figures for you, review a report together, or handle some other appropriate prop.

Leave the immediate area: suggest something which will make both of you move; go to the cafeteria for a cup of coffee, for example.

Take a walk and talk: walk side by side which offers the advantage of not having to look at each other so the two of you do not see nonverbal cues which set each other off.

Any of these actions can serve to get air into the other person's body. Mood can shift when the body shifts.

Speaking About the Other Person

When someone is angrily withdrawn and silently resentful, saying what you think he or she is experiencing can help you connect. If your intent is to "walk in the other's shoes," showing your concern by saying what the other person must be experiencing may draw him or her out, especially when you are accurate. Accuracy increases rapport, and when you misunderstand and are inaccurate, it is almost impossible for the other person to remain silent and not clarify your inaccuracy.

As you speak, watch for small nonverbal cues — eye contact, moist eyes, head nodding, shifts in breathing — which tell you that you are accurately describing and understanding his or her Awareness Wheel.

> "Joe, I think you've really been hurt by Jane's promotion. My guess is that you think it was unfair to give the job to her when she hasn't been with the company as long as you. You're probably wondering why she got the promotion when you wanted it and thought you deserved it."

Being Silent

Silence is very powerful. After you speak about the other person, be silent and peacefully wait. Let the person speak in his or her own time. Usually the combination of being on target — showing understanding of the other person's thoughts, feelings and wants — along with gentle silence will open a Straight Talk discussion. Remaining silent may be difficult for you. Most of us grow anxious with silences that last over five seconds. We break the silence with needless talk. Perhaps you believe that you do not have time to be silent, that you have to keep moving and talking. This belief will limit your effectiveness.

If the other person does not speak after a minute or so (which will probably seem like an eternity to you) say, "That's okay, take your time and get back to me when you are ready to talk." Or say, "I'll assume what I said about your experience is true until I hear differently from you," and then end the conversation — for now.

Non-Talkers

Be careful not to assign spiteful intentions to people who simply do not talk much. Here are three tips for relating to non-talkers:

1. Respect individual differences. Realize that some people have little to say.

2. Connect with non-talkers by matching — posture, breathing, and pace including comfortable silence. When they do talk, be willing to pursue their interests (comfort zones) rather than pulling them into yours.

3. Use the following approach if you must make a decision that involves non-talkers who do not give you any input or direction. Tell them what action you are going to take and indicate that you will assume they are in full agreement unless you hear differently from them by a certain time. (This can be done verbally or in writing.)

After Options 1, 2, and 3. Expand Choices: Map The Issue Together

Often your efforts to elicit the other person's negative thoughts, feelings, and wants will dissolve the other person's passive aggression. When this happens, be sure to increase the other's involvement and responsibility by responding to his or her wants with increased choices for future action. Consider mapping the issue together to create understanding and move toward a solution.

Option 4. Last Resort: Set Limits And Define Consequences

If all attempts to deal straightforwardly with Spite Talk fail, use Control Talk to tell the other person that his or her specific passive behaviors are unacceptable and must stop. Describe the behavior you want to see stop, and indicate the desired behavior which you want to see started. Spell out the consequences if change does not occur. Be sure to set the time frame for change, and follow through with the consequences as stated if change does not occur.

"Mark, I don't want to hear any more snide remarks about Carl's work. If you have a complaint, go to Carl directly and iron it out. If I hear any more cheap shots from you like 'What do they pay you to screw things up?' I'll pull you off the project."

Tips

1. Give positive feedback when appropriate. When a person who typically uses Spite Talk to handle pressure deals with a situation directly and constructively, give him or her positive feedback. Spite Talkers usually lack self-esteem and want positive attention. Spite Talk only gets them negative attention. Help break the negative cycle.

2. Recognize the dynamics. Fight Talk and Spite Talk are two sides of the same coin — each fires off the other in a vicious cycle. The more one person actively pushes and shoves, the more the other person passively withdraws and disattends. Recognize this and do not get trapped in the cycle.

IT ONLY TAKES ONE PERSON TO START RELIEVING A PRESSURE SITUATION

In most situations, the first step toward resolution is to decrease the pressure, not increase it. Pressure develops from inside ourselves and it comes from others when they put pressure on us. When we respond to pressure by focusing on others, trying to control them, we increase our own and the other person's pressure.

When pressure develops, deal with yourself first. Go to center and breathe fully to relieve your own pressure. Then invite and follow others to release their pressure; reducing pressure sets the stage for sharing concerns. Keep in mind that *creating mutual understanding is the first step toward resolving issues in ways that fit for all parties.*

Let Go

What you resist, persists. Sometimes the quickest and most effective way to dissolve pressure is to "let it go" — stop holding on.

One of the best ways to deal with pressure is not to get caught in it in the first place. We create much of our own pressure needlessly when, for reasons of ego or pride, we try to win on an issue that is unimportant and should be released.

As long as you choose to pursue something or someone, you are hooked into spending energy. Ask yourself, "Is it worth it? What keeps me hanging on?" Experience the relief of letting your desperation go.

Even some big concerns are useless when seen from a larger perspective. Many of life's biggest lessons come from recognizing the limits of our power and letting go.

15

RESOLVING CONFLICTS:
Building Self and Other Esteem

Resolving conflicts — with self and others — is a theme that runs throughout this book. Each chapter either creates a *perspective* for understanding sources of conflict or presents *principles and skills* for dealing with issues. As you encounter heated disagreements and direct or indirect aggression, many of these concepts and skills may be crucial to understanding the conflict and useful for resolving it. Here is a brief summary which will help you review how much you have already learned about resolving conflicts.

- Dance patterns — nonverbal data

- Types of issues — topic, personal, and relationship

- Styles of communication — contributing or responding to conflict

- Self and other awareness — The Awareness Wheel

- Individual similarities and differences

- Partial awareness — blind spots, incongruencies, and blockages

- Mapping Issues — contracting and steps to effective action

- Six speaking skills — sending clear messages

- Five listening skills — understanding others accurately

- Meta Talk — Pre-, Now-, and Post-Talk to alter or reinforce inter-action patterns

- System dynamics — comfort zones of adaptability and cohesion

- Relationship phases

- Managing pressure and resistance — your own and others'

With these mental concepts and behavioral skills in your repertoire, you can spot trouble early and move to prevent severe conflict from developing. Once you are in the middle of a struggle, you can draw on them to dissolve the clash.

WANTS — THE HEART OF CONFLICT

Conflict is inevitable because everyone wants to be, to do, and to have, and sometimes people have competing wants. For example, they want the same thing, but there is not enough to go around. At other times they want different things, and the conflicting wants vie for priority. Wants thrive in *scarcity or abundance* — too little or too much. Conflict erupts over who wants to *control* whom, what, where, when, and how. Wants reflect values and priorities, and they impact choices. Feelings indicate the intensity of wants, influencing the degree of conflict.

Most conflicts arise from individuals wanting others to *agree or comply* with their experience:

Sensory data — facts, perceptions

Thoughts — beliefs, ideas, interpretations, expectations

Feelings — particular emotional responses

Wants — desire for self and from others

Actions — behaviors completed or proposed

Wants come from the core of people's comfort zones. Wants are a strong motivating and energizing force. When they are thwarted, the wants give rise to immediate frustration, anger, even desperation and sometimes depression.

Conflict with another person is basically a clash or collision of *interests* (wants) and *wills* (action). The intensity of the contest depends on how strongly each person is willing to pursue his or her own interests exclusively.

CONFLICT AND ESTEEM

How people deal with conflict has a lot to do with their self-esteem and how they value others.

What is Self- and Other-Esteem?

You have a "mental image" of yourself. If you look closely, it includes both snapshots and videos of yourself physically, mentally, emotionally, spiritually and socially from the past, the present, and even the imagined future. These accumulated images create your self-concept.

As you view these pictures, you privately evaluate and judge yourself from scene to scene. You see yourself as competent or incompetent, valuable or worthless, lovable or unlovable, and successful or unsuccessful. Your judgment is also based on how you imagine or experience others' evaluation of you. Add to this your set of feelings about yourself: confidence, shame, admiration, warmth, embarrassment, enjoyment, respect, or guilt. This blend of your self-concept, self-evaluation and feelings about yourself comprise your self-worth or self-esteem.

Some self-evaluations and feelings seem to predominate more than others. People who usually feel good about themselves with approving self-evaluations have high self-esteem, while others who feel badly about themselves and generally disapprove of themselves have low self-worth. Fortunately esteem for yourself and others can be increased with positive results.

Similarly, you have pictures, make evaluations, and have feelings — based in large part on how others treat you — about the other people in your life. This composite forms your respect or esteem for others — your "other-esteem" — which ranges from high to low.

In short, esteem is *active respect* for yourself and others, and it is especially important when you are dealing with an issue that causes conflict.

COUNTING AND DISCOUNTING

Each situation you face involving a decision or conflict can be approached from a position of valuing yourself or one of not valuing yourself. We call these two self-esteem postures *Counting Self* and *Discounting Self.*

You *count yourself* when you:

- face issues and conflict
- expand, acknowledge, accept, and act on your own awareness
- take responsibility for your own decisions and actions
- disclose your awareness appropriately
- ask for and accept help
- use your talents to accomplish things
- realize your limitations
- accept corrective positive feedback as well as love and affection from others
- act out of choice

Pause for a moment and recall a time recently when you clearly counted yourself?

Where were you? (home, work, school)

Who were you with? (partner, friend, colleague, alone)

What did you do to count yourself?

How did you feel?

You *discount yourself* when you:

- avoid issues and conflict
- limit, disregard, or deny your awareness
- do not share your awareness appropriately
- disown responsibility for your contribution and response to situations
- act out anger
- fail to exercise your talents
- do not ask for or refuse help when it is needed
- reject corrective and positive feedback as well as love and affection from others
- believe you are a victim
- verbally put yourself down
- act out of compulsion

Pause and think back to a recent situation in which you did not count yourself:

Where were you?

Who were you with?

What did you do to discount yourself?

How did you feel?

Similarly, when you face an issue or conflict with another person, you can operate from a position of valuing the other person or not valuing him or her. We call these two other-esteem postures *Counting Other* and *Discounting Other.*

You *count other(s)* when you:

- attend to their awareness
- invite them to share their perceptions, thoughts, feelings, wants, and actions
- listen to them attentively
- respect and incorporate differences
- give honest and useful feedback, both corrective and positive
- enjoy them and their accomplishments
- give help
- collaborate
- connect rather than control
- create and support options

Pause and recall a recent time when you really counted someone else:
  Who was it?
  Where were you?
  What did you specifically do to count the other?
  How did you feel?

You *discount other(s)* when you:

- ignore their awareness
- operate on unchecked assumptions
- deny and reject their differences
- blame them for your own decisions and actions
- invade or assume their responsibilities
- fail to provide honest and useful feedback or give feedback in a destructive way
- claim their accomplishments as your own
- refuse help when needed
- verbally put others down
- withhold praise for their accomplishments, as well as love and affection
- emphasize control over understanding and connecting
- force agreements

Think back to a recent time when you clearly discounted someone else:

Who was it?

Where were you?

What did you specifically do to discount the other?

How did you feel?

How did your behavior impact the other person and your relationship?

Reflections of Esteem

Your Awareness Wheel reflects high- or low-esteem particularly in three zones:

1. Your beliefs — evaluations of yourself and others which become self-fulfilling prophesies

2. Your wants — what you want for yourself or for others and your values, your strongly held motivations and priorities (Values are sometimes nonnegotiable.)

3. Your actions — how you choose to treat yourself and others

In every exchange with others, your beliefs, wants, and actions either count or discount yourself, and they count or discount others. Counting builds esteem. Discounting damages esteem.

FOUR RELATIONSHIP-ESTEEM POSTURES

Your beliefs, wants, and actions reflect your general self/other-esteem orientation toward relationships in everyday transactions. However, in conflict situations, your fundamental relationship-esteem posture comes to the forefront in full strength. There are the four basic self/other-relationship-esteem postures which you can take toward another person that are readily apparent in conflict. We will look at them more closely.

Discount Self, Discount Other — No One Counts

In this posture, I believe that neither my partner nor I can do anything about our issues — we are basically passive victims. I am out of touch with my awareness or I fail to act on what I find. I have no confidence in myself or my partner to change things; we are both powerless to act effectively. Energy is dissipated or diffused. I feel discouraged and hopeless. I repress and avoid issues to protect myself from further pain. I have little concern for my partner's well being. Small Talk and Spite Talk prevail.

Count Self, Discount Other — Only I Count

With this posture, I am the person to be valued, not my partner. My concerns are more important, and what he or she thinks, feels, and wants is of little interest to me. If there is a question of who is right and who is wrong, I am right. I believe my partner must defer to me so I manipulate and use power plays to win. My solutions will be superimposed on the other person. If my partner resists my stance, conflict escalates and can even become physically abusive. Control and Fight Talk dominate this orientation.

Discount Self, Count Other — Only Partner Counts

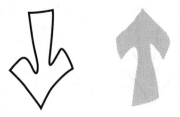

Here, my partner is the one to be considered. I am willing to defer to his or her thoughts, feelings, and wishes. My partner is right and I am wrong; my partner is smart, I am not; my partner has power, I do not. In short, I depreciate myself while attempting to please and placate my partner. I disregard my issues and accommodate my partner's instead. My conversation often sounds like Small Talk and Shop Talk, but it often contains mixed messages, and if I feel resentment, it comes out in Spite Talk.

Count Self, Count Other — Both Count

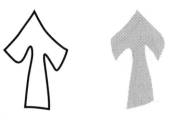

In this posture, I believe and act on the premise that "together we can work things out." Using our awareness and our skill, we can create options and find solutions to difficult situations. We have the power to do something which will fit for both of us. The challenge is to work together, not against each other. This perspective uses Search Talk and Straight Talk to resolve conflicts. It also uses the humor in Small Talk to laugh about the irony of situations in order to keep issues in perspective. If we hit into an issue that cannot be resolved, we may agree to disagree and amicably manage our difference.

RULES OF RELATIONSHIP — ESTEEM CONTRACTS

Whether you are aware of it or not, each specific relationship you have is governed by a set of informal and usually unspoken rules. These are called "rules of relationship" which influence and are influenced by self/other-esteem (Watzlawick, *et. al.,* 1967). The easiest way to understand these rules is to think in terms of *who can repeatedly do what to whom, where, when, and how?* This explains, for example, why your brother or sister can get away with murder and your parents do not say a thing, but you do not dare do it. It also accounts, in part, for your ability to talk to your boss (or a particular teacher) in ways that your colleagues cannot.

Every organization or relationship you enter — your family, school, fraternity, work place, even your bank, church and doctor's office — has informal and unwritten relationship rules in force, governing what can happen between people. The rules have evolved over the system's history to help it survive. These rules also govern how conflict is handled. For example, you learn whether it is "best" to "stuff it," collude, wait and see, withdraw, or talk straight in that system.

Over time, the rules of relationship become the basic *esteem contract* for relating to each other. *An esteem contract is the relationship posture which you and another person develop toward each other.* Two people or a group can relate out of any one of the four relationship postures.

Esteem postures may change somewhat in different circumstances and may even rotate through several relationship postures in one day. But your basic "contract" toward another person is usually quite stable over time. While one or both parties may not like the basic esteem contract between them, as long as each person maintains the relationship and continues to interact in the same way, they both consent to the basic contract — their rules of relationship.

This powerful, informal, and usually unspoken "agreement" is the foundation of your relationship dance. For example, you may be dating a person who is very attractive and interesting in many ways. When you look at the way the person treats you, you may find that he or she takes a Count Self, Discount You posture toward you much of the time. However, if you do not want to run the risk of losing the relationship, you may be willing to assume a Discount Self, Count Other posture to maintain the relationship.

It is our experience that any esteem contract less than Both Count is limited and flawed. Whether at home or work, it is handicapped in its ability to produce high satisfaction and success.

Changing Mixed Contracts

Realistically, few people operate from a Both Count posture all of the time. However, the challenge is to approach interpersonal situations from this orientation even when others do not initially approach you this way. The esteem you bring to a situation determines to a large extent how you will experience a situation and what will grow out of it.

Having positive respect for yourself and another person's well being and operating from awareness and centered energy become a strong force for changing interaction positively. The other person's put-downs or discounting behaviors will not knock you off balance if you persist in counting yourself and the other and in operating from center. From this stance you will be less threatened and better able to make legitimate requests and direct constructive actions. This type of flexible strength is tough to combat. After several discounting "tests," the other person will often recognize you as nonthreatening and begin to respond more positively.

Several things can prevent you from assuming this powerful stance. In many situations the intention to win — to fulfill your own wants at the expense of the other's wants — keeps you out of this posture. At other times limiting beliefs and negative feelings keep you from being straight with yourself and with others. Sometimes partial awareness prevents you from taking such a stance.

Why People Stay "Stuck" in a Relationship

Here are several principles about relationships that explain why individuals stay "stuck" in unsatisfactory relationships:

1. A person who believes he or she has no alternatives (for example, economic, social, or emotional support systems) may cling to the certainty of misery over the uncertainty of change.

2. The person least involved and least interested in the relationship is most in control — if the other allows it.

3. "The more dependent the relationship, the greater the resistance to clarification because of potential risk of changing or losing the relationship" (Olson, 1972, page 86).

4. "In order to feel free enough to improve a relationship, one must be willing to risk losing the relationship in the process" (Olson, 1972, page 86).

5. "Relationships that are most in need of change are the ones most resistant to change, even if change might mean improving the relationship" (Olson, 1972, page 86).

Other feelings and assumptions can also keep you from initiating change. They include:

- fear that you will offend someone else
- fear that your partner will belittle, reject, or use your concerns against you
- fear of making a commitment to the other person and your relationship
- fear that approaching the conflict might worsen things and get out of control.
- hope that things will work themselves out
- assuming that your going along with whatever your partner says or does is really what your partner wants
- assuming that your partner really knows what you mean, even if you do not say it directly and clearly
- believing that things are better left unsaid

You can see from reading over these lists of beliefs, feelings, and assumptions that low self-esteem — negative beliefs about self which generate fear — keeps people trapped in unsatisfactory dances at home, work, and elsewhere. Unsatisfactory relationships almost always stem from some discounting elements in the basic relationship-esteem contract.

Sometimes esteem contracts deteriorate over time, and in other instances they improve. What makes the difference is whether one person takes the initiative to change the relationship and both persons become involved in trying to improve things. One person's positive initiative and follow-through often, though not always, stimulates positive change in the other.

The relationship contract between two people is played out subtly in most day-to-day interactions, but it stands out in bold relief in conflict situations. Conflict highlights the basic nature of a relationship and tests its strength.

PROCEDURAL CONTRACTS

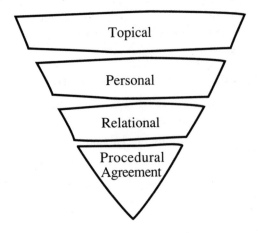

Throughout this book we have emphasized the importance of creating understanding before trying to produce agreement in decision-making, negotiation, and other pressure situations. However, when it comes to dealing effectively with conflict, establishing mutual agreement about how to proceed is an essential first step. (See the section on Contracting in Chapter 11, "Meta Talk.") Note that we are talking about agreement concerning procedures, not agreement about the substance of the conflict.

In one of our studies at the University of Minnesota Family Study Center, we identified three basic contracts that married couples display for dealing with conflict.

Option #1: Traditional Contract — Agreement Not To Talk

In the *traditional contract,* both partners are content to limit their conversations to Small Talk and ShopTalk about day-to-day topical events. There is no attempt to discuss their conflicts or to have intimate conversations about personal matters or the dynamics of their relationship. Their approach to handling conflict is mainly mutual Discount Self, Count Other.

In our study many couples with this approach reported high relationship satisfaction, due in large part to their dependence on traditional roles, and they also expressed considerable affection for each other. Aside from good will toward each other (which was a significant resource), however, these couples were poorly equipped to deal with pressures for change.

Option #2: Transitional Contract — No Agreement to Talk or Not Talk

Couples with *transitional contracts* are out of step with each other. One partner wants to step outside of the circle of their ongoing day-to-day interaction and talk about how they relate and communicate, while the other person is unwilling or does not have the skills needed to do so. The partner who wants change may try to use Search Talk or Straight Talk but is rebuffed and slips into Fight or Spite Talk. Their dissonant communication reflects their lack of consensus about a process for dealing with conflict and change.

Needless to say, among couples we studied, the relationship satisfaction was very low because of the various Discounting Self and Other postures they used.

We call this a transitional contract because parties in this state are either on their way out of the relationship or in transition to the first or third contracts. Moving to the third option may be difficult for the "non-talker," but contentedly moving back to the traditional — no-talk — option is even more difficult for the person wishing to deal directly with issues, so it rarely happens.

Option #3: Process Contract — Agreement to Talk

This third option differs significantly both in *what* partners talk about and in *how* they talk to each other. In the *process contract,* relationship rules encourage partners to talk about topical, personal and relationship matters as needed, and to deal with their conflicts from a Both-Count orientation.

In our study, the couples with his contract, similar to the traditional contract couples, reported high relationship satisfaction. A major difference existed, however, in their ability to manage change and resolve conflicts. Process-contract couples were well equipped to handle the complexity and uncertainty of daily living.

These three types of procedural contracts also exist in business and professional relationships. Some boss-employee, doctor-patient, and teacher-student relationships operate out of traditional contracts. Other people suffer in transitional contracts wishing to talk openly with their boss or colleague yet finding the other person unwilling or unskilled. Fortunately, many people enjoy working relationships and friendships which are founded on Both-Count process contracts in which parties can negotiate change and deal with conflict effectively.

If you do not have an agreement to process issues in your relationships, check the fine print in your "esteem contract" — there is some discounting going on. And renegotiate to develop a *process contract* because as we have seen throughout this book, *process affects outcome.*

RECOMMENDATIONS FOR HANDLING CONFLICT

The following recommendations for resolving conflict can be applied to a wide range of situations — from reconstructing your relationship-esteem contract (a core relationship issue) to deciding how to spend an afternoon on your vacation (a personal preference issue).

These recommendations can enhance a structured meeting in which you Map An Issue (see Chapter 8) or they can be helpful, in the heat of an argument, to shift esteem orientations and create a satisfactory resolution to the conflict.

Be Aware of Your Intentions

Your intentions are key; pay attention to your own intentions. When you find yourself caught up in a conflict, recognize if you are trying to control or collaborate, win or connect. Your intentions are played out in your actions. If you are not clear about your intentions, or if your intentions are mixed, you will send mixed messages which most people will sense and react to negatively. Look at your hidden agenda. Put your wants on the table with Straight Talk. This will enhance trust.

Line up your intentions so you can approach the conflict with the other person as a search and discover operation rather than a search and destroy mission. Seek collaboration over control. To help you realign your intentions, seek a less adversarial physical posture. Go for a walk; perhaps sit next to the other person to shift your focus from each other to a common sheet of paper with, for example, an Awareness Wheel on it or some other report of data or information. If the other person does not follow your lead, shift back to following his or her lead to get back into sync.

With Your Intentions in Mind, Follow These Recommendations:

1. Be aware that conflict occurs in a social and personal context. Many conflicts stem from, or are accentuated by, system forces (adaptability and cohesion) or individual differences (psychological types). Consider the context of a conflict. Many differences never reach the level of serious conflict if system and personal dynamics are well managed.

2. Keep an eye on your relationship-esteem postures — your own and the other person's. Regardless of how the other person treats you, do not slip into a discounting — self or other — mode. Use Search Talk and Straight Talk. The self/other-esteem you bring to a situation affects what can happen!

3. Set the ground rules (Review the section on Pre-Talk, Contracting: Setting Procedures in Chapter 11). Be sure to rule out threats such as, "I'll get even with you," or "I'll leave you," or physical abuse. Do not confuse a fight with conflict resolution! Separate fight time and serious discussion — cool off and set procedures.

4. Do not violate the ground rules you set. Consistently violating procedural rules when dealing with issues, for example, by bringing up issues at inappropriate times, in improper places, or with people not directly involved, damages other's trust of you. Respecting the procedural contract maintains essential system boundaries.

5. Get more information if the other person refuses to negotiate. Perhaps you do not have a procedural contract to deal with the conflict at that moment.

6. Recognize the meaning of being rejected by another person. Usually it means the relationship is of little value to the other person. In this situation, the "no" may be difficult, disappointing, and painful to accept. Nevertheless, use this information to adjust your own plans and count yourself.

7. Check the recent ratio of positive to negative communication. If, in the weeks prior to the conflict, good will has been scarce and genuine positive feedback lacking, negotiations will be tougher. It is more difficult to resolve conflict effectively if there are few or no "deposits in the relationship bank." It usually takes about three "that-a-ways" — positive strokes — to offset one criticism.

8. Keep your focus on the issue and watch for the other person's resistance to crucial information.

9. Use your Awareness Wheel to expand self and other awareness. Also ask yourself:

   • "How is my comfort zone being threatened?"

   • "Is there something I am defending that I can let go without discounting myself?"

   • "How can I turn our differences into a resource?"

   • "What positive thing can I do for the other person? In an intimate relationship, what loving thing can I do for my partner?"

10. Manage your own anxiety by centering and breathing.

11. Deal with feelings before facts. Explore the feelings behind anger — fear, disappointment, sadness.

12. Identify areas of agreement — what you both believe or want — while dealing with differences, and express agreement as often as you honestly can.

13. Demonstrate that you understand the other person's perspective by summarizing the key parts — beliefs, feelings, wants — of his or her Awareness Wheel. Temporarily leaving your own position — comfort zone — and accurately restating the other person's perspective cannot be overstated as an effective bridge-building step, especially during a heated exchange. When it is genuine, demonstrating understanding releases the other person's anxiety about being heard and counted, and it usually creates a dramatic shift toward cooperation and collaboration.

14. Express what you want *for* the other person as well as what you want *for* yourself. Wants *for* others become powerful building blocks to solutions. A common way people discount others is by locking in on their own wants and failing to let others know that they are taking the others' wants into account. Continually ask yourself, "What, if anything, would the other person gain or lose if my wants were realized?"

15. Focus on *interests* (wants) and *options* (possible actions), *not positions* (who is right or wrong, good or bad) (Fisher and Ury, 1981).

16. Look for a common or higher order principle — objective, fair criteria — which all parties can apply toward a mutually understandable or satisfactory resolution of the conflict. For example, parties might agree that the profits or losses from a joint venture should be shared on the basis of time and money invested (Fisher and Ury, 1981).

17. Be specific (descriptive) about what a successful outcome would look and feel like.

18. Avoid trying to superimpose solutions. Look for mutual gain. Invent options which benefit both parties.

20. Think about the benefits each person receives from a specific solution. It is probably not a viable option if both people do not get something.

21. Consider attaching a percentage to what you and the other might consider a successful outcome, adequate change, or acceptable solution. Do not get trapped on striving unrealistically for 100 percent. Set a figure for a more modest gain, for example, 20 percent, 40 percent, or 60 percent improvement.

22. Watch nonverbals which confirm real agreement with resolutions that are accepted verbally.

23. Consider your alternatives. Without threatening the other person, know what back-up action you will take if the conflict is not resolved (Fisher and Ury, 1981).

24. Take "course checks" along the way to monitor the process to see what is helping and what is not helping to resolve the conflict. Use Now Talk to reinforce what is working or to get back on track. For example, say to your partner, "I appreciate the way you are seriously treating my concern," or "I'm stuck and frustrated — how can we get back on track?"

25. Monitor your internal cues (thoughts, feelings and intentions) and external cues (other's verbal and nonverbal behavior) to be sure you

have a continuing commitment (procedural contract) to deal with the conflict. If there is any question, shift to Now Talk.

26. Allow time for Post-Talk to celebrate resolutions and to identify what you have learned from the process that can be helpful in the future. Learn from your experience.

27. Remember this principle: how people relate to each other in the *process* of a struggle determines how destructive or constructive the *outcome* of the conflict will be. The individual, pair, or group with the most good will and skills for dealing with conflict has the most options long-term.

16

COMMUNICATION STRATEGIES

In the Introduction we say that the purpose of CONNECTING is to help you become a more alert and talented interpersonal dancer by increasing:

1. Awareness of self, others, and your relationships.

2. Skills for sending and receiving messages more clearly and accurately.

3. Options for building relationships — strong, satisfying, and if relevant, productive.

All of the concepts and skills presented in CONNECTING have been directed toward this purpose. In this Chapter, we will show you how to draw on and integrate the maps and skills you have learned so far to create your own communication strategies for various situations.

CREATING STRATEGIES

The word "strategy" itself often connotes an individual's or group's unilateral, secretive, or perhaps cunning set of plans and activities to take advantage of others in order:

- to exploit
- to manipulate
- to win individually

We use the word "strategy" to mean *a planned and monitored sequence of behaviors for achieving a desired outcome.* A strategy need not be exploitive or manipulative; rather it can provide a structure to help you approach situations and judge progress — according to the sensory data generated during the actual interpersonal dance. Strategies need not be secretive; they can be disclosed in Meta Talk or developed with the other person(s) involved in a situation to produce the best outcome. Strategies can allow both parties to win.

Here again, as in most circumstances, *your intentions are paramount.* Like any resource or tool, you can use these concepts and skills to manipulate or to connect. *The choice is yours.* Keep your intention in mind — to Count or Discount — as you construct communication strategies. Your intention will color the outcome.

We hope the goal of your strategies will be to create a sequence of events that achieve outcomes that are profitable and satisfying for everyone involved. The test is this: *does everyone leave the situation feeling good about himself or herself, others involved, and the decisions made?* This does not always happen of course, but it is an ideal for which to strive.

The reason for developing a strategy is simple. If you continue to do what you always do, without any forethought, you will continue to get what you always get. A strategy which changes how your typically act, react, or interact can change the outcome of a dance.

There are two ways to formulate a strategy:

1. On the spot — as events are unfolding in the situation.
2. Prior to the situation — in anticipation of the event.

Here are some typical two-, three-person, and small-group situations for which a strategy may be useful (the situations are not listed in any order of importance):

Initiating change	Handling an impasse
Establishing priorities	Asking for change
Facilitating a decision	Presenting a proposal
Negotiating differences	Reviewing performance
Transforming resistance	Persuading boss/colleague
Gaining commitment	Expressing disappointment
Delivering a difficult message	Dealing with problem behavior
Expressing appreciation	Asking for a raise/promotion
Mediating a dispute	Clarifying a misunderstanding
Managing change	Terminating a relationship
Increasing motivation	Giving constructive feedback
Setting goals	Consulting

Allocating resources

Organizing a memo

Facilitating a meeting

Making a presentation

Confronting dishonesty

Making a proposal

Improving performance

Giving positive feedback

Handling complaints

Eliciting cooperation

Disagreeing tactfully

Asking for help

Counseling

Planning/Scheduling activities

Selling

Communicating rejection

Disciplining

Delivering good news

Coaching/Instructing

Interviewing

Asking for forgiveness

Budgeting

Bargaining/Trading

STRATEGIZING ON THE SPOT

Occasionally you find yourself in a situation where events in a specific context are not unfolding as you had hoped they would. This was the case for one of us authors when making a decision on updating the office computer system. Here is the history and context of the example.

The author immersed himself in reading computer magazines, talking to business friends, and visiting computer stores to see products demonstrated and test how he would be treated with an eye to future support services. In addition, he enlisted the services of an independent consultant, whose advice he grew to value and trust, to help him evaluate his choices.

The whole process was fun and energizing. In time he found a computer store with staff technical knowledge and availability as well as products he thought would be best.

At that point the author made an appointment with the consultant and the sales-support person for the three of them to meet at the store for a demonstration of an impressive new software package, and the author told each a little about the other's expertise. He was *feeling* excited about the prospect of bringing this "critical mass" together. He was also aware of *wanting* two things to develop from the meeting:

1. that the demonstration would provide the consultant with enough information to make a recommendation about the software program.
2. that the consultant and sales-support person would develop a relationship such that the two of them could work effectively together as backup to the programing the consultant would be doing, should the author decide to purchase the particular computer system.

As the three first met, the author introduced Mike, the sales-service person to Jack, the consultant. Mike said "hi," then turned and walked quickly toward the computer setup for the demonstration. There was no Small Talk or Shop Talk on Mike's part to connect with Jack or draw him out to get a sense of Jack's extensive background with computers and affirm his expertise.

Completely out of sync and having established no rapport with Jack, Mike led the others to his comfort zone — the hardware — and the three men took seats around the machine. The author sat at center and back from the computer. Jack sat down on the right, leaned back against the wall and folded his arms across his chest. One glance at Jack's *nonverbals* and the author *thought* Jack was *feeling* mildly offended and discounted by Mike's failure to acknowledge Jack's expertise. On the left, Mike busied himself calling up the data base program.

When the program came up, Mike began *leading* his audience through some routines which he found fascinating. Unaware that Jack was not following, there was no attempt by Mike to tune into his customers' *wants* and demonstrate the program's ability in those areas. With the exception of showing one program feature which pulled Jack momentarily forward in his chair, Mike's oblivious leading left Jack disengaged.

With this picture in his mind, the author realized, that he must shift his *actions* from passive observer to active facilitator if any of his *wants* for this meeting were going to be met. While individual meetings with both Mike and Jack were technically impressive and interpersonally satisfying for the author, the chemical elements between these two-high tech guys were not mixing. The author wondered if his backgrounding comments to each about the other's expertise prior to their meeting had set up a mildly threatening and competitive climate for the meeting.

Based on his assessment and wish to help Mike and Jack connect, the author invented this strategy "on the spot."

1. Get Mike *following* Jack.

2. *Break* Jack's withdrawn *state* by *asking* him what he would like to see Mike demonstrate *for* him that was critical to the needed business application.

3. Get the two talking to each other.

Two or three brief interventions by the author did in fact get the two of them into their own spontaneous interchange. Later, when the author saw the two of them looking comfortable, engaged, and in sync with each other, he asked Jack to raise any hesitations or objections he saw to the program. Surprisingly, Jack did not have any. Instead he detailed several positives about how it appeared to handle the critical functions we needed for the business.

Finally, when the author and Jack were leaving the store, Jack had several technical documents in hand for his further review, and he and Mike shared a warm handshake and exchanged a genuine "Nice to meet you." Seeing this, the author felt pleased — his desires for the meeting were accomplished.

There are two comments to make about this example First, once the affective components — feelings and wants — in the interchange were attended to, the more cognitive — technical and factual — aspects of the task could be accomplished. Secondly, the author's strategy and interventions were very short. When you develop strategies, *think in terms of making small changes or creating brief interventions which produce significant turning points in interaction.*

You might be wondering at this point how you can learn to be more alert in situations and develop brief strategies which will have positive effects. Here is how to begin.

Notice on the following pages the "Connecting Menu" — a summary of all the communication-relationship concepts and skills presented in CONNECTING. Scan over the Menu and then read the explanation which follows it.

CONNECTING MENU

I. CONTEXT: History and Current Situation

System Adaptability
    Chaotic
    Structured
    Flexible
    Rigid
System Cohesion
    Disengaged
    Dispersed
    Connected
    Enmeshed

Phases
    Visionary
    Adversarial
    Dormant
    Vital
Individual Similarities/Differences
    Comfort Zones
    Sensory   Intuitive
    Thinker   Feeler
    Want Closure   Want Openness
    Extroverted   Introverted

II. CONTENT: Focus

Issue
    Topic, Other, Self,
    Relationship
Awareness Wheel
    Sensory Data, Thoughts
    Feelings, Wants, Actions

Partial Awareness
    Incomplete
    Incongruent
    Blocked

III. CONTRACT: Esteem and Procedural Agreement

Change Map
Pre-Talk
    Preview
    Setting Procedure

Self/Other-Esteem
    No One Counts
    I Count
    Others Count
    Everyone Counts

IV. COMMUNICATION: Skills

Meta Talk
    Pre-Talk
    Now-Talk
    Post-Talk
Communication Style:
    Small/Shop Talk
    Control/Fight/Spite Talk
    Search Talk
    Straight Talk
    Mixed Message
Types of Listening
    Persuasive
    Directive
    Attentive

Speaking Skills
    Speaking for Self
    Giving Sensory Data
    Expressing Thoughts
    Reporting Feelings
    Disclosing Wants
    Stating Actions
Listening Skills
    Looking, Listening,Matching, and
        Tracking
    Acknowledging
    Inviting
    Checking Out
    Summarizing

V. CONDUCT: Process of Control, Competition, Cooperation, Collaboration to Outcome

Interpersonal Dance Pattern
  Together, Transition, Apart
  Space, Energy, Time
  Rapport, Control, Trust
  Action, Reaction, Interaction

Communicycle/Impasse

Understanding Before Agreement

Stop and Shift

Self Talk

Map Issue

Resolve Conflict
  Be aware of Intentions
  Count Self and Other
  Feelings Before Facts
  Interests and Options Over
    Position
  Wants *for* Self, Other, Us

Manage Pressure/Resistance
  Watch Internal/External Cues
  Go to Center and Breathe Fully
  Invite/Follow/Invite Again
  For *Fight Talk*: Accept, Blend,
    and Redirect
  For *Spite Talk*: Break State,
    Speak About Other, Be Slient
  Expand Involvement/Choices
  Set Limits and Define Conse-
    quences
  Let Go

As you can see, the concepts and skills in the Connecting Menu have been arranged under five specific categories:

  I. *Context:* History and Current Situation

 II. *Content:* Focus

III. *Contract:* Esteem and Procedural Agreement

IV. *Communication:* Skills

 V. *Conduct:* Process

These "five C's" represent the major dynamics at work in any situation. If you can master your understanding of concepts and behavioral skills associated with these five aspects, you will be equipped to create your own effective strategies, either on the spot or with some planning and forethought.

Now go back and read over the menu again to review what you have learned or what has been reinforced for you in CONNECTING. Use the menu to evaluate your own level of knowledge and competence with each concept and skill listed. Take some time to reread anything you do not understand or of which you are unsure. Choose one or two areas for which you believe more understanding and practice would enhance your people skills.

Once you have a good grasp of this Menu, the concepts and skills will come to you as needed — on the spot during an "interpersonal dance," or as you anticipate and develop a strategy for approaching an exchange.

STRATEGIZING PRIOR TO THE SITUATION

To put a game plan together before a critical event follow these four basic steps:

Step 1. Analyze the situation.

Step 2. Develop an action and contingency plan.

Step 3. Visualize/Rehearse a successful exchange.

Step 4. Act on your plan.

Again, remember that true winning interpersonal strategies must first and continually build self and other esteem.

Step 1. Analyze the Situation.

A good treatment plan is based on a thorough diagnosis. The *context* and *content* sections of the Menu will help you construct a careful analysis of the situation before you act.

As you review the history and current situation, consider the *systems* operating, the nature of the relationships in view of their *phases* of development, and the *comfort zones* — individual strengths and limitations (psychological types) — for each player.

In addition, be sure you specifically identify what the real *issue(s)* are, and expand *awareness* of self and other(s) to try and understand everyone's stake in the situation. Consider actually drawing Awareness Wheels on a piece of paper in such a way as to represent each player's power and spatial relationship; then briefly fill out what you think each player's awareness is in the situation. This will help you identify partial awareness — incomplete, incongruent, and blocked energy — and formulate important information to consider or gather, as well as determine critical points for strategic intervention.

Step 2. Develop an Action and Contingency Plan.

After you have analyzed the situation and have decided what you want to do about it, consider the *contract, communication, and conduct* aspects of the Menu. Actually jot down a specific sequence of concepts or skills to follow, an action plan.

For example, suppose you want to clear up a delicate misunderstanding which you have had with another person; based on your analysis, you might plan to approach the other person this way:

> - Establish a *contract* to talk about the misunderstanding
> - Begin by sharing your *awareness* of the misunderstanding, using *Straight Talk*
> - *Invite* the other person to tell his or her story
> - *Summarize* what he or she says
> - *Invite* more information
> - Pursue completion of any self or other incomplete *communicycles.*
> - Look for *nonverbal* indicators of new understanding
> - *Express your appreciation* for the other person's willingness and effort to clarify the misunderstanding.

Be prepared in case the process does not unfold as you anticipate. List some *contingency measures* — backups — to manage yourself and the process:

> - *Go to center and breathe fully*
> - *Now Talk*—check contract and clarify current interaction (Is the process of misunderstanding recycling?)
> - Let go

Step 3. Visualize/Rehearse a Successful Exchange.

Once you have created your strategy, the next step is to practice it.

1. Mentally rehearse the conversation by visualizing the experience like a moving picture, frame by frame. Or imagine yourself in the actual situation, thinking your thoughts, feeling your feelings, and saying what you will say.

2. Experience yourself responding effectively to the other person's reactions, possible "zingers," objections, or resistance. And when you hit a "rough spot," activate your contingency.

3. Pay particular attention to any blocks or gaps in your conversation. These signal potential difficulties. Center and see yourself working through these critical turning points effectively.

4. Do not get stranded by focusing too intently on one sequence of events or outcome. Modify your strategy if necessary by testing several scenarios. Try out several satisfactory outcomes as well.

5. If you really get stuck and are unable to visualize yourself and the others working through the issue to a successful outcome, pay particular attention to the point at which you become stuck. There lies the real issue! You must first deal with the thought or fear that is blocking you.

Step 4. Act on Your Plan.

When you are ready to deal with the situation and are feeling confident and competent, implement your strategy. Let your planning work for you. Center and breathe fully. Let yourself to be responsive and flexible while you still pursue your course.

> WHEN YOU ARRIVE AT A GOOD SOLUTION
> YOU WILL SEE IT, HEAR IT, AND FEEL IT

One word of caution: while each situation and exchange has its impact, building relationships is composed of a series of dances. Time is on your side.

EVERYTHING IS INTERCONNECTED

Now that you have reached the end of CONNECTING, you may be saying to yourself, "There is so much material here, how can I ever remember and do it all?" Fortunately, since most of the concepts and skills we have presented are interrelated, if you change one, you correspondingly change others also. For example, centering and breathing can simultaneously alter your style of communication. Or, shifting from Fight Talk to Straight Talk brings you more to center and changes your breathing as well. Likewise, transforming your self- or other-esteem beliefs from Discounting to Counting has an impact on your intentions and behavior. Altering your type of listening modifies your interaction dramatically. By changing the distance, direction, or timing of a dance step, you often see change in the other person's response too.

Do not let the apparent complexity of interpersonal communication intimidate you. Our research and experience indicate that at any point in time, most people find one particular concept or skill to be primarily meaningful or useful to them. Then when they have mastered that concept or skill, another aspect takes on special significance in their life, and they review, reinforce, or first learn that newly important component.

Remember, the more alternatives you have as a communicator, the more you will be able to connect effectively with others. Begin increasing your interpersonal communication repertoire by mastering one concept or skill at a time.

References

Bonk, J. *Perceptions of Psychodynamics During a Transitional Period as Reported by Families Affected by Alcoholism.* Unpublished Doctoral Dissertation, University of Arizona, 1984.

Campbell, Joseph, ed. *The Portable Jung.* New York: Viking Press, 1971.

Carnes, Patrick. *Counseling Sexual Abusers.* Minneapolis: CompCare Publications, 1988.

Carnes, Patrick. *Understanding Us.* Littleton, CO: Interpersonal Communication Programs, Inc., 1987.

Clarke, J. *The Family Types of Schizophrenics, Neurotics and "Normals."* Unpublished doctoral dissertation, Family Social Science, University of Minnnesota, 1984.

Curran, Delores. *Stress and the Healthy Family.* Minneapolis, MN: Winston Press, 1985.

Fisher, Roger, and William Ury. *Getting To Yes.* Boston: Houghton Mifflin Co., 1981.

Garbarino, J., J. Sebes, and C. Schellenbach. "Families at Risk for Destructive Parent-Child Relations in Adolescents." *Child Development, vol.* 55, 1985: 174-183.

Hill William F. *The Hill Interaction Matrix: Scoring Manual.* Los Angeles: University of Southern California, 1961.

Kantor, David and William Lehr. *Inside The Family.* San Francisco: Jossey-Bass, 1975.

Laborde, Genie. *Influencing With Integrity: Management Skills for Communication and Negotiation.* Palo Alto, CA: Syntony Publishing, 1984.Lowen, Alexander. *Narcissism.* New York: Collier Books, 1985.

McCaskey, Michael B. "The Hidden Messages Managers Send." *Harvard Business Review,* November/December, 1979: 135-148.

Miller, Sherod, Daniel Wackman, Elam Nunnally, and Carol Saline. *Straight Talk: A New Way To Get Closer To Others By Saying What You Really Mean.* New York: Signet, 1981.

Olson, David. "Empirically Unbinding The Double Bind: Review Of Research And Conceptual Reformulations." *Family Process,* vol. 1, March, 1972: 69-94.

Saposnek, Donald T. "Akido: A Model For Brief Strategic Therapy." *Family Process,* vol. 19, Sept., 1980: 227-238.

Sherwood, John and John Scherer. "A Model For Couples," In *Marriages and Families: Enrichment Through Communication,* Sage Issues 20, edited by Sherod Miller, Beverly Hills, California: Sage Publications, Inc, 1975: 13-31.

APPENDIX — Available Resources

THE CONNECTING SKILLS WORKBOOK

The Connecting Skills Workbook is a companion to this *Connecting* text. *The Skills Workbook* provides exercises that correspond with each chapter in the text. These include worksheets, questionnaires, quizzes, checklists, charts, observation forms, and diagrams. The exercises plus an interrelated set of guidelines help you practice and apply the communication skills and relationship processes you have learned. *The Skills Workbook* begins with a thorough pre-assessment of your current skills and processes, and it ends with a post-assessment of your progress.

Available from ICP, Inc.

OTHER ICP RESOURCES RELATED TO *CONNECTING*

Write or call Interpersonal Communication Programs for more information on communication skills programs, materials, and instructor training. These focus on couples, families, and work groups.

Interpersonal Communication Programs, Inc.
7201 South Broadway, Littleton, CO 80122
(303) 794-1764, TOLL-FREE 1-800-328-5099

ADDITIONAL RESOURCES RELATED TO *CONNECTING*

Chapters 2. and 12. Feedback Instruments for Assessing Couples' Current Issues and Relationship System Orientations

Prepare: for Engaged Couples
Enrich: for Married Couples — Each partner completes a question-naire which is then computer scored to provide feedback in the following areas: leisure activities, realistic expectations (in Prepare only) marital satisfaction (in Enrich only), personality issues, communication, conflict, family and friends, children and parenting, equalitarian roles, religious orientation, financial management, sexual relationship, cohesion and adaptability.

For more information on availability and cost, contact:
PREPARE/ENRICH, Inc., P.O. Box 190, Minneapolis, MN 55458 (1-800-331-1661). You may also inquire about instrrments on the Systems Model for research purposes at this address.

Chapter 6. Instruments and Readings About Individual Similarities and Differences

Psychological Types Framework

Myers-Briggs Type Indicator — A set of questions for discovering your "psychological type." Consulting Psychologists Press. Available from a counselor or consultant who is authorized to administer it.

Gifts Differing by Isabel Briggs Myers. The book presents insights about how behavior reflects sixteen psychological types as determined by the Myers-Briggs Type Indicator. 1980.

LIFETypes by Sandra Hirsh and Jean Kummerow. The book uses the Myers-Briggs Type Indicator to describe behavior patterns and preferences and to help readers develop psychological self-portraits. 1989.

Please Understand Me: Character and Temperment Types by David Keirsey and Marilyn Bates. After describing four basic temperments in differing aspects of life, the book portrays each of the sixteen psychological types. 1984.

These books are available in book stores.

Chapter 12. Book, Questionnaires and Exercises on The Systems Map

Understanding Us by Patrick Carnes. This text-workbook builds your Family Map by exploring how your family system maintains stability and initiates change as it moves through stages of development.

Book available from ICP, Inc.

Index

Index